Controversial

One of the most talented and certainly one of the most colourful players in the history of cricket, Shoaib Akhtar holds the record for the fastest delivery ever, clocking in at 100.2 mph. Having taken more than 400 wickets in his international career, Shoaib has seen it all—the best matches, the most exciting tournaments, the highs and lows of personal achievement and failure.

Anshu Dogra is the Director of Manana and has been leading research-based programmes for the past two decades. She is a published author and journalist. Her work has focused on gender, history and culture and she enjoys writing about her travels. Her publications include *Music of the Mirs*, Manana, 2008; *Globalisation and Women's Work—A Resource Guide*, Manana, 2005; 'Costumes of the People of India: Continuity and Influences' in *India's Interaction with China, Central and West Asia*, vol. 3, pt 2, A. Rahman (ed.).

Praise for *Controversially Yours*

'I had some great duels with Shoaib over the years... he's the fastest bowler that I've ever faced in international cricket. There's one spell that everyone can watch on the internet of him bowling to me at the WACA. That was reasonably entertaining—more so for Justin Langer, who was at the other end laughing at me all the time when I was trying to keep Shoaib's deliveries out.'

Ricky Ponting to ESPNcricinfo

'Shoaib was famous for his attitude but let me tell you, he was down to earth and never a problem for me when I was his captain. The only worry for me was his pace. Quite easily, he was the fastest bowler I kept to.'

Rashid Latif to ESPNcricinfo

'...from 1999 to 2005, there was no bowler as thrilling as Shoaib Akhtar.'

The Express Tribune

Controversially Yours

SHOAIB AKHTAR

With

ANSHU DOGRA

Harper
Sport

An Imprint of HarperCollins *Publishers*

First published in hardback in India in 2011 by Harper Sport
An imprint of HarperCollins *Publishers*
A-75, Sector 57, Noida, Uttar Pradesh 201301, India
www.harpercollins.co.in

First published in paperback in 2013

4 6 8 10 9 7 5 3

P-ISBN: 978-93-5029-402-4
E-ISBN: 978-93-5029-295-2

Typeset in 11/16 Giovanni Book
Jojy Philip New Delhi 110 015

Printed and bound at
MicroPrints (India), New Delhi

For Sudesh Rajput

Sharing so much of myself in this book was not my idea; it required a lot of coaxing from Sudesh, my partner in times of trouble—my dearest friend, who has stoically stood by me during some of the worst times I have had to face.

You went miles ahead of others to help me in every possible way. No one else could have done it. This book is a culmination of your persistence because it was you who felt I should share my concerns about the future of this game, that I love so much, in my country.

Thank you, Sudesh, for conceiving the idea for this book. I really do not have enough words to show my appreciation for all you have done for me. Allah has always sent people to help me, so you have entered my life with his blessings. You are very special.

Contents

Acknowledgements

With love to Ammi and Abbu and to all my family, thanks for all your support and faith.

To my fans across the world, whose love and affection I will always cherish.

To my friends, thank you for being there.

Thank you, Anshu Dogra, for capturing the essence of my thoughts and for giving me the words.

In appreciation to Sarang Sena for the personal pictures, the cover picture in particular.

To everyone at HarperCollins India, especially my editor Karthika V.K., for receiving this work with so much enthusiasm.

Prologue

I would like to have retired from international cricket shouting out for the world to hear, 'We won the 2011 World Cup!' But that was not to be. I wanted to bowl in the very last match that Pakistan played in the tournament, hopefully the finals, but that too was not to be. I wanted to retire with dignity, having played cricket for nearly two decades for my country. Mercifully, that wish of mine was fulfilled.

No Pakistani cricketer before me had been granted this grace. Yes, that's right, I am the first person in the history of Pakistan cricket who hasn't been pushed out or forced to languish while waiting for a recall. Aamir Sohail was one of the first to acknowledge this feat when he praised me for having the courage to decide when to retire, which probably says a lot about the state of affairs of cricket in my country. He added that I had 'set a good precedent for future generations of cricketers'.

Choosing the moment hadn't been easy. On the evening of 16 March 2011, before our match against Australia, I finally informed our team manager Intikhab Alam of my decision and said I wanted to let the team know before breaking the news to the media. Alam agreed.

Eighteen glorious years of playing cricket and serving my country. What more can a man ask for.

Even before the World Cup was over, the world had responded to my retirement with so much praise that it was humbling. When the Australian team checked into the same hotel that we were staying in, most of the players made a beeline for me. Brett Lee hugged me and said, 'What have you gone and done, man?' adding, 'it's gonna happen to me as well soon.' Grant Flower was supportive, as were so many others from all the different teams. Accolades came pouring in, directly and through the media. Imran Khan called and congratulated me on a long and brilliant career. Wasim Akram walked up to me and acknowledged my decision by saying, 'You did the right thing. Now move on.'

After our match against Zimbabwe, Vusi Sibanda shared with me a story about a 1998 tour of Zimbabwe by Pakistan when he, along with some classmates, had bunked school to watch me bowl. They were subjected to a caning for this, but they felt it was worth it. He added to those gathered around the two of us, 'Bloody hell, did he come at the batsman! He hit Murray Goodwin in the head…' Ricky Ponting said that of all the fast bowlers that he had faced, I scared him the most. Syed Kirmani, Sunil Gavaskar, and so many other greats lauded my performance as a bowler.

I must confess that deep in my heart I felt the urge to continue playing, but I knew that I had to make way for younger players. I had wanted an opportunity to move closer to my own world record and had touched 159 kmph in Colombo during the 2011 World Cup, but now I await the news of another man shattering the record. Yet, there are no regrets. It's been an excellent run.

In the course of my career, I've faced many defeats but I have also celebrated victories. Tagged as being undisciplined and having a poor attitude, I have been insulted and my moral conduct questioned on a regular basis. I have been thrown out of the side many times, fined, and had bans slapped on me. The media has highlighted my 'exploits' both on and off the field, ensuring that my personal life was well documented, even if not always accurately. But I was the first to cross the 100-mile barrier, twice, and am still the fastest bowler in the world, having set an official world record by achieving the fastest delivery ever, clocking in at 161.3 kmph (100.2 mph).

When I look back at my career, this is what I hope people will remember: That I have taken more than 400 wickets in international cricket, spearheading the pace attack for my team. I am a thinking bowler with a passion to win; as a result, my bowling spells have often won matches and even series for my country. I have taken the scalp of some of the best batsmen in the world. At my very first encounter with India, I captured the wickets of Sachin Tendulkar and Rahul Dravid, and I flattened Brian Lara with my third delivery. I have been carried on the shoulders of my fans at home in an exuberant celebration of the team's victory. Indeed, I have fans all over the cricketing world whose faith has kept me going when things went wrong. And I have always played with all my heart for my country and my fans.

When I announced my retirement to the members of the press gathered at the media centre in Colombo, almost everyone asked what plans I had for the future.

'Wait and watch,' I answered.

After all, I hadn't exactly woken up one morning and said,

'Right, it's time to hang up my boots.' The decision had been made sometime back, and now there would be many new things to do, so many promises made to myself to fulfil, so many irons in the fire. But just for now, in this moment between the past and the future, the time seemed right for taking stock, for reflection, for a look back at where it all began.

1
Growing Pains

It could be any cricket ground on the globe, but it has to be a Pakistan versus India match to get a crowd so involved. And if the ground happens to be Eden Garden, Kolkata, in India, any opposing team, but especially one from Pakistan, faces 100,000 plus eleven opponents. And if you happen to be a young and unknown Pakistani pace bowler who has just taken the wicket of Rahul Dravid, one of the world's most accomplished batsmen, you can feel 100,000 pairs of eyes boring into you while a deafening roar pours out of 100,000 throats as their hero, Sachin Tendulkar, walks in. But if you knock off his stumps with your very first delivery to him, your ears meet with a deafening and almost eerie silence. I did it, I thought, I did it, as I pressed my forehead to the ground in gratitude. I knew that I had finally shaken off the dust of Morgah.

Controversies have hovered around me since the day I was born. Take my name, Shoaib, for instance. In Arabic, it means the one who brings people together, but it can also mean the one who separates. It is one of the many words in Arabic that have diametrically opposite meanings. The name was given to my brother who was born before me; unfortunately, he did not survive. My mother loved the name and so, when I arrived, she passed it on to me. Perhaps it was a big name to carry, for my family was not sure if I would survive to bear it. I was a frail baby, my mother's fifth child, and ours was a modest home. There was not much money to go around, and a sick child could easily slip away.

My father Mohammad Akhtar comes from a hardworking, economically unprivileged family of the Gujjar community. All his life he has been a God-fearing man, and a strict disciplinarian, but he is not very worldly-wise or practical, and retains an innocence which is almost *sai*, saint-like. He was a night watchman at a petrol station belonging to the Attock oil refinery.

One of my earliest memories of Abbu is of him getting ready for work, trying to dress as warmly as he could to face the cold winter night. Ammi used to take hot food for him later in the night. He would return home in the early hours of the morning when we were fast asleep. By the time we woke up, he would be asleep and we would take great care not to disturb him. Abbu did his best to ensure that there was always food on the table. He never shirked hard work and that is a virtue that has been impressed upon me.

Abbu married my mother Hameeda Awan when she was very young. She was still a teenager when her first child, Shahid, was born. Tahir and Obaid followed, and then came my brother Shoaib, who did not live to celebrate his second birthday. I followed her string of sons in 1975, and eleven years later my sister Shumaila joined us. We lived in mohalla Jaadi, a dilapidated neighbourhood of Morgah in Rawalpindi. It was a ramshackle place, squalid and lacking any sort of infrastructure. Our home was a one-room semi-pucca house with a shaky roof. One particularly severe monsoon night, the rain came down incessantly and a large part of the roof collapsed. I remember my parents rushing around, Ammi marshalling her wet, shivering kids to collect whatever material we could lay our hands on to repair the roof. I was about four then, and being the youngest, was forced to sit outside in the rain, out of everyone's way. More than anything else, I remember feeling cold and bewildered—roofs were not supposed to fall, they were supposed to protect us!

Money was always tight but somehow Ammi managed everything for us. She faced all the challenges that life threw her way and stood like a rock, shielding us from the squalid environment we lived in. I have always had a special bond with my mother, having been the youngest in the family for many years before my sister came along. In fact, I slept with her till I was eight. She used to urge me to sleep in my own bed but I always snuck in when I thought she was asleep. My big fat ammi's ample lap was always the safest place to be in, and I still love cuddling her.

Ammi knew how to cope with adversity because she too had experienced poverty as a child. In the 1950s, my grandfather, whom I called nana, was in great financial distress and was finding it difficult to raise his children. During those days, there were a lot of British people living in the area. My nana gave away his five-year-old daughter Hameeda—my mother—for adoption to a childless English couple who were soon to leave for Britain. She stayed with them for some months and recalls being dressed in a frock, having to eat strange food like soup and bread, and being sent to sleep all alone in a room with a high ceiling. It was very different from what she was used to, and she missed her family terribly. The family missed her too, and one day her mother's brother, Riaz, decided to see how she was faring. When they met, she pleaded with him to take her away, so he smuggled her out on his cycle and hid her with relatives in another village till the couple had left for England. They came searching for her, but nobody let on that they knew where she was. It is quite incredible that Ammi emerged from this background as a good-humoured, generous and strong-willed young woman. Her positive attitude and belief in a good future for us were amazing because she really had a tough time, with three growing boys and an infant who was often very sick.

Abbu was constantly worried about our finances. 'There is no money. There is no money' was his anxious refrain, but Ammi was always positive and masked her uncertainties. As a result, we boys hated to see her looking harassed even for a moment. Of the few memories I have of Jaadi, one that stands out clearly is of the landlady constantly coming to ask for rent. Seeing how agitated my mother got every time the lady came by, my brothers and I decided to get back at her. So Tahir made a hole in the landlady's hen coop, through which I would squeeze in and pinch eggs. Poor Obaid was always terrified that Abbu or Ammi would find out what we were up to and beat him, but he would come along nevertheless and be our lookout.

How did a woman who lived in a jhopar patti and who had no formal education get it into her head that her children should be well educated, and then manage to make it happen with the very little means life afforded her? She put so much emphasis on our education that even food was second priority in our house. There were days when we starved but she paid our school fees and did so with whatever my father gave her. My parents never asked for financial help from anybody, be it friends or relatives. We may have had less but whatever we had was ours, it was never handed down to us—we never wore other people's old clothes. Ammi had too much self-respect for that. She believed that poverty was not something to be ashamed of, one just had to work one's way out of it. She made all of us see the value of a good education and made sure we got it. All her children graduated from college—a great milestone for a woman who herself had never been to school.

I was born flatfooted and, as a child, was unable to maintain my balance. I would get up and promptly topple over, but I kept trying. When I turned three, my inability to walk was no longer the most pressing cause of anxiety for my parents because I was stricken with a severe bout of whooping cough, a disease that in those days carried away many infants. As the infection in my lungs got worse, I grew weaker each passing day till my nana, convinced that I would not survive, told my mother to stop spending any more time and money on doctors and instead use whatever was left to make arrangements for my funeral. But my mother was determined not to lose another child. She continued taking care of me, carrying me in her arms to the Central Hospital, the biggest hospital in that area. She would carry me across fields and nallahs till she got to a place where tongas were available and then travel further on to reach the hospital, where I would be given injections and medical attention. For a long time, nothing seemed to work and I couldn't digest my food properly. I got weaker and weaker till, as my mother often tells me, my eyes seemed to pop out of my face. (My friends assure me they still do. I, on the other hand, think my eyes are nice and big like Salman Khan's, which isn't a bad thing because there are many who consider this popular Indian film actor a handsome man.)

I survived the whooping cough, but the doctors told my mother that my lungs would always remain weak. Fortunately for me, what actually happened was that my lungs expanded due to all that coughing and I seemed to be able to take in a lot more oxygen! I gained strength and Allah filled me with so much energy that, far from dying, I became doubly energized and hyperactive. From not being able to walk, one day I got up and started to run.

Running is the most vivid memory I have from my early childhood. Even then I could run very fast, faster than all the other children in my neighbourhood. I ran for no rhyme or reason. I would run up hills, through meadows, down the streets, everywhere and at any given opportunity. I had such high levels of energy that I just couldn't keep still.

My brothers would watch me running up and down our mohalla, perplexed. Once, I was racing down the street, my face turned up towards the heavens, when Shahid bhaijaan, my eldest brother, grabbed me and inquired, clearly exasperated, 'Hey, you son of a djinn, what's wrong with you, why can't you stay still?' But I kept running. I ran under the hot midday sun, during the monsoon, and even in the cold winter rain. I have often tried to explain to my family and friends why I felt this need to run, that it was both self-expression and an experience of complete freedom. When I ran, I felt free.

In those days, I looked forward to the kite-flying season, for it meant lots of running. I would impatiently wait for my brother Tahir to return from his apprenticeship at the refinery so he could take me kite-flying. Tahir is very much like my abbu, a sai banda. He is a generous man and good fun to be around, but he can also be very aggressive and he fights well—like me. He thought nothing of putting in a hard day's labour and then taking a younger sibling shopping for kites.

I loved going to the kite sellers. There were so many beautiful kites in those shops and fortunately for me, my brother was as enthusiastic about kites as I was. I think it was a stress buster for him. My friends, Amir, Ayub and Gulfam would gather at the maidan with their kites and we would spend many joyous hours sending them up, whoops of triumph riding the air as our opponents' kites lost their strings in battle.

I used to love collecting kites that fell from the sky. If a kite got cut off from its string, I would chase it as if my life depended on claiming it as my own. During one glorious season, I remember racing after and winning fifty kites, much to the admiration of my friends. Eventually, all this running turned out to be good training. Sprinting in chase of a kite, my lungs opening and expanding, and playing gulli-danda on the streets laid the foundation for my throwing and fielding practice on the cricket ground years later.

Ammi used to tell me that she always knew I would do well in life, not because she could see my future in anything I said or did, but because of a saint's prediction. My mother's grandmother was fairly well-off, and had her own buggy and stables. Feeding the poor was a very old tradition in the family as was the tradition of feeding saints, malangs and the like—I continue this tradition and it gives me great joy. The family used to be visited by a baba and my great-grandmother once asked him if there ever would be male children in her family, for until then there had been no sons, only daughters. The baba paused for a long, long time and then said, 'Buddiye (old woman), don't worry, there will be many sons, and one of them will make a big name for himself in the world.' He didn't tell her anything more, but predicted that in her family would be born a child who would grow up to be world famous. My mum, who was only ten years old when this incident happened, assumed much later that the child was me. She always says that my forehead used to shine in the dark, but *jab kambakhti aane lagti hai*—when mischief entered my mind—it lost its sheen and became dull. Ammi is, and always will be, a great influence on me. My confidence in my abilities, despite the disabling start I had in life, is a consequence of my mother's wisdom and guidance.

The Attock refinery where Abbu worked looked after their employees well by providing facilities such as hospitals, schools and living quarters at subsidized rates. Our family has had a long association with this organization. My brothers and I were all born in their hospital, and it was because of the facilities provided by them that we could survive on what my father earned. By the time I was old enough to join school, we were able to shake off the dust of Jaadi and moved first to Jamhra and then to C-Lines, where we were allotted House no. 16.

Ammi was determined that I should receive my education in an English-medium school. In this she was supported by Shahid bhaijaan, and as a consequence of their endeavours,

I was enrolled at Junior Model Public School, Kotha Kalan, Morgah.

I have wonderful memories of walking to school, school bag on my back, escorted by my mother—at least for the first few days. The school was some distance away from home and we would cross open fields, ditches and nallahs to get there. For the first few days I didn't really understand the purpose of attending school and felt a bit lost. Then, as I got familiar with the surroundings, being there started to feel right, and I celebrated this feeling of belonging in my usual way. I ran from room to room, bursting with energy and excitement. The moment school got over, I would strap my bag on tightly and race home, till I was breathless and could run no more.

The school yard with its swings and slides was like a dream come true for me. I wanted to play with the other children, but I think I was too physical for them. I would stand on the swing and jump off it from a dizzy height, enjoying the feeling of floating to the ground. No child was prepared to sit with me; they were too scared.

More often than not, I got slapped by my ustaadnis, lady teachers, because they were fed up of yelling at me to slow down or be careful. Though I must say this about myself—I was naughty but never got into fights. It was just that I had a high level of curiosity and energy and kept trying to engage others, sometimes putting a finger in a kid's eye, sometimes pulling a girl's pigtails and running away. I remember that I used to like teasing Khalida, a classmate of mine—her brothers were friends of my elder brothers. I used to sneak up behind her and pull her braid. Then there were Naaz and Rehana. When I look back, I think I must have been something of a Romeo even when

I was 5–7 years of age. The girls used to complain about me, but I persisted.

Somehow I just couldn't remain still for any length of time. I have a clear memory of running between parade lines on Sports Day. During assembly, I would break ranks and run from one row to another, much to the despair of the teachers. There was this haud (tank) which was very deep and about seven feet across, wide enough to drown anyone who fell in. I loved to jump across it, courting death, it would seem. Even at that age I liked the sense of danger, the thrill running down my spine. Each time I was caught doing something I wasn't meant to, I was severely punished. But nothing could stop me.

During the lunch break, I made sure that nobody's lunch escaped me. I used to crawl under the desks, take lunch boxes out of school bags and then go to a spot where I could polish off all the food. 'Shoaib! Give back their tiffins,' my harassed teachers would command from within a circle of wailing kids. I never confessed to pilfering the tiffins and stuck to the line that I did not need to take other people's food as I carried my own lunch to school from home. I used to show my lunch box as proof, its contents of half a parantha and half an egg testimony to my truthfulness.

The ustaadnis, I am sure, must have been fed up, but they were also my first crushes, so to speak. To me they were the very definition of 'ladies'—soft-spoken and erudite, interested in teaching me and encouraging me in every sphere. I remember watching an Indian film starring Mithun Chakravarti, called *Disco Dancer*. It was a huge hit in Pakistan those days. One day my teachers asked me to get up and dance, and I promptly said okay and performed like Mithun in front of all of them.

The only time there was peace at school was when I was playing a game. I loved participating in all kinds of sports and was good at all of them. I shone in athletics because I was a good sprinter and once I had learnt the rudiments of football and cricket at school, I was eagerly sought after by everyone to be a part of their team. Sport came naturally to me and I soon found a lot of friends at school because of it. My parents encouraged all of us to play some sport or the other; they believed that sport was the best way to keep us occupied and out of other people's affairs, and also to instil discipline in us. Discipline was a big deal in Abbu's scheme of things and any complaints from the neighbours about bad behaviour would invariably result in a sound thrashing. Sports ensured that no complaints were made. Except where I was concerned, of course. I ran on rooftops, climbed trees, I teased my aunts by knocking on their doors and running away. I was the naughtiest of the lot and consequently was constantly at the receiving end of Abbu's ire.

It's true, at the same time, that my teachers at Junior Model Public School found me eager to learn. I was considered to be both receptive and observant. I would watch, listen and learn—these qualities were to stand me in good stead in later years. I was rather good at studies and was often made the class monitor even though I used to throw chalks at the students sitting in front of me. Once, I was caught bursting crackers in school—I just wanted to have some fun, but right from the beginning, my behaviour and actions were judged by others as strange. I am sure that today, a schoolteacher or a child psychologist reading this would put it down to hyperactivity or something like that and know what kind of attention I needed, but at that time nobody could figure out why I was so troublesome. My parents were told at PTA meetings that I was a bright and intelligent child but required disciplining, feedback that my father took quite seriously.

Perhaps it was to keep children safe that our elders told us horror stories about supernatural beings that moved around at night, waiting to harm all those who were out of their beds or homes. They would scare us by saying that there were malevolent spirits in trees, waiting to gobble up children who climbed them. But nothing and nobody could deter me from climbing trees. And when I would tell people that I hadn't yet seen a djinn up there, they would answer, 'Djinn tu khud hai—you yourself are a djinn. Why do you need to see one?' As children we are constantly told that if you are naughty, you can't be good at your studies. I disagree. I was naughty and a darn good student. I was always in the top three in my class but yes, I was also A+ in sharaarat—mischief.

By the time I completed junior school, the money ran out at home. Shahid bhaijaan tried his very best to keep me on at Junior Model Public School. He wanted me to pursue higher studies so that I could get into a good profession and earn a decent living. But the fee was beyond our reach. Finally, bowing to circumstances, I was transferred to an Urdu-medium government school, Government Elliott High School. The new environment came as a shock to me; everything seemed different, starting from the fact that I had moved from a co-ed to an all-boys school. The quality of education was very different too. I had already covered everything that they were teaching in the sixth grade. In fact, it had been covered in class four at my previous school! I would quickly finish my class assignments and then was keen to learn more. In the beginning, when I found that the class work given to me by the teacher wasn't exactly challenging, I would ask him to teach me something new. That was all I asked. It didn't go down well with my new teachers. They started to mock me by saying, 'Do you think you are clever enough to know everything? Who do you think you are? Are you special in some way?'

This would often be followed by a sound beating, much to my bewilderment. When I tried explaining to them that I had already learnt these lessons, it only infuriated them further. They would complain about me to the principal, who would hand out another set of canings.

Tehzeeb sahab was our principal. He was an influential man in our mohalla and was respected by the community. I remember him as a fifty-year-old disciplinarian who taught two generations of my family—my uncles, my brothers and myself. He called me the black sheep of the family but was the first person to recognize that despite my lack of discipline, I did have brains and talent. I was always the first to volunteer for any co-curricular activity in school, such as debating.

Everybody looked up to Tehzeeb sahab as an ideal to follow. I too was a little in awe of him and perhaps that is why I remember him so clearly, though I don't remember the names of any of my college principals—they kept changing like the chairmen of the Pakistan Cricket Board.

This was a very troubled period for me and I remember feeling hard done by, with nowhere to go. There was no in-school counselling, and a private counsellor was out of the question. We barely had enough to eat, let alone pay a counsellor. But my naughtiness, my way of learning, and later my belief that you don't have to be a saint in order to do good work have stayed with me. I believe that one doesn't become a good person by following laws, rules and regulations—I don't think that is necessary or important.

At Elliott High, the syllabus was prescribed for each term that lasted three months. Our teachers said that you had to work hard for three months but I said, no, I will finish the entire syllabus in twenty days and then play and eat for the rest of the term. And I did. However, nobody appreciated the fact that I completed my course within twenty days. I just got punished for playing for the rest of the term. The rules at home were no less problematic. In my house we all had to go to bed early, but I never did. It seems to me now that I was naturally inclined to do the opposite of whatever the norm was, or what I was told to do. As you can imagine, I was always in trouble, always caught on the wrong side of the rules.

Even as a child, I enjoyed my own company even though I had lots of friends. I had my dreams to keep me company— beautiful dreams about the future. I dreamt about living in big cities and travelling the world. I used to share my dreams with my friends at school and they would marvel at my imagination. I would tell them, 'You just wait and watch, I will make my dreams come true.'

Then television came to our mohalla and I began dreaming in high definition. We did not have a television at home, but there were a few well-off families on our street whose children I was friends with, and I regularly watched TV at their homes. Do you remember those old-fashioned sets, with knobs and dials and dodgy signals? Very often the kids were made to take turns standing on the roof, moving the antenna about till a clear picture was received. I often joined them and we used to look down from there and watch what felt like a different and wonderful world.

Our first TV was a black and white Hitachi. Later, to my great delight, we got a second-hand Sony colour TV. I could not be moved away from the set—my parents used to scold and even beat me but I couldn't stop myself. I remember watching a programme in which people were eating chips that looked absolutely delicious.

The television was my first exposure to the world outside. I was in the eighth standard when I first saw Big Ben and some other scenes of London on TV. I was so impressed with the visuals of flyovers, roads and motorcycles. I felt this was me—I should be on a motorcycle, driving along those roads, in that countryside. I became convinced it was the place for me, it was where I belonged, and that was why I was a misfit here. Blissfully unaware that a large Pakistani community already resided there, I believed that I would be the first from my country to go to England. I imagined how I would walk down those streets in my brand-new salwar kameez, and how the lovely English ladies would stare in wonder at this exotic soul. I began to live in an alternate dream world, a world that had no boundaries.

By the time I was a teenager, I had begun to resent the environment that I was growing up in. I was constantly dissatisfied with my lot. I wanted to be free and out of the pollution, out of the despair I saw all around me. I hated my new school and couldn't get my parents to understand my problem. The lack of understanding was at the heart of it all. First I was beaten down by whooping cough, and then my teachers beat me! Like any other child, I needed guidance, needed somebody to invest some time in getting to know me, to see that I was neither abnormal nor a strange phenomenon. Throughout my childhood and most of my adolescence, however, I lacked a mentor. My father was stern with all of us and did not tolerate bad behaviour. He would constantly receive complaints from my teachers and at times from our neighbours about me. This, of course, meant regular canings. He was a tough man, tough on the kids, tough on his wife, very disciplined. I knew he loved us all dearly, but after having been punished so many times, and as a consequence of all those beatings, I would go out and pick fights.

To be honest, the unhappiness stemmed primarily from our poverty. I was getting fed up and started blaming everything that went wrong on our financial situation. It made me aggressive and I sought out opportunities to vent my frustration. So almost every day I would either get or hand out a thrashing, but at night I lay under the open sky, gazing at the stars with fascination and dreaming about my future. I still have this habit of lying on a cot on the roof of my house, or in the courtyard, staring heavenwards. Perhaps some of the answers I am looking for can be found up there.

In those days. the worst were the Eid holidays. I did not know what to do with myself. For the Akhtar household, Eid was a short affair. We woke up early, offered prayers, ate sevaiyyan, and that was the end of the celebrations. My mother used to dress me in a new set of clothes and warn me not to get them torn or dirty. That meant I couldn't play. There is a large rock outside our house in C-Lines on which I often sat mulling over things, and on it I spent most of the holiday. I recall wondering why other children could have a feast and still have money left over to spend on a cola and other delights. They had a whole day of celebrations ahead. Why would they leave all that and play with me? At such times I used to feel neglected and alone.

Even at that age I could see the difference in the way money dictated people's behaviour. Those children who had rich parents were treated differently by the teachers, were pampered more. I felt this discrimination within the school and in our mohalla. I used to tell my friends, who felt equally deprived and low, 'Never mind, one day we will make it big, we will do better, live better.' I would then draw such fabulous imaginary pictures of a shiny wonderful world that we would end up laughing.

Our life did change for the better when my sister Shumaila was born. She was lucky for our family—*Ghar mein barkat aaiyee*. My brothers got decent jobs and my father retired and was given a golden handshake with which we were able to partially build our own house in Dhoke Nawaz. It was wonderful to have the comfort of fans and a water cooler to ward off the heat. The coolest part of the house was the basement in which we all slept and as a result, even though most people feel suffocated in dark places, I love basements and am not claustrophobic at all. I have no difficulty going into, say, an MRI tunnel.

I remember being happy when my sister was born. Shumaila is eleven years younger than me and I am very fond of her. When she was old enough to go to school, it was my duty to bring her back, and for this I was allowed to take Abbu's cycle. I would wait till she came out, then I would pick her up and put her on the carrier behind the seat and bring her home every day. This was our time together and we bonded. For me she was a little playmate and we played together for ten years. Then I left home. Now she is all grown up and married and has taken to mothering me like Ammi does and I can't help laughing when she tries to scold or fuss over me.

Despite my father's beatings, I was always his favourite. Today I look after him, make sure he has everything he wants. He has worked hard for us, it is now my turn to take care of him. Parents do not want money, they want love. I remember when I was young, my parents would sit by my side while I slept and offer the tahajjud, early morning prayers, for me. Many years later, Shumaila too would wake up at two or three in the morning and join them. I am much loved by my family and though I do have my mood swings, I have nothing but love for them. Whatever I can do for them, I will. Cricket has taken me away from my family. Touring all over the world left me with little time to spend with them. But that is changing now—I am making an effort to reconnect with my relatives, both on my father's and my mother's side of the family.

As children we were deeply influenced by my mother's family—her sisters and her brothers. My uncles, Ikram, Inam and Khayam were actively involved in our lives. I love them all but Inam is someone I look up to. Inam mama is handsome, personable, full of good humour and soft spoken—*Unke lahsize mein itni shahistigi hai, itna nafees ki* it is he who keeps the entire family united. I know I would like to be like him and be able to get all of us to keep meeting, and eat together—not harm each other. All my aunts dote on their brothers, who in turn love their sisters deeply. And if anyone requires guidance or advice, they come to my mother, who is considered the wisest amongst them all.

My mother's side of the family is pragmatic and strong-willed and it is only now that I realize how much I have learnt from them. Not the least of it is a fund of traditional wisdom that I can still dip into. If there was some trouble or a problem that the family had to face, for instance, they would say, *Aag lagge te meenh nahi varde*—When there is a fire raging, don't stand around waiting for it to rain, that is, when there is a problem, you can't expect that it will get solved miraculously, you have to do something about it yourself. So our in-house nursery has always dominated my education, my attitude to life.

I loved my nana too, He passed away when I was just four years old, and I distinctly recall being cuddled and kissed by him. His beard was prickly and he would rub it against my face to tease me. My mother's sister, Khala Mussarat, in particular, has a great sense of humour. Once, somebody knocked at her door, and she called out and asked who was there. The visitor gave his name as Aashiq. Now Aashiq means an admirer or lover. So she promptly responded, 'Isn't it too late? I am married and a mother with two children.' My mother has a funny bone as well. I think our ability to laugh has stood us all in good stead and allowed us to face adversity cheerfully.

My father had a bypass surgery at the age of sixty-seven. I was nervous and even cried when he was wheeled into the operation theatre but he was very calm and as soon as he recovered, he started cycling! This attitude has genetically been passed on to me; it is in my genes to be a fighter. During the last few tours before my retirement, I heard people say that even at this age Shoaib continues to compete and contribute to his team. I know that I owe this spirit to my family. In retrospect, I know that my parents did their best and were ambitious for us, especially my mother. She was broad minded and was determined that her children would be well educated, achieve great things and be good human beings. I am thankful to them for their perseverance, hard work and all the sacrifices that have brought us to where we are today.

But while I was growing up, I was in a different space. A sense of frustration built within me, the desire to do something big. That rock outside my house became my best friend. I sat on it so often and for so many hours that I think it softened a little. Whenever I felt that I had lost control of things, I found myself sitting on it. I still go back to it and almost always, I find the answers I am looking for and am able to get on with things.

On that rock I figured out that the only way things would get better was if I made them better. Of course, there was no one to guide me or give me direction, so I kept blowing in the wind, making mistakes but constantly moving forward. Looking back, the whole of my childhood seems like a miracle because how could an infant like me, who couldn't even walk and who was a bit different from the rest, grow up to be the fastest bowler in the world? But it was Allah's will.

2

Shoaib Bhai Haazir Hai!

As I approached the end of my school years, I finally began to see some hope. I was elated at the thought of getting away from that jungle, the schooling system. Not all my teachers were harsh, though. Najeeb sahab and Naseem sahab were good to me and I was fond of my physical training teacher, Bhatti sahab. When my matriculation exams were over and the results were declared, I found that I had stood second in my school. At home though, I got punished for that. How could I have come second, my family wanted to know as Abbu cuffed me and my brothers followed suit. You see, just before I could show Abbu my results, our neighbour had walked in with his son's report card and showed it around proudly. His son had stood first! After politely listening to him gloat about his son's brilliance, my father called me and asked to see my report card. And I was in trouble.

I can safely say that I got more than my fair share of canings and thrashings in my childhood. With three elder brothers to support Abbu, I grew up on a regular diet of beatings till I told my family that it had to stop. 'I'm tired of being beaten up. Aren't you tired of beating me?' I asked. I had entered the terrible teens and rebelled against everything and everyone. While there was a lot of love in my family, there were a lot of restrictions as well, and too much preaching. I was constantly being told what I should or shouldn't do, and needless to say, I resented these impositions. My argument that it is you who want me to do this but I may not want to do it was not easily accepted. Then I would turn mulish and rebel. I am afraid I am still like that. If I am pushed towards doing something, I end up doing the exact opposite. It is not that I do not understand that there are some things in life that need regulation, and that we need to live by the laws of the land. But I can't help pushing the line a bit—it's fun. Man's law is not Allah's. Allah's law is unbreakable.

When I was about sixteen or seventeen, I ran away from home. The reason was a tiff with Shahid bhaijaan. He is the most sensible person in our family, and has always faced his responsibilities with grace and love; even now he remains involved in my day-to-day affairs. He was our guardian, and a father figure, but he was also a bit bossy and was the enforcer of rules at home. He always insisted that I come home early. As it happened, one day I reached late. The moment I entered, bhaijaan started scolding and threatening to beat me. That night, I ran away. After putting what I thought was a safe distance between home and me, I realized that it was getting colder as the night wore on and, more importantly, I was hungry. I moved towards a crowd that had gathered around a holy man at a dargah and announced to the gathering that I too was a disciple and had travelled a great distance to meet the baba. When asked about my luggage, I told them that I had walked out of home without any. The baba's disciples welcomed me and gave me a room to stay in. Over a hot meal, we spent the evening talking about Islam, a subject that I could talk about for hours, even at that age.

Our murshid, Ghulam Moiuddin Sultan, had been guiding my family from the days of my nana. He insisted upon one thing—love for Allah, and love for the Prophet (PBUH). He said that everything else came after this love. When I sat in on his discourses, I began to appreciate his erudition. He was civilized, kind and loving. He was knowledgeable and he inspired me to explore this knowledge. I began to read as many books on Islam as possible, after which I would go to him to understand all that I had read, discuss my doubts and clear my confusions. My murshid encouraged all my questions. In this way, my *ta'limaat*, my learning, had continued for the next fifteen years. So that night at the dargah I was quite comfortable as I discussed a subject very close to my heart.

The next morning, I convinced one of the disciples to give me ten rupees and went on my way. I spent another day and night with some friends before Obaid hunted me out. Obaid is like Shahid bhaijaan, strong and silent. Both of us are fond of running and often run together. We are especially partial to running in the mountains, I racing ahead and he laughing and enquiring what the tearing hurry was for. 'Pace yourself, Shoaib' has always been his advice, something that I have now begun to understand.

That morning, he tried to convince me to come home. I told him that I wouldn't go home to be beaten up. He assured me that no one would do so, and so I finally agreed. Later I learnt that my mother had scolded Shahid bhaijaan for scaring me like that. I wasn't scared, just fed up of being at the receiving end of constant beatings. My running away made everyone at home realize that this wasn't the best way to handle me.

I, on the other hand, had enjoyed my encounter with freedom—I had experienced my first few nights away from home with no one telling me what to do. As soon as I returned home, Ammi hugged me and said, 'Don't you dare leave your home like that! Don't do such a thing again.' I said I wouldn't because I could see that she was distressed, but I would eventually do it again, legitimately, by going away on tours.

My family was keen that I go to college because I had fared well in school. I remember I had such confidence even at that age that I went all by myself and got admitted to Asghar Mall College, Rawalpindi. Established in 1920, Asghar Mall had been upgraded to a degree college in 1960, offering intermediate, bachelor's and master's programmes in various disciplines including physical sciences, arts and languages. It is a premier institution for higher studies in Rawalpindi and because I had done well at school, I was accepted. When I gave the news to Ammi, I could see the pride and happiness on her face. She drew me close to her and whispered, 'Please don't fail, my son.' I promised her that I wouldn't. I didn't fail; I just dropped out. And I did finally complete my graduation through a distance-learning programme. But wait, I am getting ahead of myself.

I really was looking forward to getting out of the narrow confines of school and going to college, and I must say I wasn't disappointed. Asghar Mall gave me some of my best friends and also opened up the world a bit more for me. I used to get off the wagon at Kashmiri bazaar and walk past Pabrah

bazaar and through Krishan Nagar to reach college—a fair
distance. I recall observing other teenagers, how they dressed
and behaved with each other at college and in the bazaars,
and promptly adopted all those mannerisms that appealed
to me. Every car that passed by I wanted as my own, and
when I saw motorcycles for the first time, I can't tell you how
beautiful they looked to me. For the first time, I was exposed
to urban life and suddenly there was more freedom to exercise
my own choices.

I cruised through my college years without having to work
hard because I was so receptive that I could grasp details by
mere observation. This is true for most things even now; I can
observe you performing a task and learn from you. Nobody
has had to instruct me, whether it was in the English language,
swimming, driving, bowling or batting. Whatever I have learnt,
I have learnt through observation. But I always had questions,
and unlike at school, in college they were well received and
my lecturers began to acknowledge my abilities. Over the first
few months I found good friends—Imran Zaidi, Rashid Awan,
Faisal and Zaheer, to mention a few. Zaidi, Rashid and I were
a gang; we are still very close. We would egg each other on to
play pranks. Once, we thought it would be hilarious to drive
a motorcycle through our principal's office. Naturally, I was
more than willing to carry out this nefarious plan. I recall
saying, *Shoaib bhai haazir hai*—brother Shoaib is ready, an oft
to be heard phrase at Asghar Mall. I then swung my leg over
the bike and headed off towards the said destination.

The principal's office was spacious, with doors at each end.
I breezed right in—he was busy lecturing some students—and
wished him a polite good morning and sailed out. He caught

me within the hour. When I squared my shoulders to receive the expected caning, he just said very calmly, 'Son, get out of this college.' I immediately apologized and promised that I would never drive a motorcycle in college again. To my surprise, he smiled and let me off with a mere three-day suspension. On the third day after my return, he saw me playing cricket in front of a block earmarked for girls. Being the 'girls only' section of the college, it had a natural fascination for us, and despite it being off limits, we used to loiter or play cricket outside the wall in the hope that one of us would catch their eye. Once again, I was summoned to the principal's office and given another two days' suspension. Of course, nobody at home knew about this because I never stayed home. I just hung around outside the college or in the billiard rooms.

Those days my weekly pocket money was fifteen rupees. *Bechari Ammi*! I don't know how she managed it. She used to keep her money tied up in a corner of her dupatta and we would gauge the health of the household finances by its size. My weekly allowance was never enough to take care of my needs, and I always seemed to be hungry. There used to be a chana wala outside my college, selling a plate at five rupees, and soon I began to eat there for free. This was a great accomplishment because over the years he had become hardened to all sorts of pleas for freebies from college kids. It took me three months to bring him around. After that, he would give me a plate of rice, chana and curd every day. I had convinced him that I would become a famous cricketer and that if he became my friend, I would always remember him. I would eat my free meal in front of my friends and let them see what powerful connections I had.

My allowance also had to cover my share of the hire for my

beautiful Kawasaki. My friends and I had persuaded Anwar, the thirty-five-year-old owner of Anwar Motorcyle Store, to hire out a motorbike to us. We would pool in a day's rent and hire the Kawasaki. Each was given half an hour to ride it, but more often than not, I would not come back when my time was up and would spend the rest of the day biking all over town. I would collect the money from my friends, saying I would be back in half an hour. They would shake their heads and retort, 'No, you won't!' but they always forked out their share. I spent many wonderful hours taking the motorcycle out of the city up the mountain side. The tune from the film *Muqaddar ka Sikandar* would buzz in my head:

> *Rote hue aate hain sab*
> *hansta hua jo jaayega*
> *woh muqaddar ka Sikandar jaaneman kahlayega.*

Everyone comes into this world crying.
He who departs laughing
will be hailed as the conqueror of destiny.

I don't think it would be wrong to say that this song reflects the entire philosophy of my life. I have always felt the need to break away from gravity that pulls me down; maybe I should have been a fighter pilot. I have always loved speed. When I zoomed along the mountain road on the motorbike with the wind on my face, I thought life couldn't have anything sweeter to offer. Finally, I was at peace. On reaching the top, I would get off the bike and spend hours with myself. *Mujhe apne aap se mil kar bari khushi milti hai*—I do enjoy my own company. But then it would start to get dark and it would be time to return my beloved bike. Every evening, I did so with a heavy heart. I would talk to it and say, 'I'll be back for you tomorrow.'

I remember an amused Anwar asking me why I talked to the motorcycle. 'Does she answer you?'

I said, 'Yes, she does, when we are speeding on the road together.'

I wasn't an easy person to be friends with and often got myself and everyone around me into trouble. Naturally, my friends were a little nervous around me. They knew I could do ridiculous things like hand over wrong assignments to teachers. But they had great affection for me and stood by me throughout my college days because they knew that basically I was harmless and good fun to hang out with. I did get into fights, but not serious ones and certainly not of my own making. Not that I shied away from them. Sometimes I got beaten up too. Once, for instance, I was singled out and roughed up by six seniors, but I took my revenge on them. I had a bet with my friends that I would scare them silly by posing as a lecturer. It had to be a lecturer on Islam because I was very good in that subject. A friend found out that their Islamiyat lecturer was unwell, and that was my cue. I strode into their class with supreme confidence, introduced myself as the assistant lecturer, and announced that I had been instructed to take a pop-quiz. I then proceeded to single out the students who had beaten me—you should have seen their faces—and asked them questions that they were unable to answer. So I punished them, threw them out of class, threatened to inform their teacher about their poor progress.

I guess the boys soon figured out that something was wrong; perhaps they recognized me.

I went again the following week to give another lecture. By then the boys had asked their teacher about me and he had told them, *Woh saala to khud mera student hai*—That scoundrel is himself my student! So I was caught and while I was being handed another three-day suspension, the astonished lecturer asked me how I knew so much about the subject.

Now when I meet my college friends, we spend most of the time laughing at all the silly mischief we got up to. They tell me that whenever they saw me walking towards them, they would warn each other: 'Here comes trouble!' Each one has their favourite Shoaib story, but there is a general consensus that the episode with Koda sir was the best. Koda sir, as we called him, had a habit of not letting us go when the class got over. He would continue his lecture well into our lunch hour, much to our dismay. Something had to be done about it and as usual, *Shoaib bhai hazir tha*. I bought some fire crackers and lit them just as the bell rang. BANG! The poor man clutched his heart and began to crumple to the floor. I jumped forward and grabbed him before he hit the ground, saying, 'Sorry, sir, it was me. Please don't die, but you never leave when the class gets over!'

When he got his breath back and his heartbeat returned to normal, he said, 'Shoaib, you will never change.'

The last few years of school life had deprived me of access to sport. Being able to play again was perhaps the greatest gift I received in college. Cricket was very popular in Pakistan. We had won the World Cup in 1992 and I began to follow the team's performances seriously. That brilliant cricketer, Imran Khan, was leading Pakistan through a glorious phase. My inspiration came from watching him, and so in the beginning I tried to copy his run-up and bowling. But very soon I began to develop my own rhythm and began playing for the college cricket team. Earlier, I had played a match or two but only with a tennis ball, so this was my first real attempt at the sport. Shahid bhaijaan watched me bowl in some of the college games and recognized that I had talent. He used to play cricket at Rawalpindi Club—the locals called it Pindi Club—and one day he took me to a local match. It so happened that one of the teams was a member short, and they asked me to join them, adding, 'This is a leather ball, don't get hurt or your mother will scold us.' I was about sixteen years old and was confident enough to assure them that nothing would happen. When I was given an opportunity to bat, I saw the ball clearly and began to punish the bowlers mercilessly. Everyone was surprised and remarked how well and stylishly I was playing—I wish I could still say that about my batting! Then they wanted to see me bowl.

When I started walking up to my seventy-yard mark, one of them yelled, 'Oye! You're required to bowl, not field.' I told him that this was my normal run-up and that I bowled really fast. The captain of my team looked quite unconvinced when I added, 'Just let me do my thing. Whatever I do, I do it like a star.'

He replied roughly, 'Get on with it, and don't waste time.'

The first ball hit the batsman on the head, the second on his chest. The opposition looked anxious but my captain had a broad smile on his face. The result of this game was that I gained a reputation as a very fast bowler and was often invited to play with the local team. During one of these matches I caught the eye of Majid Khan, who called me over at the end of the match. I was only sixteen years old and there I was, in the presence of the great Majid Khan. He said, 'Son, what is your name?'

I replied, 'Shoaib. Very soon everyone will know my name.'

He responded, 'Son, I hope you have your head screwed tightly on your shoulders.'

Abashed, I hurriedly answered with due respect, 'Yes, sir.'

Whenever I look back at this period of my life, some of my fondest memories come flooding back. I was happy and doing what I truly wanted to do. I love Rawalpindi. There is something about this city that encourages sport. Its topography—the fields, the hills, the fresh air—makes it a natural gymnasium and the region has produced Olympians, and hockey and cricket stars. It is also a great town for training, with endless bike trails and back roads to run on. Developed by the British, the area where I was growing up had hockey stadiums, open fields, badminton courts, football fields and cricket grounds—everything I needed—and I made sure I availed of all the facilities.

In the early days I had to walk rather a long distance to reach the bus stop. I lugged a kit that I had created by cramming all my gear into an ordinary bag and taping my bat firmly on it. Many times, there was no room in the wagon—if there was space for me, my odd and bulky bag would not fit in, and if I could find space for both myself and my bag, I would not have the required fare. So most days, I used to travel sitting on the roof. The ground was a forty-minute walk from the stop, and I used to trudge onward stoically under the afternoon sun. Through all this, I never lost my enthusiasm for the game but things really looked up when Shahid bhaijaan gave me a bicycle of my own—my first set of wheels. I was over the moon! The cycle became my personal symbol of liberation and independence, for it allowed me to roam without supervision by adults. I would ride it at top speed without holding the handle bars, eyes closed and arms spread as if I was an eagle or an air plane. I felt reborn.

Getting to the club grounds became less of a hassle now that I had wheels. Net practice used to start at about three in the afternoon, but I was always early and would immediately get on with my sprinting and exercise routine. I was fit and ready to go, and it was for the others to catch up.

I embraced exercise with a passion. Shahid bhaijaan had enrolled me in a gym in the hope that it would help me expend some of the energy that kept getting me into trouble in college. At the gym, I worked on strengthening my legs so that I could run faster. I was in very good physical condition and with a little effort could surpass everyone else. When my cricket colleagues used to show up at around four or five in the evening for practice, I would get quite upset. I would ask them, if you guys keep this up, how are you ever going to become cricket stars? Their usual response was a mocking 'You go ahead and become one!' to which I would respond, 'I have absolute belief in Allah. He knows I am working hard, so I *will* become one.' It is true that whatever I had asked of Allah until then, I had been given, but only after a *phainti*, a caning.

I was now playing regularly at the Pindi Club grounds which were nestled in the General Headquarters (GHQ) area. By the time my classes got over, it was well into the afternoon. I used to reach the ground by half past two, change into my very brief shorts, a thin singlet, and top it off with a pair of plastic sunglasses. They had cost me a week's allowance and were my pride and joy. I was the only wise guy there who diligently, some say crazily, did fifteen or twenty laps in the mid-day sun, and I ran regardless of the weather. When I finished my training on the field and was done practising with the ball, I would start racing up and down the club's stairs. For the first time, I found a way to channel all my energy, and I felt so good and confident about myself that I became convinced I was the next best thing for Pakistan cricket. But for now, I focused on training hard and bowling well, hoping that someone would spot me and take me away.

In the end, that is exactly how it happened. The club was a regular meeting place for army officers of various ranks, many of whom enjoyed the game. All those colonels and majors would look at me and wonder, *Yeh cheez kya hai?* Who is this creature? But they were impressed with my hard work and passion. Over the years, they began to acknowledge me and I even played with some of them. As they moved up in their careers to become generals, they watched my changing career graph with great interest and empathy. As a result, I am on first-name terms with many of the army's top brass. There were several amongst them who cared for me and I remember with appreciation the guidance of Col Muqtadar, who was a doctor in the army and used to run the nets at Pindi Club. But of them all, I owe the most to Lt Gen. Tauqir Zia, Corps Commander Mangala.

It was during one of my crazy practice sessions at the club that I met Sir Robert Cross, a man whom I learnt to respect deeply. A small community from Jamaica had migrated to Rawalpindi in the 1920s. Robert Cross was from this community and like all Jamaicans, he was keen on cricket. He started coaching at GHQ, the Test cricket ground in Pindi, and everyone had a healthy respect for him. We addressed him fondly as 'Sir'. And so he became Sir Cross.

Sir Cross had been observing me for a while, had gauged my

talent and was impressed with my enthusiasm for the game. So he took me under his wing. He introduced me to his sons Robert and Geoffrey, both good cricketers. In fact, Robert was very talented and could have played for Pakistan. They used to speak to me in English and encouraged me to respond in English as well. I believe that their entry into my life was ordained by Allah. I was to rise and play at the international level, so Allah had appointed people to help me communicate with the world outside.

Sir Cross was perhaps one of the first to recognize my potential and he found the time to coach me. He always told me that I needed to channel my talent and when I asked him what that meant, he had the patience to try and explain that my energy needed to be focused on the game and nothing else. But hot-headed as I was, I kept telling him, 'Sir, I am a big star, don't you understand?'

He would earnestly reply, 'But I do understand.'

I remember him once asking me when I thought I would make it. I confidently replied, 'Sir, by the time I turn nineteen, I will be a star.'

He was fairly anxious on my account for even though he was convinced of my talent, he was a pragmatic man and knew that the road to success was not easy. But Sir Cross believed in me. He commanded a lot of goodwill at the club and he kept promoting me and pushing my name forward when it mattered.

My friends, too, had faith in my potential and would escort me daily to the ground on their cycles. By then I had convinced everyone that I was a star and whether I walked or biked, I always had an escort. We were a like-minded bunch, optimistic and cheerful. I disliked bickering and whining and used to consciously avoid people who talked negatively. I hated such talk, for I refused to believe that good things didn't happen. If Allah exists, you are not alone, this I believe. How can you believe in Allah and not have the conviction that he stands with you? Where is your belief then? If Allah has given you life, he has also ensured that you are never alone. There are angels to protect you. If, while driving, suddenly a tree falls in front of you, automatically your steering-wheel turns to avoid it. Did you steer it on your own? Did you save yourself? No, it is the strength of Allah. It is that which makes you brake spontaneously when a child comes in front of your car. This happens to you all the time, doesn't it? There are powers that align with you. Why are you disappointed, how can you give up? If you truly believe and depend on Allah, he will open doors for you.

When I told everyone around me that I would be a star, they responded, 'Abey, you haven't even got a cycle, saale, how can you become a star?'

I would answer, 'So what if I don't have a cycle, one day I will have a plane.'

They would want to know what special ability I had that others did not. I would respond, *Mere mein ability khuda ki dein hai, meri jaan.* I have been bestowed with a gift from God, dearest! I have capabilities born of conviction and belief, which you don't have.

One evening, when the lights at the Pindi Club grounds were switched on, we saw the Pakistani team practising there. I remember my friends and I were standing far away, near the railings, and there were Imran Khan, Wasim Akram and Waqar Younis practising in front of us. I watched them for a while, then turning to my friends I said, 'Remember this day. In the next few years, I will be standing right next to these cricketing giants.' They hooted with laughter and tugged my sleeve to pull me away from the railings saying, 'Theek hai, right now let's fill our cycle tyres with all this hot air inside you and then we will see what the future has to offer you. Let's go home now.'

But my conviction never wavered, and their friendly mockery only served to strengthen my will. I decided then and there that I would play in the national team with these greats, come what may. Of course, I had no idea how to go about it, not even how to get into first-class cricket. I had till then played more often than not in the hope of impressing girls, and had used up most of my energy playing pranks. But now I was determined to play for Pakistan.

With this goal in mind, I began to withdraw from almost everything else and played cricket wherever and whenever I could. One day, I was playing in the college grounds when Ishtiaq Shah, the head of Rawalpindi Division Cricket Association (RDCA) and president of Rawalpindi Cricket Club (RCC), saw me. He had an amazing eye for new talent, was passionate about the game, and totally dedicated to his division. In 1993, he had organized Super League matches for the RCC. Only a visionary like him could have organized such events and enhanced the reputation of his division, which in the coming years gave Pakistan many promising Test cricketers, including Mohammad Wasim, Mohammad Akram and Azhar Mahmood.

When Ishtiaq sahab sent a boy over to ask me if I wanted to play at the college intermediate level—there was a match to be played in Lahore—I said, yes please! I took my mother's blessings and headed off on my first trip to Lahore. I recall

staying in a hostel at the Minar-e-Pakistan Complex; the match
was played in the Lahore University campus. There were many
other hopefuls—what they had I lacked, and what I had they
lacked, but I think I had more belief and conviction than they
did, for despite my team losing, I did well. I kept my idol Waqar
Younis in mind when I was bowling, and had a great match.

While I was there, I was keen to see this wonderful city where
all the cricket action seemed to be. I wanted to visit Minto Park
and other prominent sights of Lahore. It didn't matter that I
had no company. It also didn't matter that my sightseeing tour
started at two in the morning, don't ask me why. I just decided
to set out towards the park, stopping to sample the delicious
fare at the food stalls, just me and my thoughts. My head was
buzzing with plans and strategies on how to move further up
to district cricket, and then into the national side.

My performance in the Lahore match must have remained
in Ishtiaq sahab's mind because when the New Zealand Under-
19 team came to play in Pakistan in 1994, he put my name
down for a side match that was to be played against them at
Pindi Club. I didn't let him down, and took eleven wickets. I
remember thinking then that I really was a star player and I
needed to push forward in my career. I needn't have worried
because Ishtiaq sahab proposed my name and I got selected to
play for the Pakistan Under-19 Test team that played against
New Zealand in January 1994. I remember how excited we
all were, my family and friends, when I made my Youth Test
debut at the Rawalpindi cricket stadium, where I bagged two
wickets. My Youth ODI debut followed the very next month at
National Stadium, Karachi, where I took two wickets for thirty-
two runs. This was when my family really began to believe in
my talent, and gave me the freedom to play cricket.

3

Trial by Fire

I was a good student, so my family wanted me to continue with my studies, but my Youth Test and ODI debut made them realize that cricket had become my sole interest. I now knew that I wanted to play the game professionally and as a result, my attendance in college became erratic. I am sure many people heaved a sigh of relief—peace was restored at Asghar Mall at last.

It wasn't easy convincing my family about my decision, though; they were concerned about how I would fend for myself while trying to break into the game at the national level. I knew I needed a job to sustain myself but hadn't found anything that interested me. One day, my friend Ijaz Arshad told me that Pakistan International Airways (PIA) was holding trials in Lahore for their Karachi division team. This seemed to be a perfect solution—a job doing something I really wanted to do—so I decided to try my luck with them. I grabbed a bag, convinced Ijaz to accompany me, and we headed off to Lahore by bus. We were not going to pay for a ticket; we didn't have enough money on us. So we waited for the bus to start, ran behind it and scampered on to the roof. The conductor was wise to such tricks and kept popping up to check if anyone was travelling at his company's expense. The entire seven-hour journey was spent dodging him. He would poke his head up from one side and peer over the top, and we would hang down the other. We would jump off before every stop, and then run and jump on just before the bus picked up speed. I remember this journey well simply because the conductor's determination to make us pay the fare matched our determination to travel free of cost.

In this furtive and, if I may add, adventurous manner, we reached Lahore railway station late in the evening. Our late arrival posed another challenge. The trials were to take place the next morning, so we needed shelter for the night. I had Rs 12 in my pocket and Ijaz the princely sum of Rs 13, a grand total of Rs 25 which was, as we found out, about the same as the amount required for a night's stay at a cheap hotel. But if we paid for the accommodation, we would have to forgo dinner, a dismal prospect for two growing lads. Ijaz got a bit stressed out but I wasn't worried. I told him that we would find a safe place to spend the night—with a tongawalla. I picked out a tonga that looked new and shiny, walked up to its owner and said, 'Salaam! I am going to treat you to a good meal tonight.'

He looked at me and said, '*Tu hai kaun?*' Who are you?

I replied that I was a cricketer from Pindi.

'Do you play for Pakistan?' he asked immediately.

I answered, 'Allah *kare* that too will happen, but right now, I am standing in front of you.'

I remember him smiling and asking why he should oblige

me. Because, when I joined the Pakistan team, I would come back to meet him, I said.

'Do you really believe that will happen?' he asked.

And I said, 'Yes, look into my eyes and you will see it.'

'It's a deal,' he said.

In this manner I managed to convince Aziz Khan, the tongawalla, to share his bedding and sleeping space with us, and that night we slept peacefully on a footpath in Lahore. Next morning, Aziz Khan in his generosity took us to the ground in Model Town where the trials were to be held. Tongas were only allowed as far as Mall Road and as I got off, I reiterated my promise that when I became a member of the Pakistan team I would come back to meet him, and that if he ever heard from someone that a cricketer was looking for him, he should know that it was me.

'Naam yaad rakhna,' I told him. Remember my name.

The Nawab Grounds were a two-hour walk from Model Town. We had had no breakfast and were starving, but an excitement was rising within me, which peaked when on arrival I set eyes on Zaheer Abbas sitting at the selectors' table. I was in a state of awe and I recall thinking that if I got the opportunity to say salaam to him, it would be wonderful. Sitting next to him was Moin Khan, who was the captain of the PIA team. There were many aspirants that day but I knew that I had to outshine all of them and somehow catch the eye of the great Zaheer Abbas. I was determined to play so well that he and everyone around him would be forced to focus their attention on me. I wanted to announce—Look at me! I have come! I have arrived!

I began running laps of the large grounds and soon noticed

from the corner of my eye that Zaheer Abbas was observing me.
I ran faster. Then came the wait for my turn, which seemed to
take forever. A good part of the day had passed when finally, I
was given the ball. The pitch was made of cement, and to add
to that, I was really fast. *Bas!* What more did I need? I took over
the game and had everyone running helter-skelter. By the end
of it, I had succeeded in doing what I had set out to do, and
when we assembled in front of Zaheer Abbas and the other
selectors, he addressed me directly. 'You are the man I want.
Do you want to play for me?'

With my usual confidence, I replied, 'Yes, I will play for you,
and soon I will be promoted to play for Pakistan.'

He was quite taken aback.

The PIA team had stars like Moin Khan, Wasim Akram and
Rashid Latif, some of whom had represented Pakistan and
had brought home the World Cup in 1992. And there I was,
amongst these stars. Perhaps I appeared to them a misfit—the
whole dressing room would look at me in my brief shorts and
plastic sunglasses as if I was an alien. But I didn't care because
I had a job that was taking me in the right direction. Soon
Zaheer Abbas started sending me with the team to play in
casual tours in places like Singapore, Hong Kong and Malaysia
and I felt that all my dreams were coming true. This was a
step towards official tours and matches, I thought, as I played
unofficial matches at different destinations. The world was in
my hands and it looked very glamorous to me. I was ecstatic
at travelling abroad and especially remember my first night in
a hotel. We were in Singapore and after a full day of playing
and sightseeing, I went straight up to my room and fell asleep.
Hunger pangs forced me up at midnight but to my dismay,

the hotel's restaurants were closed. We were not allowed to use the mini bar and I wondered how I would pass the night. Fortunately, I had some crisps and peanuts left over from the day's shopping and I munched them to keep from starving. Next morning, the senior members of the team hooted with laughter when I complained that I had spent a hungry night. They then explained the concept of room service to me.

I was young and naïve but my innocence didn't last very long. PIA is a Karachi-based organization and Karachi is the financial hub of Pakistan, the country's largest city and its only port. I did not realize then that moving there would cause a lot of problems; in fact, it could have cost me my life.

My stay in Karachi is etched in my mind as a time of terrible anxiety and grief. The early 1990s were witness to political tensions between various ethnic groups and the city was wracked with violence. Karachi was in turmoil and I was there in 1994–95 when it was going through its worst phase of unrest. The army had been ordered by the then prime minister, Nawaz Sharif, to commence Operation Clean-up; it was given a free hand to get the situation under control. The period is regarded as the bloodiest in Karachi's history, with thousands killed or gone missing in the fighting. I didn't know anyone in the city except my uncle, my mamu, but he moved out of Karachi a few weeks after my arrival so I had to find independent accommodation. It was then that I began to feel the pinch of a meagre salary, Rs 500 a month. To add to that, PIA rarely gave it on time. There were two or three other boys from Lahore who found themselves in the same plight. We didn't know where to go. There was always a curfew in place, but did PIA care about our safety or worry about how we would manage? How were we supposed to travel or find shelter in a city in which we knew no one? How were we supposed to survive on such a low salary? How were we supposed to manage it all, we were only kids!

Perhaps this callousness towards a few of us stemmed from the fact that we came from poor families. With no support from my employers, I began hunting for a place to stay, one that my pocket could afford, which of course seriously limited my options. The places where I could afford accommodation—Al Karam, Lalu Khet, Dus Number Market, Sharifabad—were at the centre of the disturbance. There was violence on the streets everywhere, including firing and rioting, and I was forced to live in the middle of it, cowering amongst strangers.

' But it was these strangers who ended up caring for me. I had managed to get a room in an area where most of the residents were migrants from the Chitral region of northwest Pakistan. They lived as one community in Karachi. Fortunately, I spoke Urdu well and made friends easily. Financially I was in a mess; after paying rent and commuting to the cricket grounds and back, I barely had enough money left to eat. Fifty rupees in my pocket, that was all. You can imagine how difficult it was. I felt lost and unprotected. Given the terrible law and order situation, PIA should have taken care of its young players and arranged for a safe place for us to stay but they showed no concern, felt no responsibility towards us. To complicate matters further, I had convinced my friend Saqlain Mushtaq to try for a berth with PIA and when he got in, he made a beeline for me.

Both Saqlain and I rose from the Rawalpindi cricket circuit. We had played together for the Under-19 team as well, so it was natural for us to stay together in a new city. But I felt responsible for his safety, since I was the one who had convinced him to move to Karachi. Fortunately for him, he stayed with me for a few months and then shifted to his friend Hasnain Qazim's place. I didn't have a choice, so for a year and a half I slept on a marble-chipped concrete floor with just a pillow and a sheet. The chips dug into my flesh with every movement I made, so I didn't get a restful night's sleep as long as I was there.

It was not the PIA sports board but my friends from Chitral who looked after me. They ensured I got hot meals to eat, taking turns to invite me to their homes. They and others— some of whom were actively involved in the unrest—would escort me out of the troubled areas, all the way to the ground, and sometimes hang around to escort me back. I will always be grateful to them for looking after me during those harrowing days. They cared for me as their own, kept me from starving, and made sure I survived all the madness that was unfolding all around us.

The army had been given shoot-at-sight orders, and I survived bullets flying past me as I sat next to my window. I saw people being blown up by rocket launchers. When curfew was imposed or a hartal took place, you couldn't see even a bird outside. I lived in a constant state of fear. I was still in my teens and had already spent many nights on the roadside; I had seen people around me dying in the rioting and sniper fire. It was the worst time of my life, but I never complained. Honestly, I would have undergone anything for the sake of playing cricket.

Things started becoming unbearable only when the sports committee of PIA refused to let me play any official fixtures.

They were getting negative feedback about me from some of the other players, who were having difficulty pushing me around, and said that I had to sit on the bench because of my 'attitude'. This was a word I would hear for pretty much the rest of my cricketing career.

I clearly remember that for the entire duration of my stay in Karachi, I had to walk for four hours every day from Lalu Khet to National Stadium. I would reach there and then they wouldn't let me play. All day I was used as the 'water boy', and I was by far the quickest bowler they had. In fact, I was the quickest bowler in all of Pakistan. I used to tell them that I should be given a chance because I was faster than anybody else. Even when everyone used to mock me, I would keep insisting, 'Nahin, yeh sach hai—no, this is true, I am the quickest.'

But they continued to ignore me; they would harass me and use foul language, abusing my mother and sister. I was made to sit out in the sun and was only allowed to eat when everyone else had finished. It was only when the rest of the team went home that I used to start sprinting and complete my exercises. I would train all by myself and then start the long walk back to my room. Because of this gruelling routine, I was tired all the time. I couldn't, and to some extent still can't, figure out why they behaved the way they did. Perhaps some of them wanted to stop me from getting ahead, from progressing. This is not uncommon—people try to keep those who are more talented than them down and out.

This state of affairs went on and on. I wasn't playing any games that went down as official, or getting enough to eat, and as my misery increased, I began to get frustrated. It was already close to two years of not playing, not eating properly, watching people get shot and through all this, trying to keep alive and positive. I was feeling drained, physically and mentally. One day, after a week of severe rioting in my neighbourhood, I called my friend Asfand and asked him to get me out of there.

'Take me to some other neighbourhood, please,' I pleaded.

Asfand is still a great buddy of mine and whenever I visit Karachi, I stay with him. He was concerned about my safety but I had asked him for help at a time when the streets were burning. He tried to keep me indoors, away from the madness on the streets by saying, 'Bhai, the conditions are really, really bad right now. Let's do this another time.'

Asfand was right because anyone attempting to enter the area where I lived was going to get killed and similarly, getting out of my room meant flirting with death. But I had had enough and suggested meeting up at a safer place. When he realized that he couldn't persuade me to hang on any longer, he finally agreed.

I had to get through Lalu Khet and Al Karam. These were, as I have mentioned before, very dangerous neighbourhoods that I had to pass through every day to get to the ground and back. Many times, I had walked back home over dead bodies and now I was determined to leave this hellhole permanently.

Bullets were coming out of nowhere, everywhere. I tried to stay as alert as possible and slowly began to inch towards our meeting point. Looking back, I was probably too young to understand the consequences of what I was doing, but as I have said before, I had friends among those who were an active part of these disturbances and they escorted me from one neighbourhood to another till we came to a particular corner where there was continuous crossfiring. I remember thinking, if I try to walk through this, I will die. I just couldn't do it, so I spent the night in the neighbourhood, trying to build up the nerve to go through. Asfand, too, spent the night in great anxiety because I hadn't kept our rendezvous. He knew that I had left my room but when he called his home in the hope that I was safe, his folks told him I wasn't there either. Somehow I managed to contact him later that night and told him to go back home.

The next morning, I managed to get out of Lalu Khet, which was at that time the epicentre of the disturbance. The moment I crossed the area, I threw my bag over my shoulder and broke into a run. I reached Hasan Square, only to find that the whole market was burning. Shops were on fire and rioters were out on the streets. I remember joining the throng so as to not stand out. I moved with them till I could cross the square, and then I broke away, jumped over the nallah which divided chaos from safety and finally reached Asfand's sister's house, much to our shared relief. It was the first time since my arrival in Karachi that I had a comfortable bed to sleep on. I stayed with them for four months, my last months in Karachi.

I continued to try and adjust to the situation but finally reached a dead end. I knew I couldn't carry on like this, I was getting nowhere. So I decided to quit. But I wasn't going to slip away quietly, was I? They needed to know that I was leaving not in despair but in defiance. I hadn't been bowled out; they hadn't broken my will or self-belief. I had only one thought in my head—because you have hurt me, I'll hurt you back. Taking things lying down was not in my nature. I wanted revenge.

I managed to get six months' advance pay out of them. This covered the dues that they had been withholding for one and a half years. I pocketed the money and then marched into the PIA office where all the big guns were sitting. I stood in front of them and said, I am leaving this team and I am leaving with my rightful wages. *Kameenon*, you rascals! You didn't give me a chance to play. Now you just watch what happens. Within a year I will be playing for the Pakistan team, try and stop me. I will be the star of the Pakistan team. Write this down so you won't forget it. I handed over my resignation letter saying, '*Laat bhejta hoon is naukri par*—I wipe my feet on this job, I spit on this job, I spit on you people and I spit on this sports body.' I swung on my heel and walked out to the sound of their mocking laughter. I was so mad that I walked to the airport—it took nearly seven hours to get there—and took a flight back home.

The feeling of satisfaction at having been able to get back at those who had given me such a hard time began to subside as Rawalpindi drew nearer, and I began to think of the consequences of what I had done. I had left a job to which I couldn't go back because of the way I had stormed out. I didn't have any other options in hand and didn't know what my next move could be. But I knew that what I had done was right. Something inside of me was saying, it's okay, it had to be done, and it's going to be fine. I knew I had talent. They said my attitude was not right but I refused to accept that. I had done everything I was supposed to do. I went to the ground regularly, trained properly. I spent the whole day giving water to the team and completed all the work assigned to me. The only thing I didn't do was *khushamad*. I was never a sycophant and I was not about to start becoming one for anything or anybody. To become a 'yes man', one has to kill one's self-esteem and this I couldn't do, for it was this belief in my self-worth that had brought me thus far. I have been called egotistic and arrogant because of this, but that is both untrue and unfair. I believe that one has to do more than one's best. Be proud of who you are and what you do.

By the time my plane landed in Pindi, I was feeling calm. It was no use crying over spilt milk. I was going to get it from my folks when I reached home, so what was the hurry to get there? I had many friends to welcome me back and we had a great time together, visiting our favourite haunts. The next morning, I went home to face the music. I remember my mother was home and happy to see me, but when I told her that I had left PIA, she was shocked. 'You left a job worth a thousand rupees,' she exclaimed. I told her that I had lied, that it had only been five hundred and that I couldn't afford to live in Karachi on that sum.

I never told my family how hard it had been and all that I had been through. They sat me down and asked me what I wanted to do next, hoping that I would agree to study further. I said, 'Nope! I am going to continue playing cricket.' Born worrier that he is, Shahid bhaijaan found it difficult to accept my decision. He had different dreams for me. He wanted me to finish college, get a degree and find a well-paid job. I did eventually earn a degree several years later because I too believe in the importance of education, but at that stage, wild horses weren't going to pull me back from my goal.

My brothers wondered how I would be able to pursue my goal. There were the financial constraints and I had no agent or manager, no clear way by which I could achieve what I wanted. But they accepted all my arguments. Besides, they knew that I was too stubborn to be pushed in a direction I didn't want to go, so they let me be. Though I had received innumerable canings from him, I knew I was still my father's favourite. At this critical juncture in my life, he supported my decision and stood by me.

In that uneasy winter of 1995, I woke up early every morning and ran from 3 a.m. to 5:30 a.m. I knew that this in itself wouldn't get me anywhere but I had to remain fit and keep my spirits up, so I ran. It was the only thing I could do at the time. My mother used to get up early too, and when she looked out of the door she would see me running back towards the house. She used to say that I looked like some ghost or spirit steaming towards her on foggy mornings. It made her grieve, seeing her troubled young son running on cold winter mornings while the rest of her brood were tucked warmly in their beds. She once asked me what was wrong. What was it that troubled me so much that I had to put myself through such discomfort? But I never shared my troubles with her; she had enough of her own.

For a whole year, I got up every morning and ran. Then I would pick up my cycle and bike three hours to the Pindi stadium and do my exercises and training. I never stopped working. I was not the only talent in the area. There were others who were definitely better than I was but not as hardworking. They did not have the *junoon*—that obsession, the kind of passion and belief that is needed to succeed. I am convinced that is why they fell by the wayside and I went through.

I wasn't untouched by depression, though. This was a difficult

time in my life and I desperately needed guidance. I remember
once looking up to the heavens and shouting, 'Boss, are you
there? Is someone going to talk to me, advise me?' But Allah
doesn't work that way, he sends down people to do his work.
Over the years, many people have supported me and helped me
carry on. This time, too, I was rewarded with a second chance.
I had spent most of the year exercising and training and
playing for Pindi Club. I had learnt the art of reverse swing
bowling by closely observing Waqar and Wasim on TV. I had
been struggling for four years. I had paid my dues, now it was
my turn. *Allah ne mera haath pakra*—Allah took my hand, and
I was selected to play for the Agriculture Development Bank
of Pakistan (ADBP). Mansoor Rana was the captain and he
was the one who picked me in 1996. Presently he coaches at
the National Cricket Academy (NCA) in Lahore and is a good
friend. I value his counsel.

To my great satisfaction, that same season ADBP played
PIA. Oh ho! I was waiting for this moment. I was so fired up
and raring to have a go at them that I reached the ground
at six in the morning. When the ball was handed to me, I
probably had a terrible smile on my face, a true reflection
of my inner feelings. I got two of them on the helmet and
in all, injured five. I remember them saying, Bhai, we aren't
responsible for the bad blood between you and the sports
board, why are you taking it out on us? I retorted that I was
just not in the mood to spare anybody.

I had a brilliant day with the ball because of which we won
the match, but I wasn't finished yet. After the game, I went
and stood under their dressing room window and swore at
them. 'How many of you did I get?' I yelled. 'Did you see what

I can do?' The past had taken hold of my mind, and I couldn't help myself. I just kept shouting and swearing at them till my teammates dragged me away saying, *Khuda da vasta*, for God's sake, come away or you'll get into real trouble.

That year I was taken into the Pakistan team. What I had said would happen, happened.

It had been a tough period, but I will say this, even in the worst of times I always found ways to enjoy myself. Life was, and still is, an adventure. Besides, I was young and nothing could break me. I had got what I wanted: freedom from being told what to do. If someone tries to curb my freedom, I tend to shut down and not function. Even at the height of Karachi's period of unrest, I had found moments of happiness, fun and enjoyment with my new-found friends, and I dearly appreciated their company. I often asked them why they did what they did. The question usually came up when someone died—and many did. They had their own logic and conviction. I was told that I too was fighting, finding a way to resist the torture meted out to me by PIA. I had reasons for my fight and they had theirs, and we left it at that.

As an aside, I must mention that I encountered something similar later, when I was in Ireland. I was out sightseeing and found myself walking into what looked like the beginnings of a street fight between Catholics and Protestants. A group of Protestants were defiantly marching through Catholic neighbourhoods, looking for trouble, and I joined them for the heck of it, reliving for a short while the memory of days long gone.

Life is a great teacher. There was nobody to fight my battles for me, so I learnt to take things as they came. There were times when the chips on that hard floor in my room in Karachi burrowed into my back and I had to get them out in the dressing room the next morning. I recall this not to get sympathy but in the hope that my life lessons might be of use to youngsters. If even one youngster learns something from my account, I will consider my job done. Making a name in one's field doesn't happen by fluke or luck, it's the result of sheer hard work and dedication. It's not about parties or girls; it's about perseverance against all odds. I have seen the Pakistan team having a good time—and what I have done is nothing in comparison, believe me. If you are doing well, everybody wants to know you, otherwise they drop you like a hot potato. One should be prepared for this and not expect that life will be only about bouquets, without any brickbats coming your way. I have seen all this and more in the last eighteen years that I have played cricket.

4

A Few Hiccups on the Road to Glory

I had been playing on the domestic circuit for Rawalpindi Cricket Division and as a member of the ADBP team for about a year now. I'd had a haul of seventy-five wickets in one season alone. My reputation as a young fast bowler was growing and I had caught the eye of Majid Khan, who was at that time the chief executive of the Pakistan Cricket Board. I knew that very soon a call would come for me; everybody around me was talking about it. Then, in 1996, to my great delight, I was selected for a tour of England as part of the Pakistan A team.

Throughout my childhood, Ammi had talked to me about the days she had spent with the English couple who had adopted her for a short period of time. Consequently, I felt a connection with England, although I had only seen the country on television. I remember being greatly excited about the tour and when we reached there, I wasn't disappointed. I loved everything about England—the cool weather, the lush green countryside dotted with pretty cottages, the way people smiled and greeted you when you passed them by on the street—everything! And I adored London, its cosmopolitan flavour and its rich history reflected in its architecture. I spent all my free time roaming the streets and I did it with ease, as if it was my hometown. It's the same today. I don't feel a stranger there. I am very comfortable living and playing in England.

I performed extraordinarily well during the tour. As usual, I was working hard and playing hard. The team manager was Justice Azad and our coach was a weird man named Agha Akbar. I don't think I have come across a stranger man than him. He was rather proud of his fitness and had a distressing habit of banging our heads together just to show how strong he was. None of us appreciated his behaviour but nobody knew how to stop him. A few of the boys wrote a letter to the board complaining about him, on the basis of which he was finally dropped.

Apart from fitness, Agha Akbar had another fetish: the morning shave. He forced us to shave every morning, come what may. We used to grumble; we barely had hair on our faces those days. At some point, an idea began to float amongst us that his shaving kit should be confiscated, and soon a consensus on how it could be done had emerged. All that was required was a volunteer. And who was the first to come forward? Yours truly, of course! I said, no problem, brothers, I am at your service—*Shoaib haazir hai*, and promptly set about getting a duplicate key made for our coach's room. I snuck in while he was out, opened his suitcase and pinched his shaving kit. Then I put everything back in place and strolled out of the room, locking the door behind me.

That morning, an unshaven coach joined us. He looked so funny walking around with bushy green stubble that I couldn't resist saying, 'Sir, you haven't shaved today. That's unfair! You force us to shave every morning. Double standards, sir!'

He told me to stop talking nonsense, but I kept needling him the whole day. He got pretty irritated and began to suspect that I had something to do with the condition he was in.

The next day, of course, he found his shaving kit in its place. But somebody had confirmed his suspicion about who the culprit was and I was to discover that he had no sense of humour. I was fined £55. That hit me hard. It wasn't as if I had committed a theft, it was just a prank. I also wondered how he had identified me in the first place, and so started my own investigation into the matter. It didn't take long to locate the tattler. Payback time, I thought, and got a large box gift-wrapped. I tied a bright red ribbon around it, stuck on a bow and added a rosebud as a final touch. Then I went up to the traitor and said that somebody had left a gift for the coach but since he wasn't talking to me, it might be better if somebody else handed it to him. When my treacherous teammate did so, the coach was a tad suspicious and inquired who had left the box for him, to which the boy replied that he didn't know, but Shoaib had received it. I shook off all knowledge and the deed was done. Agha Akbar tenderly peeled the wrapping off, opened the box and peered in to find it full of gutter brushes, waste and toilet paper. The first name he yelled out was—Shoaib! I said, 'It wasn't me, sir, it was him', pointing to the other boy, who tried denying it. Akbar was so mad that the boy was fined £100.

Despite such distractions, I did very well on the tour and by the time all the matches were over, I was immensely satisfied to learn that I had been selected to go with the Pakistan team to Toronto. There were a couple of days left before our departure from England, so the coach gave us some free time to shop or do whatever else we pleased. I took his permission and went to spend a night with some friends in Birmingham and came back as scheduled the following morning. Akbar had sanctioned my night away from the team. However, in the tour diary report that he presented to the board at the end of the tour, he complained that I had left the team to spend the night elsewhere. As a result of this report, I was dropped from the upcoming Toronto tour. What was worse, his report ensured that my Test debut was delayed by a year.

Missing out on the Toronto tour was deeply frustrating but I was young and resilient. I swallowed my disappointment, put a lid on my anger and worked furiously. I played domestic cricket and trained hard at the Rawalpindi Cricket Academy. In fact, I overdid things and nearly burnt out in the process.

That was the year of the World Cup and Pakistan lost to India at Bangalore in the quarter-finals. Losing to India, as always, had serious consequences back home. Waqar Younis's career was on the wane, and in the background Mohammad Zahid and I were emerging as Pakistan's new pair of fast bowlers, ready and waiting to step in if called.

Then it happened. I was given my first Test cap when the West Indies came to Pakistan in 1997. The West Indies at that time were considered a weaker side, so the board thought it was a good opportunity to play a few youngsters, give them exposure, while preparing the Pakistan team for the next World Cup. But I had to wait a bit longer. I was not picked for the first Test, and finally made my Test debut on 29 November 1997 at the Rawalpindi cricket stadium, my home ground.

It was, of course, a momentous occasion for me, especially

when I received my first uniform. I recall immediately changing into it—I now had a huge star on my chest. I did not take it off for three full days. But I was still seething with anger against Agha Akbar. He probably thought he had finished me but he was wrong, I couldn't be finished that easily. So when I was selected to play my first Test match, I called him up at his home and showered abuses on him. I said that I was playing for Pakistan despite his bullshit adverse report. 'Now watch me become a star,' I told him.

These days Agha Akbar is a curator with the PCB and doesn't look me in the eye if we happen to pass each other. It was because of him that I joined the Pakistan team a year late. And it was because of him that I became known as the lad who was selected for the team and then quickly dropped on disciplinary grounds. That was my introduction to the Pakistan team; I started with entirely unnecessary baggage that made everyone wary of my reputation as an undisciplined player.

What can I tell you about my first Test match! The one I had prepared for all my life. Wasim Akram was the captain and he told the board he wouldn't play Shoaib, come what may. Perhaps he wished to continue with the previous team because he was satisfied with its performance or perhaps he didn't want to encourage the emergence of a new fast bowler. Perhaps the memory of my outburst in Karachi held him back. Whatever the reason, Wasim succeeded in keeping me out of the first Test but the board insisted that new blood be given a chance; they wanted him to try me out in particular. The result was that I became the discordant note within the team, the bone of contention between Wasim and the selectors.

The Pakistan Cricket Board had announced that I would play and the team's captain had responded by threatening to quit if I did. But the board held on. So Wasim pushed the issue further and said five other members of the team were threatening to not play if Shoaib was allowed to. There was a division in the team even before the match started, and a controversy arose in which I unwittingly played a part. On one side was me, a mere youngster, and on the other side were the senior players, all of them in a state of mutiny. I sat quietly at the back of the dressing room, horrified at this turn of events. I didn't want to exacerbate matters by being visible or audible.

Majid Khan phoned Salim Altaf, who was the chief selector at the time, and told him to ask Wasim if he would abide by the board's decision or else he was sending replacements and would accept Wasim's resignation as captain. Wasim backed down but was furious with the decision and came back to the dressing room, shouting and swearing. I was to bear the brunt of his ire. I wanted to ask if anyone could explain to me how all this was my fault but I kept quiet. This was my first Test match, so you can imagine my state—I was all nerves! It was only when I saw Wasim striding out for the toss in a ferocious mood that I allowed myself to believe that I was going to play.

We were to field first and I nervously got ready to go out on to the ground. The atmosphere in the dressing room was horrible; the rest of the team ganged up against me and made things as uncomfortable as they possibly could, peppering every phrase aimed at me with abuses. The result was that I felt messed up and terribly unsure of myself. This feeling heightened as the day wore on and I wasn't asked to bowl even once. I did get my first chance after lunch and got two wickets, but I knew that I had underperformed. I just couldn't shake off the tension that had built up in me, and as a result I bowled far below my own standards. I remember feeling that perhaps I was not good enough to play at this level. I was completely demoralized and my dreams seemed to lie shattered around me. Despite the fact that we won the Test by an innings and twenty-nine runs, I was dropped for the next Test, which to my mind wasn't a rational decision either. If the aim was to give more exposure to new players and groom them for the future, surely you needed to give them time to let them come into their own.

Whenever I think about that Test, I wonder why my teammates were so quick to believe all that had been said about me. I was a newcomer and yes, I had already had to face disciplinary action, but I could have been given the benefit of doubt. Someone could have asked for my side of the story. My teammates chose to make me feel like I was an outcast. In retrospect, I think it was because they could see that I would ultimately secure a berth in the team and they felt threatened; they could see that I would make it through. I would face this alienation from the team throughout my early days because I could never bow down to my seniors saying, yes sir, no sir, or bring food for them, or make their drinks and suck up to them. I didn't have it in me. I was never rude to any senior player but I couldn't do what others did to secure their place. So I was told throughout my career that I had a bad attitude, was arrogant, and that I never listened to people. Is maintaining your self-respect equivalent to having a bad attitude?

I have never been rude, or insulted or talked down to my senior players in the Pakistan team. This is a fact. No one, Wasim, Waqar or any other senior player, can say that I insulted them. And believe me when I say that my teammates never held back from using the choicest of abuses. They would talk down to me, swear at me, lobby against me constantly, spread wrong and hurtful rumours, and write terrible things against me. Their attitude was clear for all to see—who is this person and where has he sprung from? He is not one of us. I only responded with my bowling.

I had to struggle in that hostile environment for almost two years. My teammates did not talk to me. I was punished for my belief that Allah alone has the power to give anybody anything; it is not in the hands of mere human beings, *Insaan ke bus mein kuch nahin hai*. I always believed that Allah is the one you must ask for what you need. Respect human beings but know that they are not the givers. But my senior colleagues wanted me and others to ask them for favours. 'What can I ask of you?' I often queried. 'I do not get involved in petty intrigues or politics, or carry tales. Nor do I gamble my country's hopes away. I do not say things to hurt you, so what is your problem with me?' No answer. Has anyone ever heard or read that I engaged in politics within the team or conspired against anyone? Are there any rumours of my involvement in match fixing? Do you think that large and tempting offers did not come my way? There was a time when allegations of match fixing cast their shadow over the whole team with the single exception of myself. What was I collared with—being undisciplined! They didn't seem to require any other pretext to keep dropping me from the squad.

So I wasn't the least bit surprised at not being a part of the Pakistan team that went to play the Akai Singer Champions Trophy in Sharjah in 1997, a week after the West Indies series.

Once again I was forced to cool my heels while the Pakistan team went about playing their scheduled matches. In the meantime, things got rather ugly for Wasim Akram as allegations of his involvement in match fixing did the rounds in Sharjah. In fact, our whole team came under a cloud of suspicion and was quite demoralized. As a result of these allegations, Wasim was dropped for a while and did not go to South Africa for the Test series. I went instead. Aamir Sohail was given the captain's cap. He was a very positive, good-humoured man and almost immediately began to encourage me. I began to feel rather good about myself and the mood in the dressing room was definitely better, perhaps because our new captain was taking care of us for a change.

Mind you, we nearly didn't play the series. The night before the first Test match at Johannesburg, Mohammad Akram and Saqlain Mushtaq came back to the hotel crying that they had been mugged and beaten up. The next day the media splashed the news that Saqlain and Akram had been mugged. It was a stupid story that nearly jeopardized the tour. The truth was that Akram was unfit, so he enlisted the support of our good friend Saqlain and concocted the story—I gave Saqlain an earful afterwards. The incident resulted in an unnecessary delay of a whole day; the Test actually started on day two. I managed to get a wicket and the game ended in a tame draw.

The second Test match at Durban was perfect. It was the match in which I made my first major impact on the international scene by taking 5 for 43. I remember having to wait a long time to bowl. When the ball was finally tossed to me, it was shiny on one side and rough on the other. Naturally, it swung like crazy and I got my first five-wicket haul while giving away a mere forty-three runs. My speed and skill with the ball were immediately applauded and everyone acknowledged that it was a match-winning spell. It was Pakistan's first-ever Test win against South Africa and boy, did we celebrate! Suddenly the papers were talking about my speed and skill and saying that I was the reason we won. I began to be recognized wherever I went, and that in itself was a big high. Finally the world's attention was on me.

I always enjoy visiting South Africa. Not just because it's the country where my prowess in the game came to the fore but also because it is a beautiful place with friendly people who enjoy sport. And I must say that the crowd there is always rather distracting for the players. The most nudity you will ever see is at a South African cricket ground and the youngsters in our team end up turning their attention to the crowd when they should be keeping their eye on the ball. Unfortunately, the playing conditions in South Africa are not the best as far as I am concerned. Over the years I have realized that my muscles always hurt when I play there and so whenever I can, I run in the water on Cape Town's lovely beach and that helps.

But in 1998, it wasn't just about my aching muscles. I was actually a worried man when we left for Port Elizabeth for the third Test. My knees had always troubled me but I had thought that it was part of the customary wear and tear that a fast bowler had to live with. Without a professional trainer to guide me, I had no way of knowing that this was not normal, so I had continued playing without seeking proper medical help. Now my knees were swollen and hurting. I was advised to do something about them but once again, I had no idea what to do. Dan Kiesel, the team's physiotherapist, took one look at them—they had swollen up like balloons, were raw, and so painful that I could barely walk—and rushed me to a doctor who explained that there was an immense build-up of fluid that needed to be drained immediately. The doctor went on to stick a huge needle first in one knee and then the other, drawing out half a cup of fluid from each knee. The problem, he explained, was that my joints were hyper-extensive. This caused excessive friction between bones and led to the build-up of fluid.

I was to go through this painful procedure many times, usually before a match, and the pain would linger even though my mobility improved. I bowled in that third Test with sore knees and felt I couldn't give it my best.

Immediately after the South Africa tour, we were to play a series of ODI matches in Zimbabwe. What no one knew was that I was bowling with knees that kept threatening to give way. My left knee in particular was in a terrible state but I wanted to prove that I was good enough to play in this format as well. Dan Kiesel, however, had seen the state of my knees and warned me that I was in trouble if I didn't take care. But I begged him to let me play, I wanted that ODI debut. I wanted to wear the Pakistan colours. He gave in and got me to take some painkillers, and I was in the series. I had to negotiate one Test match at Bulawayo in which I took four wickets; I sat out the second Test. The memory I have of my ODI debut in Harare is of being in intense pain. I went out to bowl, managed to take a wicket, but after the fourth over, Dan's prediction came true—my left knee broke. I was declared unfit to play and sent home. I was in so much pain that I had to crawl to the bathroom and it would be six months before I played for my country again. I wasn't, however, going to sit around doing nothing.

Before I left for South Africa, a gentleman known to us as Dr Aslam had approached me with an offer to play for the Strabane Club in Ireland. This was something he had organized for several players, including Mohammad Wasim and Mohammad Akram. I liked the idea of playing league cricket so when I felt a bit better, I set off to join Strabane Club in Northern Ireland. Within a month of playing in Ireland, to my delight and relief, my knees improved without any medical attention whatsoever. Over the years I began to connect the state of my knees to the physical environment around me. The pain was unbearable when I bowled on the hard and dead pitches of the subcontinent. The hot and humid climate did nothing to improve the condition.

The four months that I stayed in Ireland not only healed my knees but exposed me to a very different culture than the one I had grown up in. Terence Patton ran Strabane Club and initially, I was the only foreigner playing for them. I guess I must have appeared young and lost, for Mr Patton invited me to stay with his family. I was made to feel very welcome by them, particularly by Mrs Patton, a warm and affectionate lady who introduced me to some fine Irish cooking and went to great lengths to make me feel comfortable in their home. She is a great cook, and served all kinds of different dishes—chicken, vegetables and puddings—that I was unfamiliar with. Thanks to her, I can now enjoy food from any country, including seafood. The Pattons have three sons and their second son Terence and I played cricket together at the club, so we started to hang out. I also remember making friends with another player called Michael Gillespie. Thus my days passed very pleasantly. We often went out together and I recall an occasion when we walked into a restaurant. I was dressed in my finest—white trousers, white shoes and a canary yellow shirt, the kind you need to shade your eyes to look at. But I thought I cut a fine figure, just like a Hindi film star—Govinda at the very least. In the restaurant I noticed a white girl looking at me and giggling. Ever hopeful, I thought she liked me and stood a little straighter, but then she began walking towards me and any knowledge I had of the English language flew out of my head. She stopped in front of me and said, 'How are you?'

'Good,' I answered.

'What you been up to,' she continued.

'Good,' I replied hopefully.

'Would you like to have a drink with me?' she asked.

Main kya, 'Good!'

'What would you like to drink?' she asked.

I pointed towards some orange juice and said, 'Good.'

She started giggling and asked, 'Do you know any other word in English?'

'Good,' I grimaced back.

She collapsed with laughter. We became very good friends, and today I am comfortable with the language because of her and the Patton family. My accent is, of course, a source of great amusement to folks around the globe who are unfamiliar with this unique blend of Irish-laced Punjabi English.

I went back to Pakistan to play in the home series against Australia and Zimbabwe and continued to pick up wickets. In those days, there were no contracts—the PCB started contracting players only in 2003. We used to be given Rs 8000 per Test. I proudly gave my first cheque to my mother and received her blessings. I was now able to earn my bread and it felt good.

One of the first things I did upon receiving my first pay-cheque was to rent a car, an Alto, because I felt awkward going around on a cycle after having played for my country. I had never sat behind a wheel before, so I didn't know how to drive. Using my instincts as a driving instructor, I had the basics under my belt within a week. Once, I was entertaining my friend Zaidi, showing off Islamabad to him, when suddenly I lost control and drove the rental up a high curb. The radiator was damaged and I was in a fix because I didn't have enough money to get it fixed. Somehow I got it patched up and quietly returned it to the shop.

By 1998, I had managed to save up enough to buy my first car, a white Suzuki Margella. I loved that car, she was my prized possession. It was so easy to move around now. My friends and I would zoom around town and marvel at how the city had shrunk. It sure hadn't felt this small when I had to walk or cycle to my destination. The Margella was the first car in my family, and I treasured it. After the World Cup in 1999, when I received close to six lakh rupees, I gave the Margella to my brothers and bought myself a Honda VTI that still stands in my garage.

At the end of that year, I felt that my family had begun to believe I could make it; my friends were as sure as ever that I would continue to rise and I had regained my belief in myself. I recall feeling that finally things had begun to look up. What I didn't know was that Allah was about to shower his mercy on me.

5

A Star Is Born: The Rawalpindi Express

In the first quarter of 1999, I was to tour India for the first time. There were two fixtures before us, a two-match Test series to be followed by the Asian Test Championship in which India, Sri Lanka and Pakistan were to participate. Our team was packed with young blood—Shahid Afridi, Saqlain Mushtaq, Azhar Mahmood, Abdul Razzaq and I, and we were all terribly excited. We knew how high the stakes were: A Pakistan-India cricket encounter is incomparable to any other. Yes, Australia and England have the Ashes but the subcontinent's history ensures that cricket assumes a much larger significance than perhaps it should. A successful team and successful players are treated like heroes for months after the victory. On the flip side, a loss at the hands of the other is considered nothing less than a national failure. The tremendous pressure this puts on both teams can make for an exciting game. For me, it's the best high in the world. The stadium is always packed with people who will cheer you on; you can feel their enthusiasm, and you can sense that they too have a stake in the game. In fact, India was the first place that *mujhe kuch apna sa laga*—where I felt somewhat at home. They love my talent, but hate losing to Pakistan, just as we hate losing to India. I am very passionate when I play for my country, so there is something special about playing in India.

I have discovered over the years that Indian cricket fans are warm and generous and know their cricket. As a result, I love playing and touring in India and apart from my fan following in Pakistan, I'll be honest with you, I have really been touched by the Indian crowd. They have huge cricket memories, which makes you feel you never really left after the last time you played there.

At the same time, playing in India, against India is a serious task. The crowds stand right behind their players. And the crowds that attend India-Pakistan matches are huge. As far as I am concerned, I forget everything and go out to win the game. Pakistan has often come out of these fixtures victorious and I think the reason is that we are the more aggressive side and gel together the best when we play India.

The first Test match at Chennai was a thriller. India needed 271 runs to win in the fourth innings and looked comfortable till Tendulkar got out when the score was 254. We then pulled off an amazing victory, winning the match by a mere twelve runs. I hadn't been played, so was a bit restless and anxious, but Afridi had held his own amongst the seniors and that was something to be cheerful about. Our excitement at snatching victory in Chennai was, however, quelled when Kumble ran through ten of us in Delhi. The consequences of losing to India are always severe and the blame game started. Waqar Younis had not done particularly well so far and was at loggerheads with Wasim Akram. Before the series began, it had taken the selectors a long time to decide who should lead the team and finally, Wasim was made captain. He had picked me for the tour but didn't play me in either of the Tests.

I was, of course, aware that getting into the team was not going to be easy because between Waqar and Wasim, there was no place for another seamer. Six or seven fast bowlers had tried to find a place in the team before me but had failed. Their careers were finished in the attempt, leaving them broken. When I reflect on why the others failed, I think it was because they didn't have the strength to battle on. Fortunately, there was an additional factor that led to the opening of the gates for me, as it were. In 1993 several team members, led by Waqar, had revolted against Wasim's reign, resulting in his temporary absence from the scene. When he came back as captain, he wanted revenge against Waqar, Asif Mujtaba and anyone else who had turned against him.

Wasim continued at the helm till 1999–2000 and the consequence of his revenge was that a few youngsters, including myself, got a chance to join the team. Saqlain was taken in and Asif Mujtaba was left out, Waqar was replaced by me. Mohammad Zahid got in, and a few others did too. At one stage, too many were dropped, but more about that later. When I saw an opportunity, I firmly decided I would push my way in and hang on.

Many of my teammates as well as some who did not play for Pakistan have called me a madman and an actor—a B-grade actor, according to Steve Waugh. They would even say that Shoaib is not training, he is just acting. But I always had a goal ahead of me and I made it. I wanted to play and win for Pakistan, and earn money while doing what I loved the most. As for madness, a little madness is necessary at times to reach your goal. And yes, you have to work hard. There are no shortcuts and you have to be mentally strong.

I had been selected for the India tour but, as I said before, I'was not played in the first two Tests. In fact, I was not even allowed to enter the dressing room. If I went inside, I was told by my seniors, *Tu andar kya kar raha hai? Bahar baith.* What are you doing here? Go, sit outside! Without taking any names, I can only say that these were my seniors and there was nothing I could do other than go out and start running and exercising.

Our dressing-room environment is undeniably tough for youngsters. You do all the right things and are polite, yet they make you suffer. Here we were on an important tour and I was in the team but not a part of it. I was treated so badly that I got seriously depressed. Then one day, Salim Malik walked up to me and said, 'Listen, you will get a chance to play in Kolkata, keep your spirits up.' Afridi had by this time already made a positive impression in India and gained a large fan following. But no one knew me and I was determined to change that.

Meanwhile, we lost the Delhi Test and Wasim got into an argument with Waqar. It got so bad that rumours started doing the rounds that Waqar was to be sent back home. But the entire squad left for Kolkata for the first Test of the championship. Inside the dressing room, things got uglier. I do not remember it ever being as tense as it was then. The two seniors were at war and we were a young and fresh team. Everyone was stressed out and amidst all this, it was decided that I would play.

Waqar always spoke softly and was known to be of a gentle temperament. I was very fond of him. Unfortunately, I was responsible for him losing his place in the team and I do not think he has ever reconciled himself to that. When he returned to the side as coach in 2010–11, he kept everyone abreast of his opinion about my fitness and ability as a player. But back then, Waqar was my idol, and there was no getting away from the fact that I was being played and he was being dropped. It was a very awkward position to be in. I went up to him and said, 'Sir, I am not of your calibre. *Aap ke pair ki juti ke barabar bhi nahin hoon.*' He quickly said, 'No, no, you go out and enjoy yourself and make sure you do well.' This was a huge tour with one hundred thousand spectators watching us at the ground and as many outside. The whole of India and Pakistan would be watching. But let's not talk about the atmosphere. Let's talk about the pressure.

I had a major attack of nerves and walked into the stadium on knocking knees and wobbly legs. I had to shake off the nerves and I did it the only way I knew how. The Indian batsmen were warming up, just knocking around with their bats. I walked up to Sachin Tendulkar and asked him, 'Do you know me?'

He looked up and said, 'No.'

I told him, 'You will, soon enough.'

I got him with the first ball he faced and later he said to me, 'I will remember you now.'

Some years later I asked Sachin if he remembered this incident but he said that he didn't. But look, that's me! I play the street hood, the big brother because it's the only way I know to boost my confidence. My legs were shaking but I knew that Sachin was the guy I had to snare. Actually I wanted all of them, that's how hungry I was.

Before the match started, I had a bet with Saqlain—he told me that he would get the much prized wicket of Sachin Tendulkar and I said, 'Nope, it's mine. You can't take it because it is my time now.'

He said, '*Really?*'

And I replied, '*Yes, really!*'

And the bet was on. I remember I kept waiting anxiously for the ball to be thrown my way. When it finally came to me, I knew it would swing on command. I got V.V.S. Laxman's wicket and my nerves began to steady. My next victim was Rahul Dravid, who had built up a fierce reputation over the years as a man who didn't like giving up his wicket to anyone. He and I had had a few words on the field—I do play a very aggressive game, it's not personal—and I guess he was carrying the memory, for he was pretty nettled. One of my deliveries swung like a banana and off went his bails. Then Sachin walked in and the stadium erupted. I have never heard such a high level of noise. I recall thinking, *Yeh kaun aa raha hai, bhai*—Who is this walking in? Saqlain dug me in the ribs and said, '*Woh dekh, aa raha hai prize wicket!*' Look, here comes the prize wicket.

I nodded and waited for him to settle down. I looked up and prayed, 'Boss, I need this one! I need to get him out with my first delivery.' I remember this prayer distinctly. And then I ran as fast as I could and heaved the ball at him. He played his stroke rather casually and missed the ball by a mile. The prize wicket was mine! I fell to the ground in *sajda* saying, 'Thank you, Boss! Thank you!'

I had really swung the one that got Sachin's wicket but

in my opinion, the one that I bowled to Dravid was a better delivery. Eden Gardens had gone quiet when Dravid got out, and when Sachin followed, you could have heard a pin drop. But when I finished the over, I received a standing ovation from the spectators and I felt my heart swell with gratitude.

I must add here that there is a history behind these two balls as well. Wasim had done something similar in the World Cup and I had wanted to do the same; I had a point to make. Those two wickets of Dravid and Tendulkar turned the match right around in our favour. Had they formed a partnership, we would have lost. I now knew that I had the capacity to be a match winner and this really boosted my game further. I took eight wickets in that Test match.

I was also involved in getting Sachin run out in the second innings of the same match. He struck the ball and it raced towards the boundary. I had my back to him and was concentrating on the return throw. I didn't know he was behind me and somehow he got entangled between my legs. The throw was a scorcher that came in right from the boundary and was a direct hit. Yet again, I was involved in a controversy as the crowd felt I had deliberately obstructed Sachin. This was absolutely untrue. I didn't see him and it wasn't deliberate, but they went berserk with anger and set the stadium on fire. We went off the field in a hurry, not knowing what would happen next.

The stadium had to be cleared before the match could continue and we ended up victorious. I had never known such elation amongst us before. There was a club in the hotel where we were staying and the whole team went clubbing and danced the night away, delirious with joy. We came back to our rooms at six in the morning, we were so happy. My performance in

India was sweetened later when we defeated Sri Lanka in Dhaka and won the championship.

A month later, we were back in India for the Pepsi Cup to be played by India, Pakistan and Sri Lanka and we won the finals against India. At that time we were rated one of the best, if not the best side in the world. The Indian team was unable to hold us off and we smashed them easily. I remember that our side was very bored because there was hardly a challenge to meet. The Indians were certainly not as aggressive as we were. In fact, I have yet to see any Indian batsman except Virender Sehwag playing aggressively against me. I do enjoy watching Sachin, Sehwag and Dhoni bat. Dhoni is one of the nicest and smartest people I have met but, on the whole, I get bored if there is no aggression on the field. It's the same while playing against England: cool temperaments and a cold game. That's why I enjoy playing against Australia. They play an 'in your face' game that I relish. I feel truly challenged. It keeps me charged and interested in the game.

This aggression and desire to dominate are natural to Punjab. There is more frustration to contend with here, and the result can be seen in our manner, our faces. I believe that our battle is not with any outsider. I am not fighting the opposition, I'm fighting against all that has built up inside me, all that frustration—he is not good enough for the game, he is not fit, he is not disciplined, he is not good for us. I have all this to battle against. I have played with a team that knew no fear. I have bowled out the finest batsmen from India, Australia, England and the rest, with aggression. And I am aware that this aggression on the field is what, strangely enough, draws my fans to me.

I also think my bowling abilities made Indian fans a bit nervous—their team had to survive my bowling spells and they watched with trepidation, and yet they loved me. It's amazing! Perhaps it is because I have a passion for the game that they recognize and empathize with. When I run in, I feel that the whole country runs in with me. I received a standing ovation from the crowd when I knocked out Sachin and Dravid in Kolkata with two successive balls. And I felt the same love when I went out to play for the Kolkata Knight Riders. I could feel them respond to my positive energy.

After our Eden Gardens victory, when we went back to Pakistan, I could not have imagined the way in which I would be greeted. I knew I had been instrumental in our victory but it was the team that had won. I stepped out of the plane and the crowd literally picked me up and carried me to our coach. I reached Lahore to find that it had virtually shut down and people were lined up along the streets that we were to pass by. Fans followed in their cars like a convoy.

I knew that I had played a part in our victory, but I didn't realize how those two wickets would make me so important in everyone's eyes. I was a star and became the most wanted cricketer for the media as well. When I went for interviews, I was mobbed, and at times it took me hours to reach my destination. Advertisements followed. I was able to complete work on our house in Dhoke Nawaz. It was raining money. I had, however, a promise to fulfil. The very first night I got back to Pakistan, I put on a disguise—a false beard and dark glasses—and left the house. I first went to Daata Sahab, a revered shrine in Lahore, to offer thanks for the benevolence shown to me. Then I headed towards the railway station to look for Aziz Khan, the tongawalla who had given me shelter six years ago when I was trying to get into the PIA team. It took me quite a while to search him out but my perseverance paid off. I found him sleeping in one corner of the street. He was startled to be woken up and looked up at me with bleary eyes. When they focused, I said, 'Main kya si ki main aavanga—I told you I would come back to see you when I was a member of the Pakistan team.'

He jumped right into my arms like a kid and hugged me, murmuring blessings. For a long time he just kept repeating that he couldn't believe it was me. After a while we went to a nearby tea stall and had tea. All the while, he kept marvelling at Allah's grace saying, 'I can't believe it has happened. Miracles do happen. Miracles appear in the world just like that and you are one of the miracles.' He said he found it surreal that a person who had slept alongside him on the footpath was now a beloved celebrity. We raised a toast to each other on the streets of Lahore.

By now the crowd knew I was there and the station virtually shut down. He pointed at them and said, 'Look how many people recognize you and are dying to take you to their homes now.'

I said, 'Yes, but you were the one who gave me shelter when I was unknown, so I recognize you alone and am here to meet only you.'

I kept trying to push some money into his pocket but he wouldn't let me. Aziz Khan was a poor man in the eyes of the world, but to me he was rich with self-respect and dignity. Later that night, once again we shared a meal and he refused to take money for it. He said, 'Us din bhi maine tujhe khana *khilaya tha, aaj bhi main hi khilaunga. Us din bhi tu mere liye Shoaib tha, aur mein chahata hoon ki tu hamesha Shoaib hi rahe, kabhi bhi na badalna.'* To me, you will always be that Shoaib I met years ago, don't ever change.

He asked me if I would ride in his tonga and I said, 'Of course!' So we took the same route we had taken six years ago when I was trying to enter PIA. At the end of the ride, I saw tears of joy in his eyes. Aziz Khan and I kept in touch after that day, until he passed away four years ago.

Another old friend is Rashid at Imperial Saloon. Ever since my college days, I have gone to him for a hair cut. He works out of a barber's shop at Sadar Bazaar in Pindi. It's a small shop but everyone there is always happy to see me and more importantly, they don't treat me like a star—just a favoured customer. It's a nice feeling to know that there exist people who wish you well because they care for you and not because you are a celebrity. Therefore I often go back to Pindi and visit my old haunts. These places and the people there are my support base. I follow a set routine, beginning with a walk down the road, a little ahead of the barbershop, and visit a vendor there, who since my college days has given me a glass of sugarcane and cheeku juice. He used to tell me that he was investing in my health and knew that it would come in good use. After downing the juice, I take a round of the city that I grew up in.

There was a beggar that I used to pass by daily. Initially we greeted each other as I passed him by on the way to college or to Pindi Club. Then we started asking each other how the day had been, and finally we became friends and have been so for the last eighteen years. So he is the next person I visit. I remember he would sing to me and would motivate and encourage me in my pursuit of my goal. Everyone called him 'Yaarji', and I still don't know his name. Sometimes, when I was in a pensive mood, I used to sit next to him on the footpath. He would continue to beg and I would just sit quietly and listen to him. I am fond of him and am concerned about his health. Strangely, he won't take any financial assistance from me, though sometimes I send some money to his family without his knowledge.

After leaving Yaarji's corner, I go to the club. Pindi Club holds a very special place in my heart, for that's where it all began. I honed my skills on its grounds and made lasting friendships there. At least three of my good friends found their way into the Pakistani side—Azhar Mahmood, Mohammad Akram and Saqlain Mushtaq—and we faced some tough times together while trying to find a place in the team.

I also like to roam around in the Pabrah and Kashmiri bazaars, ending with a visit to my friend Zaidi. Below his house are two eateries. Sheikh sahab's samosas are delicious and never to be missed. And the moment Saada Ali sees me, he makes a huge glass of his famous *dudha* (milk) soda for me, which I drink sitting on top of the fridge, like I did when I was in college. The next thing on my agenda is to meet up with my college friends. There is a huge picture of mine in the college assembly for all to see. They are very proud of me. There are still some professors there who taught me. Koda sir is around too, and once when we met, we laughed about the cracker incident. He told me, 'Shoaib, yaar, eighteen years back you nearly killed me. I'm a heart patient, you know.'

I normally end the evening by visiting my mohalla where I am warmly welcomed by all. I know the young girls of my mohalla are intrigued by me. Very often I visit my school, usually late at night so that nobody knows I'm there. Jumping the locked gate has never been a problem for me. I get very nostalgic as I walk from classroom to classroom. Then I sit on the old, familiar rock and start reminiscing about all that has happened to me and about my future. That mound is almost in the middle of the road but nobody moves it because the locals know what it means to me. They have actually encircled it with a railing and affectionately call it 'Shoaib's thinking rock'.

All these guys who knew me in my struggling days don't seem to want anything from me. They just feel happy to be acknowledged; it's humbling. One of the reasons I look back with affection upon my years in college is that in those days, I did what I liked—playing and eating—and there was no pressure. Today, whenever I pass by the college, I eat dahi chana from Arif—yes, he is the same guy who used to feed me for free. He has done very well for himself and now owns a large eatery. Incidentally, all these friends drop in at my home whenever they come to Lahore and have quite a lot to say about all the problems I have had to face. I relish their criticism for it is for my own good, and their accolades mean a great deal to me. Looking back, I realize that I was pampered by all of them. And that includes my tongawalla, who would ensure, at my request naturally, that he picked up at least three female passengers before taking me on board—*maine saare apne liye set kiye hue the*. I think they liked me because I was approachable and friendly, and used to joke and tease them.

Years later, when I was given the title Rawalpindi Express, I felt honoured. I truly believe that all of these friends from my youth taught me a lot about life, they were my murshid.

In April 1999, I continued my winning streak in Sharjah at the three-nation Coca Cola Cup that featured Pakistan, India and England. I got eleven wickets in five matches and was declared the Man of the Series, for which I won an Opel car. It was only after this string of successes that the management acknowledged that I had a career ahead of me.

1999. The World Cup was here. I flew into England feeling very positive. I was peaking, my form was good and I remember telling my teammates that this tournament would belong to me. They must have put it down to my arrogance but I know that it was confidence and self-belief. I have been given speed and smartness as a gift from Allah. I am not just a fast bowler; I am a very smart bowler. I use my brains and therefore I don't give runs easily.

When my teammates mockingly asked me how it would be my tournament, I told them that the very first ball that I bowled would be of such speed that the world would say the fastest bowler in the history of cricket had arrived. As usual, their response was a derisive, 'Really?' Yes, really!

My very first ball in our first match versus West Indies at Bristol had Campbell hopping and fending it off. He merely touched the ball and it flew over the wicketkeeper's head and out of the stadium. Campbell is a good friend of mine and he looked at me, bewildered. I said to him, 'Friend, you are in trouble.' They all were. I was on fire, performing in every match and bowling really quick. Before this, everybody hailed Alan Donald as the quickest. He was a great fast bowler and a great ambassador for the game. There were no two opinions in our dressing room about him—he was really good. But now everyone was talking about my pace as well and then Tony Greig named me 'Rawalpindi Express'.

For the first time, at this World Cup, the speed gun was officially used. I crossed 97 mph, 98 mph and then 99 mph. It was a dream run. I had a haul of sixteen wickets. There was excitement all around me. As a team we were doing well and our bowlers were doing us proud. Wasim had taken fifteen wickets, Saqlain had taken seventeen, Azhar and Razzaq had thirteen each. But it was my speed and flair that caught everyone's imagination. Fans followed us in caravan lines.

And there were girls everywhere. I was the star performer, so you can imagine how many of them crowded around me. They would follow us on the motorway and crowd the hotels we were staying in, yelling out my name almost without a break. Ooof! I just loved all the attention but I had begun to dream of taking the World Cup back to Pakistan. So I was really focused and kept to my room. That was a good decision because there were girls lining up in unending queues outside my door. I don't remember a single day during this World Cup when there were less than a hundred girls standing outside the hotel, especially in Manchester and Birmingham. If I had walked out of my room, I doubt I could have got back in. I was being hounded so aggressively that I had to keep my door locked all the time. The noise outside was so distracting that I used to take sleeping pills to go to sleep so that I could be well rested in the morning.

It was the perfect summer. The sobriquet Rawalpindi Express caught everyone's imagination and Pakistan won all the important matches that led us to the finals. I was one of the leading wicket takers and the media had begun to acknowledge that the tournament was mine. The night before the final, I lay in bed thinking about the next morning. I imagined the sheer ecstasy of winning, I imagined the winning lap—I couldn't stop thinking of victory and how much joy it would bring me. What happened the next day was a downer, to say the least.

Things went horribly wrong right from the start. Wasim won the toss and chose to bat. Bowling second was a rather ignorant decision. We should have studied the wicket more carefully and chosen to bowl first. Pakistan's batting is known to collapse, and it did—we were all out for 132. A pitiable score that was very difficult to defend because we needed about 200 to 230 runs on the board to keep the Australians at bay.

The loss was devastating and we came back to the dressing room a deeply dejected lot. It was so quiet *ke hamare saanso ki awaz aa rahee thhi ek doosre ko*—we could hear each other breathe. Most of us were in tears and emotions were running high.

I was heartbroken. We had missed the opportunity, and my dream of bringing the World Cup home had come to nothing. I couldn't breathe. To lose the final match after playing so well throughout the tournament was nearly too much to bear for me and the other junior players. You win and you lose, that's the nature of the game, but at that moment, losing the World Cup was like the end of the world. I remember thinking, What went wrong? This shouldn't have happened. Why did this happen?

Nobody felt like leaving the dressing room. *Kis moonh se bahar jayen?* We felt that we had let Pakistan down. We had collapsed for 132 runs—if we had got some decent runs, we would have been seen to have gone down fighting but our batting performance was shameful. We had started the tournament with a bang and went out with a whimper. We just stayed indoors and nobody came in to call us out either. I guess they all knew how hard we had taken it. It was one of the worst days of my life.

Back home, we were greeted by the news that a new accountability cell had been set up to debate the World Cup defeat. It was said to have come into being at the behest of Prime Minister Nawaz Sharif. This is the usual pattern of behaviour in Pakistan. If we lose, almost every official makes it his personal duty to insult and run down the team. They hauled up Wasim Akram and Ijaz Ahmed and treated them like shit, keeping them waiting outside their office for four to five hours, before interrogating them. They wanted to find out why we had lost and whether there was any possibility of match-fixing.

Then, all of a sudden, the cell wanted me in as well. One day, out of the blue, they called and asked me to appear before them—I, who had played my heart out. When I asked them what I had done, they answered, 'You were undisciplined, that is why we lost the World Cup.' Can you believe that? They called me three or four times but I told them to buzz off. I said, 'I'm not coming, do whatever you want to do.' So they sent me an official letter which stated that this was a national matter and therefore I could not refuse. My family was rather bewildered but Shahid bhaijaan advised me to go, so I finally did. It was to be the beginning of many such encounters, all of them ridiculous in nature and content.

I sat before the panel and they accused me of not concentrating on the game. They said they knew for a fact that

I had been out partying with girls the night before the final game. I said, prove it. They had no proof but kept pressing for a 'confession'. I was livid and also very hurt because I had given it everything I had. It was bad enough not to have won, this was unacceptable. I asked them who the hell they were to ask such questions and was told that they were the Pakistan National Cricket Accountability Cell and that I had to answer all the questions put to me. So I tried reasoning and said that winning and losing is all part of the game—we lost, it happens. The stuffed shirts said, No, that's not it. You were looking tired on the morning of the big match; therefore you were out the night before. I responded, If this is true, the manager should be held responsible. And in any case, where is the proof? Show me the videos.

Then they switched tracks and told me that I had to be careful as the prime minister himself was angry with me. I said, angry for what? What wrong have I done? They kept saying that I was partying with girls. They kept trying to pin something on me that had nothing to do with cricket. What puzzled me was, where had they heard all these rumours? Later, I came to know that this ridiculous information had come from one of my own teammates. Some of the boys told me that Wasim had been talking about me, saying that I was out partying with girls instead of concentrating on the upcoming final. I promptly confronted Wasim, but he denied having said anything about me to the panel so the truth continues to be elusive, regardless of my suspicions. The panel finally gave up and let me go, with a warning that I might have to go back if any new findings turned up. I lost my patience then and told them I wouldn't—I had come in once and that was quite enough. That didn't go down well with them and they said I would have to face the consequences. Disgusted at the pettiness of it all, I told them not to waste my time with threats and go ahead and do whatever they wanted. Then I got up and left.

The year had begun with such promise, it ended on such a sour note. My entire career has followed this pattern of highs and lows. Success was often rewarded with some sort of disciplinary action. I never got used to it and probably never will understand why it had to be thus. In this case, for instance, I had done my very best, played with all my passion and integrity, for I was playing for my country. The world had sat up and noticed my abilities, and I had scalped some of the best batsmen in the world. What more did I have to do to make my own teammates and my board believe that I was serious about my game? I was a match winner and had consistently got results for my team. My private life was surely my own business. I didn't poke my nose into other people's affairs. Nor did I indulge in petty politics. And everybody else in the cricketing world acknowledged my worth. Nottinghamshire had offered me a county contract worth a fair bit of money, in fact, the highest they had ever offered to any cricketer. They had been particularly impressed by my bowling spell in the semifinals at Old Trafford, Manchester, where I had bagged three wickets for fifty-five runs. But at home, all I faced was inquiries!

6

Highs and Lows

My experience with the accountability cell had left a bad taste in my mouth but it hadn't taken away the sense of achievement, the feeling of success that I carried within me. It had been a terrific year and I was looking forward to going to Australia towards the end of 1999 to play a three-Test series, which was to be followed by ODIs. My bowling form was excellent and I was surprising myself. I kept taking wickets and was causing a buzz in Australia. When I walked in a little after the rest of the team, the crowd would roar out my name or welcome me as the Rawalpindi Express. I was enjoying my fame immensely. It was crazy—the crowds, the media, the women. They would ignore the rest of the team and make a beeline for me. It was a dizzying experience and I must say there were ample opportunities for me to spin out of control.

I did have a great time. And rather obviously, my colleagues did not like this very much. I could hear some of them mutter, this newcomer, *kal ka bachcha*, has taken away the limelight, all the money from sponsorships and endorsements.

Many years ago, when I was just a teenager, my murshid

sahab and I were travelling together when our car broke down in the middle of nowhere. We got out of the car and he told me to sit beside him on the roadside. I settled down next to him and together, we sat gazing up at the stars. After a while, he told me that someday in the future, he would still be sitting there but I would rise and shine like the stars. He foretold my success, but he also told me that I should never lose sight of the ground. Perhaps it's because of him that despite all the attention that I suddenly got, I managed to stay on my path.

The first two matches at Brisbane and Hobart had gone by with me riding on a high. Then a controversy arose at Perth during the third Test when umpires Darrell Hair and Peter Willey questioned my bowling action. John Reid, the match referee, agreed with them and they lodged an official complaint with the ICC. When we came back to Pakistan after the series, there was a cloud hanging over my head.

Towards the end of December, we went back to Perth for the three-nation series between Pakistan, Australia and India that was to be held later in January–February. We were to play some warm-up matches in Perth, Adelaide and Brisbane.

During the first warm-up match, a teleconference took place between the ICC and the PCB and a ban was imposed on me. They called a press conference and announced to the world that my bowling action was suspect and that I couldn't play any more. Thus began the darkest phase of my career. The first two years of the millennium were to be overshadowed by chucking allegations that left me in a state of shock. I had been bowling with this action for the last four years, why was it being questioned now?

The chairman of the PCB, Lt. Gen. Tauqir Zia, instructed

me to stay behind and await his call, so when the team left Perth and headed off to Adelaide to continue with the series, I was alone, miserable, and convinced that my career was over. I didn't leave my room for seven days and seven nights. In a state of abject depression, I called up some friends in England and asked them to help me find a job there as my career as a cricketer was finished, and had ended in such shame. When I did walk out of my room, the media hounded me with questions I had no answers to. I didn't know how to defend myself. What was to become of my career, was their favourite query and I remember replying defiantly that I would return with a bang, but for once, I wasn't convinced myself.

In the meantime, I started training with Daryl Foster and his team of experts at the biomechanics department of the University of Western Australia. Daryl is a great guy and was a terrific support to me during this very trying time. He did his best to help me get out of my depression while concentrating on trying to correct my bowling action. The experts at the institute studied my bowling action carefully and asked me to straighten my elbow. I couldn't, because the inverse bend at the elbow is natural, I was born with it. On top of that, my elbow had too much elasticity. I confess I wasn't very enthusiastic about what was happening around me, for all I could think of was that I was finished and somehow I didn't think anything or anybody could help me.

This was the state that I was to be in for the next fortnight or so when suddenly, one evening, I got a call from my manager to pack my bags immediately. I was to catch a connecting flight for Adelaide from Perth that was scheduled to leave in two hours and was to rejoin the team at Brisbane and play the match the following morning. I couldn't believe my ears and asked him to repeat what he had said. He patiently told me that the ban against me had been lifted; I wasn't allowed to throw bouncers but could go ahead and play. I recall falling to my knees in prayer and saying, *Ya Allah, yeh kya?*

Much later, I got to know that Lt. Gen. Tauqir Zia had excellent relations with Jagmohan Dalmiya, who was the president of the ICC at the time. He must have requested Mr Dalmiya to lift the ban, which he did. The bowling panel comprising Michael Holding and others observed that while bowling a short-pitched delivery my arm bent extensively, so I was not allowed to bowl short deliveries, but I could play. With one ruling, I got back everything that I had worked so hard for.

The immediate problem that loomed in front of me was how to get to Brisbane from Perth, and then to the match on time. I had been rushed to the airport but was still mid-air as the time for the start of play drew near. On landing, I was quite surprised to find several people there to see me through the formalities. They even sent me through special protocol, only because a delay would affect the match. That's why I have so much respect for Australians—they love sports and sports people.

The feeling of amazement continued as I walked out of the airport and found myself being cheered on by people, and even the media. When I walked on to the ground, the crowd stood up and greeted me, giving me a thunderous welcome. They seemed so happy to see me back, and their enthusiasm and affection infused a sense of belonging in me. I immediately wanted to return their kindness by playing my heart out for them. I got Steve Waugh lbw with the first ball—he went back without any runs on the board—and I received a standing ovation from the crowd.

I will never forget the spectators who came to see that match. They seemed to respect my courage in coming out to play after such a traumatic experience. The only way in which I could return their love was by playing well and taking wickets; I took sixteen wickets in all. The ruling against my action had killed my desire to play, but the support of the Australian people resurrected me. Thousands of letters poured in as fan mail, each saying, 'Don't you worry! We are with you'. They were even planning a walk along Sydney Harbour for me, the message being, you've got to get this guy back into cricket, cricket needs him. Wherever I went, I saw a sea of fans shouting words of encouragement and support. They were everywhere, even outside my room—men, women and kids. Because of their love and Lt. Gen. Zia's faith in me, I felt motivated to play cricket again.

I am truly thankful to all my fans across the globe who stood by me, backed me and inspired me to play the game once again. I was touched because I had never received this kind of attention from my teammates—with the exception of a very few—and certainly not from my seniors. It is no wonder that wherever we went, I sought out and found friends outside the team, and made sure I spent as much time as I could with them. As a result, I have wonderful friends on every continent.

Another incident occurred after the second match in Brisbane that drew everyone's attention to me. As we were getting into our coach, I noticed two children, a boy and a girl, running towards us, unmindful of the traffic. The boy was racing ahead and I saw that he was going to be hit by a taxi, so I dived towards him, grabbed him and rolled out of the way. The traffic came to a screeching halt. The media was there and saw it all. The next morning, I was all over the news—I was given epithets like 'superman' and 'son of Australia'. I was surprised at this fervour. I mean, almost anyone from my part of the world would have acted in the same way, without thinking twice. Kids are always playing on the streets or wandering about and as we pass them, we keep warning them of the danger. *Oye! Idhar ho jaayein kanjara, thhale naa aaeen*—Get to one side of the road, young one. Don't get run over. Besides, I am a bit more careful because when I was a child, my classmate Amjad had been run over by a car and died on the spot. I remember being saddened by the news at first, but when I went to his funeral, I felt terrified—a sense of my own mortality hit me. It was my first encounter with death and I couldn't sleep for three nights.

Back in Brisbane, I had scraped my elbow rather badly and hurt my knees in the process of saving the little boy, but thank goodness he was unhurt. His parents grabbed him and hurried off. I recall saying jokingly that I was bleeding and the kid didn't even say thank you. Now, that got picked up! Honestly, I wasn't serious, but the media was quick to hype it up. We left for Perth, but they were still talking about it. Can you imagine, the kids had gone back to Melbourne, and they had them flown in to thank me! I was so embarrassed. When I met the boy again, I hugged him and gave him my shirt, and we had lunch together.

Immediately after the Australia tour, Sri Lanka visited Pakistan to play a set of ODIs and a three-Test series. I was serving a one-match ban for violating curfew hours in Sydney so I missed the first and played the second ODI only. I wasn't all that fit but wasn't going to tell anyone about it and so managed to play in some of the games. Perhaps I should have rested but I was determined to go with the team to Sharjah in March for the three-nation Coca Cola Cup in which we were to play India and South Africa.

Once again, my bowling made a difference to the side. I took three wickets and turned a losing match around. But, in the process, I developed a rather painful groin injury that I ignored and continued playing with. An immature decision, as it turned out, because I ended up damaging my groin severely. Imran Khan was in Sharjah as a commentator and was very concerned about me. He knew Pakistan would be touring the West Indies in April and he said to me, 'Shoaib, please don't go for the West Indies tour.' Imran suggested that I should instead spend a season playing county cricket in England as it would be beneficial for my health and would also improve my bowling.

Javed Miandad was our coach and he said, 'No, I'll take him on the tour. I'll get medical attention for him and take care of him.' Because I was very young and enthusiastic and wanted to play every game that came my way, I listened to Miandad—a big mistake!

I was left unsupervised on those islands that had so many beautiful beaches. Nobody advised me to take care and instead of nursing myself back to health, I went ahead and had a great time running on the beaches, jet skiing and parasailing. Pain or no pain, I was hellbent on having a good time. I loved wandering around with the friendly West Indians. I loved their sense of humour. On one occasion, my friend Rich and I booked a car at the hotel and went out to eat. Rich is a journalist from Britain whom I first met in Sharjah and affectionately call Ritchie. He is a gregarious guy and, within minutes, struck up a conversation with the driver. The driver mentioned that he followed cricket, so Ritchie asked his opinion on the current West Indies versus Pakistan series. The driver got a bit agitated and started criticizing me, saying, 'Why isn't Shoaib playing? I bought tickets to watch him play and he isn't.' I couldn't resist asking him what he thought of my bowling, to which he replied, 'He is very quick, man, very quick, but he doesn't play cricket!' Ritchie said that perhaps the reason could be that Shoaib was injured. This didn't cut ice with the driver, who nearly yelled, 'What injury? He's fine and just bullshitting!' He continued in this vein right up to our destination. When we got off, I went up to him and said, 'Thank you very much. I am Shoaib.' His jaw dropped for a second and then he jumped out of the cab, laughing, and gave me a hug. I was laughing as well and then I said, you have had your say about me, now show me some Caribbean dance moves, and he did.

It was a fun-packed month and a half before they decided to play me in the last and crucial match at Trinidad. Miandad and Moin Khan dropped Waqar and put me in without making sure I was fit enough. I bowled beautifully, got three wickets and helped us win but while doing so, I broke my rib in three places, so they just spat me out and left me to my own devices. You might say this was entirely my fault and that I should have had the sense to rest. I would agree with you to some extent. But it is my contention that if a youngster is not guided properly, he will make mistakes. For Imran Khan I was a main strike bowler for Pakistan, his country, so he advised me to stay away from the tour. For Miandad, I suppose I was a mere instrument to achieve glory. He was our coach and it was his duty to take care of his team, especially a player who was carrying an injury. There is absolutely no doubt that Miandad was a great batsman but I think as a coach he left much to be desired. In fact, he has been our coach three times and has been sacked three times. He never guided any of us, never cared for anyone. Surely some responsibility for my condition should fall on his shoulders as well?

The truth is that a similar callousness resided within almost all the senior players in our team. Waqar Younis had been dropped for the last game and was very upset, and as usual he let everybody know. Now that he has become a coach for Pakistan, he talks about team discipline and manners as if he was the epitome of it all.

I have seen that whenever a senior cricketer becomes the coach, he talks about discipline *jaise unhon ne ise ijaad kiya hai*—as if he invented it. In fact, I can vouch for the fact that most of them were never even in their hotel rooms the night before a game, all through their playing days. I won't talk about what they did, what they drank, but none of them taught us juniors by example how to play cricket in the spirit of the game or how to behave on tour.

I wish I had played under Imran Khan and that he had been around to guide us as youngsters. He was the last man who cared about the game, about the Pakistan team. Our seniors set the example of going out, having a good time—girls were always coming and going out of their rooms. This was the prevailing culture in the Pakistan team. This is what we saw and learned. But when one of the seniors became our coach, he preached what he never practised in his own time. I know people who were drunk and came out to play. This is a fact. And now they call me undisciplined—it's unbelievable!

I wish now that I had never listened to Javed Miandad. I should have gone back home, trained, and then gone to England for the county season. That would have helped me become a better bowler. Towards the end of 1999, Nottinghamshire had invited me to play for them and had I joined them, I would have been the highest paid cricketer of the season. But I lost the contract because I didn't recover from my rib injury in time. I also lost an opportunity to play for Somerset. When I did get better, I tried but couldn't get another contract. In my eagerness to play everything, I had become injured and on recovery, there was no berth for me anywhere. I hung around doing nothing for months. I desperately needed to get back to some form of fitness and that was when Dr Tauseef Razzaq entered my life and for this, too, I have to thank Lt. Gen. Zia. These are two men to whom I owe half my career.

Initially I thought Tauseef was a bit of a nerd and he thought the same about me. Both of us are Gujjars, very aggressive people who don't have it in our genes to back down. But very soon, our opinion about each other changed and I now love him like a brother. He took me in hand and started my training with the object of getting me back in shape. The first two weeks, he had me exercising in water, and then we began working in the gym. I had never had this kind of training before and very soon my knees and shoulders gained strength and to my amazement, I started feeling better. There wasn't enough time for me to lose weight but I trained hard with him and after almost a year, I was selected for the New Zealand tour in February 2001. Tauseef had built me up and I was feeling so good that in my first match I got 5 for 19 and was declared the Man of the Match.

Immediately after the game, however, I began to feel that there was a problem with my hamstring. I needed to be rested for a game but once again our coach was Miandad, just my luck! He insisted that I play despite my telling him that I was unfit. When I dug my heels in, we got into an argument. Finally he said that he needed me and that he had spoken to Lt. Gen. Zia about it, so I had to agree. It was the final ODI match at Eden and I had managed to bowl one and a half overs when my hamstring seemed to snap.

I had worked very hard to get back into the team but the rest of the year was to be an agonizing one. I was sent back home after the match, not because I was injured but because I had come under another cloud of controversy, thanks to Stephen Fleming, the captain of the New Zealand team at that time. He had complained about my bowling action to the umpires and Doug Cowie, the match referee, called me for chucking. Moin Khan made an attempt to prevent him from doing so, but to no avail. I had gone to New Zealand with happiness in my heart and played really well, but returned home carrying an injury and worst of all, once again under the immense pressure of having my bowling action questioned.

This time, I was really stuck. There was no way out of the mess. I landed in Pakistan with Tauseef Razzaq, who had been thinking about how to get rid of the problem once and for all, but I could see no solution to it. I had been saved in 2000 but how could I be saved in 2001? I knew I had to face Lt. Gen. Zia, who was Corps Commander Mangala and a very powerful man. The Lt. Gen. had known me since the days I played at Rawalpindi Club, much before I entered the national side. He was very fond of me, had invested a great deal of his time in my career, and had looked after me. He had wanted me to win this series for Pakistan. Instead, I had returned unfit and facing charges. He wasn't happy with me at all. But I had to meet him.

I have vivid memories of the long drive from Lahore to Mangala. Tauseef was with me, of course. My friend Asad Bukhari also came along for moral support as I was horribly nervous. Lt. Gen. Zia had backed my selection but instead of winning games for him, I had been sent home under a cloud. I knew I was going to face a very frustrated man. The drive seemed unbearably long, giving me ample time to morosely mull over what was to become of me. I had full faith that Lt. Gen. Zia wouldn't let me down but I knew he was facing a lot of criticism for backing me and that I had disappointed him, and I hated that feeling.

We drove through the huge security lines at Mangala and the moment I walked into his presence, I could see that he was really cheesed off, and that's putting it mildly. He shouted at me for what must have been half an hour, barely pausing to draw breath. I guess he needed to let out his frustration. When he calmed down a bit, he looked around and said, 'Okay, what is the solution? How do we get him out of this one?' O, *main kya*, thank goodness! My first thought was that he hadn't forsaken me.

Then Tauseef took over and calmed him down. He had done his research. Tauseef said, 'Sir, this is the way out for

Shoaib. He has hyper-extensive joints that do not allow him to straighten his arm.' I quickly showed my arm to Lt. Gen. Zia and he understood what was being said. Tauseef continued to explain that Muttiah Muralitharan too had double jointed wrists and he'd had to face similar allegations, so there was Murali's precedent for us to follow. Tauseef had already asked around and found out who had handled Murali's report and who his physician was. Lt. Gen. Zia agreed that this was the best way forward. The first step was to check into the School of Human Movement and Exercise Science at the University of Western Australia in Perth. He nodded encouragingly at me and I went back to Lahore in a better frame of mind.

Next day, I presented myself before the PCB and asked them to help me with all the formalities, but nobody was interested. One of the officials actually said, 'No, you are a chucker—a word that makes my blood boil. Your action can't be corrected, so don't waste our time.' Then they suggested that I should stop playing cricket. This is what the guys on the Pakistan Cricket Board are like! They kept delaying my getting on that flight to Perth by not booking my tickets and not making any arrangements. Finally Tauseef called up Lt. Gen. Zia and said, 'They are not ready to follow your orders, sir, and aren't doing anything for Shoaib.' Lt. Gen. Zia then took over. He blasted the officials and abused them like hell. The result was that when I walked in the next day and asked if my ticket was ready, they said, 'Yes, sir, it is'.

I then set off to catch the flight to Perth. In the air I was again bogged down with doubts, but Tauseef was dead sure I would come out of it—he had studied all the cases, spoken to all the doctors in Perth. I checked into the Human Movement

Institute and was attended to by Bruce Elliot, Jackie, Dennis Lillee and Daryl Foster, as well as many other doctors. I owe so much to these men for being so good to me at a time when I was feeling very low and nervous.

Dennis Lillee is a wonderful, larger-than-life character whom I have always admired. He nearly had to bow out of the game because of a severe back injury but worked on his action and went right back to collecting hapless victims. He understands the problems a bowler can face and generously shares his knowledge. He strode into the room in his usual style, spitting and cracking jokes. He looked at me and drawled, 'What's going on, man?' I showed him my arm and he said, 'What the fuck is that? Is your arm broken?' I told him that this was how it always looked. He said, 'Sorry, sir, I came to fix your action but I can't do anything with that arm. Jesus Christ! I don't think I can help you. You have a medical problem and you'd better get it assessed by doctors.' To me, that was the beginning of a vindication.

The next ten days were extremely stressful. I was under the care of Bruce Elliot, who is a specialist in human movement, or biomechanics. He has written several books on the subject and was the first guy to defend Murali. I was his second case but being a thorough professional, he needed to be absolutely sure that he was defending a legitimate case. The doctors at the institute stripped me down to my underwear, plastered my body with electrodes and placed a helmet studded with wires on my head. This was connected to various machines that would graphically record my movements. I was then asked to bowl. So I did. When the first footage came out, their mouths fell open, as did mine. The video recording showed that when I swung my arm, my shoulder joint popped out of the socket and then popped back in, hindering any movement at the elbow. My elbow became useless, almost dead, when I bowled.

Then they set about observing my knee joints, ankles and hip joints and found that everything moved a little abnormally. My joints moved at almost 180 degrees. Bruce then explained that my hyper-extension rate was twenty times more than what was considered normal. A week later, they gave in their report, which stated that I was in no way controlling my bowling action. The report from the University of Western Australia concluded that my action was a result of *unique physical characteristics*. It was as normal a movement as my joints allowed and therefore it was a *natural action*. They all said, 'Shoaib, no one can help you. This is God's creation. That's what makes you the fastest bowler in the world. We can't fix your joint movements. Even if you put it in a plaster, things are still going to move inside.' These were the most beautiful words in the world as far as I was concerned—it's a natural action! They added that I was in the clear and that I now had the university's backing.

By now, I was flying high with happiness and relief. I had been deeply uncomfortable with this accusation hovering over me all the time and had even begun to ask myself, am I cheating? The findings of the School of Human Movement came as a huge relief.

Being called a chucker is probably the worst insult for a bowler. It is so demeaning that it used to make me mad with anger. I remember a headline in 2001 that was written by a Kiwi media person: 'Chucker leaves for home'—that really hurt. I now resolved that if anyone called my action suspect ever again, I would sue them for millions. The chucking allegation and repeated injuries had deprived me of a whole year of cricket. If it wasn't for the support and belief of Lt. Gen. Zia and my dear friend Tauseef, I would have had to walk out of the cricket arena in shame. I owe them more than I can express in words.

We sent the report back home and I was permitted by my board to join the team for the England tour but the ICC still kept me under observation. As a result, nobody would leave me alone, and they kept questioning my bowling action. So I showed my arm to the world for the first time and read the results of the report to the gathered media and requested them to please stop calling me a chucker. No one took me seriously. Why would they when our international governing body was not doing anything about it? Throughout the tour, umpires kept threatening to call no-balls off me and the ICC did nothing. Towards the end of the tour, I got unfit again and went back home, where things continued to be unpleasant for me. Even my relationship with Lt. Gen. Zia wasn't what it had been, though he didn't abandon me.

The straw that finally broke the camel's back was when I heard my own countrymen discuss my action on television. I had recovered from my injury and had been selected for the Bangladesh tour. I had started to regain my momentum and was picking up wickets at will. After Bangladesh, the team went on to Sharjah to play the West Indies and it was there that I heard commentators from Pakistan talking about my bowling action. I had the report with me, evidence that I couldn't help it, but they just wouldn't shut their mouths. I hold the ICC responsible for not taking immediate action. They should have at least sent a letter to all the umpires, giving them the details of the report and asking them not to penalize me.

Finally, Lt. Gen. Zia and I decided that with the help of the School of Human Movement, we would press the ICC into taking appropriate action. We consulted some lawyers, who were quite certain that if we decided to take legal action, we could get a large compensation from the ICC. In the meantime, rumours of my intended action reached members of the ICC. I guess they quickly understood that if they didn't start taking reports like mine seriously, they stood to lose a lot of money. They could and would be sued. I'm sure that made a great difference to their way of thinking. Finally, the ICC issued an official letter to every umpire, informing them that my action was legal. Until then, their legal department had not heard the word 'biomechanics' in relation to human beings. I forced them to recognize the findings of the institute and got my action cleared. These institutions have spent years researching the subject and it is not easy to negate their authority. So the ICC finally realized that my case was unusual, and needed to be studied. Once they understood, they let me go.

On the basis of the report on my bowling action, the ICC actually launched a new biomechanics section and hired more people to study the actions of players. It was an eye-opener and an education for them and I am sure that a lot of bowlers will benefit from it, so I am rather satisfied. But at times people still can't help themselves and comment on my action. For example, in 2009, while playing against Australia, Billy Bowden came up and told me that when I was tired, my arm did bend a bit. I recall telling him, please do report this—and I will ensure that you feel the consequences of your reporting. He backed off instantly, saying that he was just joking, airing an opinion. Yeah, not funny, Billy!

The events of the last two years had taken their toll on me. I had just got cleared for chucking when I was selected for the team that left for the England tour in 2001. I had had to clear a fitness test because my hamstring was still troubling me and I really wasn't hundred per cent fit, but I got through the test and joined the team a little later. As usual, our manager didn't bother to oversee the arrangements for my departure. On the day I was to depart for England, there was no car to take me to the airport, but having foreseen that, I got a friend to drop me off. This mismanagement is typical.

It was an important tour for Pakistan and for me and I trained for two days at Derby before the first Test. I played the match half fit and though I didn't bowl particularly well, I did beat a couple of batsmen. In fact, I bowled a sharply rising delivery that broke Nasir's finger in that Test. I was dropped for the second match.

In the first ODI of the three-nation Natwest series, I suffered a hamstring injury again. I knew that it would get better within a week but the atmosphere around me wasn't exactly congenial. Many of my teammates continued to make it clear that they were not happy that I had been cleared of the chucking charges. I had been stubbornly fighting off all the many allegations and negative team decisions, but after the first one-dayer, I broke down—it was almost a nervous breakdown. I felt depressed and sick and was of no use to the team, so it wasn't surprising that I was dropped. For me, it was a wake-up call: I needed to get away from it all.

Osama, a friend of mine who lived in Kent and worked

with David Folb, owner of the Lashings Cricket Club, rung me and suggested that it would be beneficial for me to play in a no-pressure environment for a while. He invited me to join his club. I grabbed the opportunity. It was what I needed, and gradually I began to heal, both mentally and physically.

Meanwhile, Lt. Gen. Zia arrived on a visit to England. Barely two months ago, he had sent me to Perth to fight my case. He had spent time, effort and money on me and was facing criticism back home for supporting me. He had depended on my performing well in England and winning a couple of games to ward off further criticism. By getting unfit, he felt I had let him down, and he was very upset and angry, but *O'mere haath vich nahin see main ki karaan*—it was not in my hands, what could I do? I was trying my best to climb out of the spiral I had fallen into but I was only human and had broken down physically and mentally. He once again vented his anger on me and I had nothing much to say. Then Mrs Zia, who was with him, intervened on my behalf and calmed her husband down. She rescued me and I was forgiven again. Perhaps he finally saw that I needed some space. And eventually Lashing's easy environment, the lack of pressure, the company of my peers and many light moments helped me to mend.

7

The 100-MPH Club

While I was in Australia in 2000, a journalist friend fulfilled a long-standing desire of mine by arranging for me to meet with Jeff Thomson. I have always considered him among the best fast bowlers in the world and it was his record of 99.7 mph, bowled in a 1975 Test against the West Indies, that I wanted to shatter. I was invited to have tea with him, so I travelled to Brisbane where he lived with his family. I was warmly welcomed and very soon, cricket took up most of the conversation. The great man smiled at me and said, 'Well! Are you going to make a bid for my record?' I answered, 'It's not a pressing goal but the day I feel good and strong, I will break it.'

It may not have been a pressing goal but I certainly wanted to be known as the fastest bowler in the world. This was something that I had determined very early on in my career. I had since proved myself to be a match winner for Pakistan, but I wanted more.

Right from the beginning, I had been convinced that I was unusually quick but when I entered the international arena,

I knew that I was not the fastest. In 1999, when I first got Sachin out at Kolkata, I wasn't bowling out of my skin but I knew I was bowling fast. So I began to concentrate on speed. I had often been told that I was slower than Waqar but I didn't quite agree with this assessment. Then, during the 1999 World Cup held in England, it became evident to everyone that I was genuinely quick; they couldn't ignore it because a speed machine was recording every delivery. At that time Allan Donald was considered to be the fastest, but I had begun bowling consistently at 96–97 mph. This was a period when I was feeling good about myself and was gaining a momentum that should have ensured that I soared even higher. But the truth was that I was holding myself back.

My knees continued to trouble me, but then they had always been a problem, so that wasn't enough to hold me back. My self-restraint stemmed primarily from the constant queries about my bowling, which had started getting to me to such an extent that I became a bit uncomfortable with my action. Murali had been called already. I hadn't wanted my action to be questioned and when it was, I lost faith in myself. A whole year went by in struggling to overcome these allegations, and during this time I was constantly being told I could do this, I couldn't do that, a process that unnerved me. These should have been my peak years but I couldn't find my rhythm. Instead, I began to doubt myself, wondering if I was cheating the game. Confused and worried that my action would be penalized, I ended up playing half-heartedly.

In January 2002, I joined the cricket camp at Karachi but was still struggling to find a place in the team. We were to tour Bangladesh for a two-Test series. In the first Test, on the first delivery, Wasim Akram's hamstring tore. He was devastated, I recall, crying his eyes out in disappointment because he knew his career was winding down and this injury would hasten its end. He wasn't in the good books of Lt. Gen. Zia either, so he was really worried. Despite our very public differences, I have always respected Wasim's talent and perhaps I was more mature now and able to understand his situation. I remember empathizing and trying to reassure him by saying, 'It's okay, you will play the next World Cup, take it easy.'

Wasim was frustrated and annoyed with himself but his injury opened the door for me. I played in the second Test and took four wickets for forty-eight runs. After that we went on to play the West Indies in Sharjah. My hamstring was still tender but I soon regained my form, performing well in the Tests and ODIs, thus vindicating Lt. Gen. Zia's continued faith in me. But it had taken me a year to get back the rhythm I was known for.

A year is a long time in a sportsman's life, especially when he is a fast bowler. But when it all finally settled down, and the ICC cleared my bowling action, suddenly my mind began to regain its focus. I found that once again I could concentrate on what I ought to be doing. I did not hold myself back any more and successfully recorded the fastest delivery in a one-day match, against New Zealand in Lahore—it was in April 2002 that I finally crossed the 100-mph barrier. But naturally, this feat almost immediately became controversial.

The top speeds in those days had all been recorded on a system developed by Electronic Development House in South Africa. The fastest delivery recorded on this system was 96.75 mph (155.7 kmph), bowled by me against India two years earlier. When I clocked 100.05 mph (161 kmph) in my second over against New Zealand, I was pleased to know that I was the first to slip into the 100-mph club. But soon afterwards, we were told that the 100-mph delivery had been measured on a device supplied by a Lahore hi-tech company, Cybernet, because the 'official' speed machine was out of order. This was enough for the ICC to decide not to endorse the new record. I had no doubt that the speed machine used was authentic and the record was accurate. I recall telling the press that I had regained my fitness and could easily generate the speed to deliver over 100 mph any day. I was being honest when I added that I would be delighted if the record was accepted by the ICC but it didn't really matter to me whether they recognized the speed gun or not. I was convinced that I had bowled the fastest ever delivery.

The next morning, Brett Lee phoned to congratulate me and over the next few days, I heard from many of my friends. Some of them, like Justin Langer, spoke to the media, telling them that I was 'lightning quick', while Tony Greig openly chastised those who continued to question my capabilities, especially from within the commentary box.

Meanwhile, Brett Lee announced to the media that while he was excited for me, he too was aiming to break the speed record and that he was looking forward to June 2002, when he and I would have the chance to outpace each other during the coming series in which Australia and Pakistan would play three one-day games in Melbourne and Brisbane. Adam Gilchrist went to the press with the opinion that he did not think Lee's record of 97.81 mph (157.4 kmph) in South Africa was actually his fastest ball of the innings, and all of a sudden Brett and

I were in a competition that was being discussed with great interest by the media.

I think Brett actually enjoyed all the hype but it ensured that the excitement, if any, about my yet-to-be endorsed record fizzled away. Actually, since nobody had really acknowledged my previous efforts, I thought, *kya bakwaas hai*—this is all rubbish. Everybody is making such a noise about the record but nobody recognizes that it has already been broken. I told myself, Right! Let's make it clear once and for all that I am the fastest. And suddenly a fierce competition came alive between us.

This competition stayed on the field. Off the field, Brett and I are good friends. The first time we met, he told me that I was his inspiration to join cricket as a pace bowler. Apart from being a superbly talented bowler, Brett loves music and dances without any inhibitions, just like I do, so we have a number of things in common and get on very well. I enjoy his company immensely. We often went for parties together and caused quite a stir. When the ladies would see two of the fastest bowlers in the world walk in, they would make a beeline for us. We have had some good times together but there always has been a friendly competition between us on the field. And at the back of my mind the thought took shape that the ICC was likelier to acknowledge his pace as opposed to mine and he would receive credit for being the first to break the record. He had his whole country behind him while back home, nobody really cared about supporting me. So I thought to myself, I am the fastest. I know that, now let's get the world to acknowledge it. I was aware now that this could only happen at an ICC event where they had 'authorized' speed machines.

So 2002 began with me taking up the hunt in earnest. The Australian side had, over the years, come together as a strong unit. At one time, they had raised the bar really high with their excellence in batting and bowling and their incredible fielding. They worked together as a team with the sole objective of winning and were always a tough opposition. In fact, they were the toughest opposition I ever faced. Though Justin Langer is a good friend of mine, we were at war on the field. He was often uncomfortable facing me, playing and missing and getting hit, but he is one of the toughest openers I have had to bowl against. I could never get him out; he was always too good for me.

Gilchrist is an amazing person and a tough opponent and I consider Ricky Ponting one of the best. Hayden was also a tough batsman to bowl out and Andrew Symonds could and did cause a lot of damage.

Off the field, the Australians were great fun to be with but on the field they were aggressive and loud. They gave no quarter and used every method to dominate the batsmen, including abusing and sledging. Frankly, they play my kind of game. It's all about intimidating the opposition and fast bowlers are naturally good at it. During this series, under Waqar Younis's stewardship, I consistently bowled the fastest ever in my life and we won comprehensively. I was on fire and bowled beautifully, picking up two wickets in the second and a fiver in the third ODI and despite not playing the first match, I was awarded the Player of the Match and Series. For the first time, the Australian top order seemed nervous and flinched when I bowled at them—believe me, it was hugely satisfying. I returned home feeling that good things were about to happen.

In August, Pakistan was to go to Tangiers to participate in the Morocco Cup but I thought I needed some time off. I was beginning to listen to the needs of my body, which was clearly in need of a gentle phase, so I went back to play a couple of matches for Lashings instead.

Playing at Lashings Club was an interesting experience, I must say. We played cricket all right, but rarely. It seemed to be more of a social club with a bar, and girls who wanted to pamper the players. But whatever cricket we played was fun and drew crowds. It wasn't serious cricket and mostly guys ended up chatting with girls on the boundary lines. Probably a win-win situation for all of us as we got to party and received money and David Folb got publicity. We got cars and good accommodation. Mostly, guys were there to have a good time. That's what Lashings was all about.

I recall playing a charity match with Kent in which several Pakistani cricketers participated—Wasim and Waqar also played for Lashings. I stayed back, they left for Tangiers, and I rejoined them to play our matches in Kenya.

The Kenya tour was disastrous. We played badly and lost the series and when we lose, the Pakistan dressing room is the worst place to be in. Our run of collective bad form also ensured that we got knocked out of the Champions Trophy in Sri Lanka the following month. We were to face the Australians for a three-Test series, the first of which was held in Colombo. I tried to shrug away all the negativity around me and did rather well—I took 3 for 51 and later, 5 for 21 in 8 overs. I don't know how I managed to do it because it was so hot and humid that I was struggling to breathe. I can never understand why matches are scheduled in non-conducive environments like the hot and humid summer months in the subcontinent. It's incredibly hard on fast bowlers, and opposing batsmen get the advantage. Imran Khan used to tell the board that he could not play in such heat because his body just did not function. He used to advise me not to play in such high temperatures because it was against the labour laws! If it's above 47°C, you should not be working anyway.

I bowled nevertheless in these trying conditions but it took everything out of me. The next two matches were to be played in Sharjah. It was 50°C on the first day of our match and I had managed to bowl a couple of overs when my body temperature shot through the roof and I blacked out. I spoke to the management and said I couldn't do this any more, my body was collapsing, and so I came back home. Unfortunately, Pakistan lost that series. It was a dismal batting performance once again: we scored a mere 59 runs in the first innings and in response to their score of 310, we got out for a mere 53 runs. As a consequence of our poor performance, Lt. Gen. Zia gave in his resignation. He was embarrassed about the way we were losing matches. But we all got together and convinced him to withdraw his resignation.

The year ended with me struck down by knee injury and penalized for throwing a water bottle at a spectator in Zimbabwe. Throughout the Zimbabwe series, in November 2002, I'd had trouble with my knees. Playing on a hard surface and in the heat had taken a further toll on them. I was in pain and struggling to contain my frustration. And then, during the first ODI, I lost control of my temper. I was at the boundary, re-hydrating myself, and there was this one guy in the crowd who was consistently hurling the choicest of abuses at me.

Now, this isn't an isolated incident. There are always a few bad apples in a largely sports-loving crowd. Normally you shut them out from your consciousness but it isn't always possible. On this occasion, the man succeeded in getting on my nerves. As it is, I have a temper and it only gets aggravated when I am bowling. I turned around and hurled the bottle of water that I was drinking from. It hit him squarely on the face, hurting him badly. The match referee saw what had happened and I was banned for a match. I deserved it. I actually expected to be taken to task even more severely.

2002 ended with me in a state of worry about my fitness because I didn't want to lose my place on the team for the 2003 World Cup which was drawing nearer. But my knees had collapsed on me. I was already injecting painkillers directly into them and Lt. Gen. Zia, appreciating the urgency, sent my dear friend and physician Tauseef Razzaq to attend to me. Tauseef was able to get me back into some sort of form and I was able to play the World Cup that was held in South Africa early next year.

It was during the 2003 World Cup, on 22 February, that the moment I had been waiting for finally arrived. Pakistan was playing against England at Newlands, Cape Town, and early in the match, I realized that I had just bowled unusually fast to Nick Knight, who was at the batting crease. So I began to observe my own speed—it was well into the 90s. I began to push myself harder then, and the speed gun—an official one, if you please—started registering speeds ranging from 94 to 97 mph. Then I began to touch 99 mph and I told myself, this is it, you can do it, run in with everything you have—let's set a record. The moment the thought sprung into my head, I slowed down a bit. At first I couldn't figure out what I was doing wrong but then I began to concentrate on my run-in—where I landed, how I took off. I realized that the problem lay in the last few yards. I made a conscious attempt to sustain my speed till the very end, twisted and swung my arm appropriately and released the ball at the speed of 161.3 kmph; I had broken the 100-mph barrier. *Again!* I looked towards the pavilion and signalled to those inside: Look, I have done it again. *Allah ka vasta hai*, please recognize it. And they did. There was excitement all around but, you know, I am convinced that I could have bowled even faster. At that moment, though, it was enough to have broken the record. Later that evening, I walked across to Knight and asked him if he had felt the impact of my deliveries and he answered, 'Yes, of course; every ball!' Limited edition pictures of the delivery were released and Knight asked me to autograph one for him. I was touched. I have signed a couple more for other friends who still have it up on their walls.

The record was the only satisfying moment of the tournament because our performance was awful. The 2003 World Cup was a disaster for Pakistan. I didn't do anything spectacular, nor did any of the others, and we fell out of the tournament. We should have won the match against India but the pitch at Centurion Park was a batsman's paradise and Sachin and Sehwag hammered us. They played beautifully and won the match for India. I did get Sachin's wicket finally but it was too late for us.

Lt. Gen. Zia felt letdown by me because we hadn't won. He believed that I was the only person who could have run through the opposition's batting line-up. I am glad that I was seen as a match winner but one has to accept the downside as well—you can't always be a winner.

Even though I had taken a fiver against Kenya, and wickets in almost all the matches that we played, it was not enough for us to win the Cup. The dressing room reflected what was happening to us on the field. Tempers were short and fights and squabbles kept breaking out. Once again we were on the losing side, and that is never conducive to Pakistani team spirit. The whole lot of us were rubbing each other the wrong way and I got involved in a verbal conflict with Waqar, which of course was the only thing the board remembered later—not my record, mind you. I was sacked along with other players, including Waqar. As an additional fallout, I lost my contract to play for Hampshire because the board did not give me leave to join the county, even though they themselves had dropped me.

It didn't feel so bad—though I still don't think it was right—when people from a different part of the globe refused to recognize my feat of breaking the speed record at Lahore. Perhaps it was galling for them to think that the record was owned by a guy from the subcontinent. But the sad truth is that when I returned home after the World Cup, it was as if nothing had happened. Forget about being honoured for it, my achievement wasn't even acknowledged. Instead, I was sacked from the team.

My grouse is with my own board. If a batsman gets out of form, he is given some time to regain it. If a bowler bowls poorly, he too is given a chance to find his rhythm. After all, no one can play brilliantly all the time. But no one had the patience for Shoaib. Today, if somebody comes up—and he will—and bowls faster than I did, he will be hailed as the one who broke Shoaib's record. What about Shoaib who set the record? Nothing! At one stage, Shaun Tait got close to my record and made more news than I did when I set the record.

Look at my country. What does Pakistan not have? What do we lack? Our rice is long grained; we have sweet water to irrigate our crops. Seventy-five per cent of our land is agricultural and can feed all our people. Pakistan can become debt free by merely selling its high-grade coal to the world. We have oil, coal, rivers, the ocean and natural harbours. Our food is delicious, the mangoes are sweet and our people are talented. What else do we require? If you ask me, Pakistan has everything but *qadar*, the ability to value what we have. Allah has given us both a gift and a curse and the curse is that we will never be valued by our own, whether we are in politics or sports. Benazir was shot dead—whoever wants to work for the good of the nation is bound to be finished. We have produced outstanding players in squash and hockey and have consistently produced valuable cricketers. Ironically, eighty per cent of our population, the proverbial man on the street, loves us deeply but the twenty per cent who are in power don't care. I have studied the case histories of ten of our best cricketers and found not one who was not plagued by some controversy or the other. Younis Khan won us the T-20 World Cup in 2009 and was repaid by being forced to face inquiries.

Even Imran Khan. A person of his calibre is a boon for the world. He has built a university, the Shaukat Khanam hospitals; he has done so much for the people of Pakistan. In turn, he is dearly loved by them, I have heard people praying in gratitude, 'Ya Allah, bless Imran and forgive all his sins, forgive any mistakes he has made because he has done so much good.' He has built an education city and so many poor people are employed and receiving health care because of him, but what has happened to him at the instigation of the uncaring few? He was beaten up by politically motivated rogue elements in Punjab University in 2007—children were instigated to hit him. Can you imagine something like that happening just across our border, a mere thirty-minute drive from where he was so heartlessly treated? Can anyone imagine this happening to Sachin Tendulkar in India? Is it possible that Sachin Tendulkar or Rahul Dravid have not made mistakes? They are protected because they are national treasures belonging to a country that has invested national pride in them. The face of India is Aishwarya Rai, Sachin Tendulkar, Amitabh Bachchan. The face of Pakistan is controversies. We are unique in this.

And while I still have my tongue on a raw nerve, will someone tell me why so many Pakistani cricketers are dying of hunger? We have produced some of the finest players in the world and they are starving. I know a former Pakistani captain who drives a taxi in England. When is this going to change? When are we going to start looking after those people who have played for the country? Yes, the country has given so much to us, but we too have given it reasons to be proud of us. But we are never recognized; *mujhe aitraaz hai is baat pe*—this is my objection and complaint. When will there be a change in the attitude towards players, when will they stop insulting them? *Kab tak zalil karte rahenge? Hamare jitney bhi star hain, sab zalil ho ke nikle hain.*

8

A Bowler's Dilemma

After having been dropped following the 2003 World Cup in
South Africa, I rejoined the team to play the Three Nation
Bank Alfalah Cup in Sri Lanka in May the same year. It was good
to be back but I had already used up the year's quota of luck
granted to me by Allah. I had set a world record. The rest of the
year was all downhill and, of course, full of controversies.

I remember it being very hot and humid in Dambulla and
as is customary with the pitches of the subcontinent, it was
an awfully slow track. We were playing New Zealand and we
needed results. Out of desperation, I began fussing with the
ball. Yes, for those of you who want to know, I did tamper with
the ball during that match. And yes, I know it's against the rules
and it's not something to be proud of—I apologized for it. I
have tampered with the ball on many occasions, have been
warned several times, and even been caught twice—Dambulla
was one such instance. I was suspended for a match and
fined seventy-five per cent of the match fee. But I can't seem
to help it; I've got to do something with the ball. I know this
will make a big noise, but I won't lie about it.

Almost all Pakistani fast bowlers have tampered with the ball. I may be the first one to openly admit to it, but everybody is doing it. I won't name him, but one Pakistani cricketer actually switched the ball in the umpire's pocket with one that reversed like crazy! Umpires usually keep the ball in their coat pocket and then hang their coat up for lunch. That was when the transfer occurred. After this incident, they now leave their coats in a locked room. To be honest with you, every team in the world tampers with the ball. We probably started it, but today, *koi team dudh ki dhuli nahin hai.* No team is innocent, and virtually every fast bowler does it. That is the only way to survive because the wickets are so slow. After years of not allowing bouncers, in 2001, the ICC ruled that only one would be allowed per over. The pitches are dead and slow, and are made to order for batting. It's the bowlers who are curtailed. It's like giving match practice to people: we are hit all over the ground.

Back home in Pakistan, bowlers have very few options other than learning how to 'take care of the ball'. If, by some chance, a track that assists fast bowlers is made, everybody protests. *Jab aise pitches aati hain tab aapko batting ka art nahin aata kya?* Shouldn't the batsmen have the skill to play in difficult conditions as well? The result of all this whining and complaining by the batsmen is that most of the pitches are made for them, and to hell with the bowlers! We have never complained. Do we not give our best on pitches that are made to give batsmen the advantage? This is why I respect batsmen who played in the 1970s, on uncovered pitches.

Cricket fans love fast bowlers, but their heroes do not have the freedom to perform to the best of their abilities. While a batsman sets records making runs, bowlers need wickets. And the team needs wickets to win. So bowlers are bound to do something with the ball in order to help their case a little.

There are so many ways to prepare the ball; it's not just a matter of scratching it. I have used my boot nails and the zip of my back pocket. Many bowlers put Vaseline or gum on the ball. The only way to stop this is for the ICC to ensure that at least some pitches are prepared in favour of bowlers. That would make the game less one sided and more balanced. The game, especially now, has become very unequal and only favours the batsman—if you bowl a no-ball, the batsman gets a free hit; bouncers have been curtailed; and a bowler can't even touch his hair before picking up the ball. They have restricted us so mercilessly that I find it very difficult to feel entirely guilty about ball tampering. Since we can't seem to stop doing it, maybe it's not a bad idea to legalize it and set rules for it. After all, it's still an art to use that ball. You need the pace and the skill. Not everyone can do it. Perhaps some manipulation of the ball, like scratching it with your nails, could be legally allowed... sigh! I know I am going to get it in the neck for saying all this.

Groundsmen, of course, have a very important role to play in the way a pitch behaves, and I, for one, have the greatest respect for them. I have always had a very good relationship with them, and they would often tell me beforehand how the wicket was likely to play. Sometimes, in order to please me, the groundsmen would make a net pitch that had bounce. Batsmen hate such pitches and I have seen them chase the laughing groundsmen with their bats, complaining that they had been hurt by the rising ball. I know that when there is a bit of bad blood between a bowler and a batsman, the bowler often lets it rip in the nets, sometime even busting the batsman's nose. I think this is very unprofessional but it often happens at net practice in Pakistan. Despite being the fastest of them all, I have never hurt anyone in the nets—never.

At home in Pakistan, I make it a point to enquire how the groundsmen are doing. I have found that just by acknowledging them, I get to hear about the possible behaviour of the pitch and can adjust my bowling accordingly. In fact, captains often asked me about the state of the pitch because they knew I had more information than they had!

Coming back to 2003, after the heat of Dambulla, it was a relief to get to cooler climes and play away from the hot and humid venues. In the Natwest Challenge in England, we played good, competitive cricket but lost 1-2. We gave them a good fight, and I played well.

I had earlier received an invitation to play for Durham, so I stayed back to play for the rest of the county season. Bangladesh was to visit us at home for a three-match Test series and to my delight, Rashid Latif, who was the Pakistan captain, called me back to join the team. I played two Test matches and bowled my heart out, and in the second Test at Peshawar I got ten wickets. However, that Test was nothing less than a physical battle. It was so hot in Peshawar that every time I completed a delivery, I had to literally concentrate on refocusing my vision so that I could see the other players on the pitch. By the time I was into my third or fourth over, I had to wear an ice jacket around my neck to keep my body temperature down. I was feeling so ill that I remember wondering when the match would end—*udde pehle main mar he na javaan.* I thought I might die before the match ended. I had felt like this once before, in Sharjah. Being asthmatic doesn't help either, in these conditions. It is almost impossible for my lungs to cope with so much heat and humidity.

Somehow, I got through that second Test match where I was declared the Man of the Match, and then immediately went back to continue my stint with Durham.

I did enjoy playing for Durham and achieved some success, especially when I got 5 for 35 against Somerset in the National League (2003). I was playing with a good bunch of guys—Paul Collingwood, Graham Onions, Phil Mustard, to name a few. We enjoyed playing together and because I had performed well for the team, they invited me to come back for the next season. The biggest difference between playing for a county or a club and your country is pressure. It's almost non-existent while playing for a county. You just have to look after yourself and concentrate on your performance. It's liberating, and a good way to hone your skills.

October brought the South Africans to Pakistan to play a set of five ODIs and two Test matches. We were determined to do everything right as a team. I was in good form and bowled really well, and we were two-nil up when Duckworth Lewis struck. The third match was abandoned due to poor light and South Africa was awarded the match. This was the turning point of the ODI series. South Africa came back strongly and we lost the series. But I put our loss behind me and concentrated on the two Test matches ahead. The first Test saw me finding my rhythm, I was bowling quite fast. At one point, Gary Kirsten was batting and he hit me to the boundary, so I threw a fast bouncer at him. It struck him on the face, cutting him wide open. I remember running as fast as I could right across the pitch and catching him before he fell. He bled all over my shirt—I still have that shirt. Later, I called on him because he wasn't able to speak over the phone. I remember him telling me that he didn't know what got into him to try and pull the fastest bowler in the world at his age, and we both shared a laugh. Gary was in his mid-thirties then and I was at my fastest. I felt terrible about hurting him but in the very next match that he played, he scored a century and won the Test for his side. Kirsten and Langer are two of the bravest batsmen I have ever played against. Tough and gritty, and both perfect gentlemen.

Coming back to that first Test match against South Africa, I had succeeded in leading our team to Pakistan's first victory against South Africa on home soil. However, the match didn't end on a positive note for me; I let my aggression get the better of me during the game and shouted at Paul Adams. I ended up with a two-Test ban. I had lost control again, and I shouldn't have done it. I am aware that kids watch us play and it's not a good example to set. But it happens in the heat of the moment and I was embarrassed about it and apologized.

In December that year (2003), New Zealand came to Pakistan for an ODI series. We considered them, along with South Africa, to be the biggest chokers in the game. Both these teams appear to lack faith in themselves. They seem unable to shrug off the pressure that's natural to a big tournament. The only way to get over it is to produce wins in major tournaments at regular intervals. Unfortunately, they click at the wrong time. They have no dearth of talent and personally, I think A.B. D'villiers is brilliant. But in 2003, we thrashed New Zealand easily. Then we followed them back to New Zealand to play a Test series. As usual, my body needed time to adapt. Annoyingly, I always pull a muscle at the beginning of a series and then have to deal with it quickly.

Yet again, our coach was Miandad, who realized that I couldn't be used for the first Test match. So, all of a sudden, he was thinking of pulling me out of the series and sending me back home! That is the way it is in Pakistan cricket. For our management, handling a situation means sending people back. They aren't there to help or guide you—certainly not to manage things for you. So Miandad wanted to send me back but Inzamam intervened and I was able to play in the second Test. I took eleven wickets in that match, which incidentally was the only Test Pakistan won in the series. Miandad promptly did a volte-face and was all over me, praising my abilities. I wonder if he took me for a fool.

I had played with a pulled calf muscle and had also been hit in the groin while batting, so I bowed out at this stage. Now, here is how I understood what followed. While I was not fit enough to deal with the stress and demands of bowling, I wasn't crippled, so I went jet skiing, something I love doing. The media caught me flying over the waters and then all the fuss began. 'Shoaib is not playing due to a groin injury but he seems fit enough to jet ski,' the headlines screamed and the hullabaloo that followed was unimaginable. I guess it was a stupid thing to do—I left myself open to one more controversy. I never seem to learn. Of course, the controversy overshadowed the fact that I played rather well in the three ODIs.

What I was really looking forward to at this point was going home and playing against India. The Indians were coming after a very long time and as always, there was a huge buzz of anticipation amongst our fans and therefore a huge responsibility on me to perform well.

We did do well in the ODIs against the Indian team led by Saurav Ganguly, though there were some anxious moments. As you know, Pakistan always makes a mess of one or two crucial games—*saaddi batting collapse kar gayi*. And sure enough, our batting collapsed in Karachi. Thankfully, things rarely go wrong with our bowling and we were able to snatch back the lead in the next two games.

The Pakistani team cements together when we play against India. But the Indians, though they always have a great selection of talent, especially in the batting department, often play for themselves first and then for the team. In our dressing room, when we sat around discussing strategies, we always remarked upon the fact that some of the Indians would play to get runs for themselves and this would help us win the match. We, too, have had great batsmen like Inzamam and Miandad, and we almost always had the edge when it came to bowling—we've had terrific bowlers like Imran, Wasim and Waqar, all match winners. Although we had differences with each other, we held together better as a team because we were always passionate about winning. Nothing less would do for us.

I could be wrong in my judgment but I do believe that batsmen the world over are to some extent selfish and play for records. Pakistan, too, has had selfish batsmen. They play for themselves more often than not, and do not really contribute to a win. Most bowlers tend to criticize them for this. India has had great batsmen, but whenever one of them walked in, we used to feel that he was going to waste many overs searching for records. I think players like Sachin Tendulkar and Rahul

Dravid weren't exactly match winners to start with, nor did they know the art of finishing a game. Things changed when younger players like Virender Sehwag and Yuvraj Singh arrived on the scene. These guys didn't play for records, they played to win.

I know our whole team gives Sehwag the credit for being the one to lead India's winning streak. Gautam Gambhir and he have given India quick and wonderful partnerships. Before that there was only Sachin; the poor man carried the entire burden on his shoulders. With him was Dravid, who has a great technique but has never been a match winner.

With the coming of the younger players, the Indian team took the No. 1 Test spot—that's the difference they have wrought. And Sachin has started scoring quickly, and playing the role of a match winner for his team. I can't recall a series from his earlier playing days when he helped win matches. But now, with the help of Sehwag, Yuvraj, Gambhir, Virat Kohli and others, who are terrific batsmen and keep things moving, he wins matches for India. He has taken a leaf out of their book and bats beautifully. Now he is a complete batsman. Please don't get me wrong. I think he was always a great batsman, if not the greatest in the world, and I admire his extraordinary skills. To me, however, winning is everything. Vivian Richards, Ricky Ponting, Brian Lara and the likes of them are great batsmen who dominated with the bat and were truly match winners. Initially, when I bowled against Sachin, I found these qualities missing. He might have had more runs and records but he lacked the ability to finish a game. *Apne run liye aur out ho gaye.* But in the last three years, I can see that he has changed his game. In this new Indian side, the responsibility is shared and he is more at ease. Look at him now: he scores 200 runs in a match and his team wins. In 1999, in Chennai, the same batsman scored 150 runs and yet his team lost. That's the difference. The kind of culture I come from, people need us to win matches. Staying on the pitch is not appreciated.

An important thing that happened to Indian cricket was the captaincy of Ganguly. I think he was a superb captain, a giant of a man in a slight body. One of his greatest gifts to his side was the very brave decision to bring in youngsters, and he backed them as well. This has changed the face of their team. Dhoni has benefited greatly from taking over Ganguly's team. He is a very smart man, an intelligent captain, and manages his resources perfectly. Plus, he wants to win. India is blessed to have someone as level-headed as him at the helm. I admire the way he overcomes problems, and on the field he is calm and collected, and means business. He knows how to lead, and the Indian team were deserving winners of the 2011 World Cup.

But back to 2004, where we were in Pindi, playing our third Test match against India. I was bowling to V.V.S. Laxman when I felt a sharp pain in my ribcage. I ignored it and carried on bowling till I felt it give way. I had to retire hurt and told Inzamam I couldn't bat. Almost immediately, rumours started flying around the dressing room that I was faking injury. The problem I have constantly faced is that people don't believe me if I say I am in pain. And, of course, nobody waits for medical reports, they immediately speak about it to the media and one more controversy is spun out of thin air.

Nothing is confidential as far as the PCB is concerned and nobody cares about another man's reputation. The PCB loves leaking news to the media. To say that I was cheesed off is to put it mildly but I have never taken these battles to the press so I went back to play for Durham as soon as I healed. Back home, the controversy got hotter and louder till I wasn't able to ignore it any more. It was being said that there would be an official investigation into the matter. I then got a dye test and bone scan done and sent the report to the PCB. It clearly indicated that I had had an injury—my rib had snapped in two places. Rameez Raja was the chief executive of the board and also the main accuser, and he was backed by Inzamam. Raja's insistence had forced me go through a bone scan—I wonder if he or anybody else was even mildly embarrassed when they discovered that I had been telling the truth. I was really cross with Rameez and did not speak to him for a number of years. But that is how it is. You lose the game and they need a scapegoat. Unfortunately for me, I seem to be the one they want to pin everything on.

I continued my stint with Durham but was carrying around a lot of anger against the management. I was thankful to be away from it all and thought it might be a good idea to stay on in England for a while. But Bob Woolmer had other plans. He had been appointed as coach to the team by the PCB and he expressed a desire to meet me. We met once in Kent and then in Northampton. He kept making notes and told me that he needed me to come back and play for Pakistan. I said no, I didn't want to go back because they had treated me badly and had accused me of faking injury. I didn't want to be subjected to any more humiliation. Besides, I wasn't on great terms with Inzamam. But Bob persisted and in the end, the desire to play for my country overrode all the rubbish that had come before. In July 2004, I left Durham for Sri Lanka to play in the Asia Cup.

I was back in England in September for the ICC Champions Trophy. Until then I hadn't got an opportunity to bowl to Brian Lara, even though we had played a couple of series against the West Indies. To me, Lara is the most elegant, most beautiful person—a fabulous batsman, the best batsman I have ever seen. I was dying to bowl to him because he was my favourite batsman, apart from Vivian Richards. Finally, in Hampshire, I got my chance. I took a catch and Lara walked in. As he came towards the wicket, I walked up to him and asked if I could say something to him. He said, 'Please do, but don't be nasty to me.'

I laughed and said, 'No, I won't. It is an honour for me to bowl to you. I have been waiting for this for so long.' He replied, 'Thank you very much, how about going easy on me then?'

He went on to take guard, when Sarwan walked across and asked him what I had said. Lara jokingly replied that I had told him to watch out, I was going to kill him!

Providence had ordained that on the third ball that he faced from me, he got hit on the head and had to be hospitalized with a concussion. I couldn't believe that I had knocked the great Lara down. For some reason, Sarwan told the press at a briefing that Lara had informed him of my murderous intentions. That bit of misinformation spread like fire over the wires. The next morning, Lara himself cleared the misunderstanding and personally apologized to me. All I was interested in was that he sign the ball—the one that had a bit of the great batsman's blood on it—for me and he kindly obliged. It's a pity I only bowled three balls to him. I admire him greatly and would have loved to match my skills against his. Recently, we played together at a charity match at Lord's and I was charmed by him.

Most of the batsmen I have bowled to were uncomfortable facing me. Rightly so—I was bowling at close to 100 mph. I felt that half the Indian batting line-up was uncomfortable, and surprisingly, even the Australians shuffled. My fans always yell for blood: I guess it's exciting to see a fast bowler hitting someone. For me, it has always been about scaring the batsman into playing bad shots, but over the years I have hurt and damaged several batsmen, leaving them with broken bones, a broken jaw, a broken leg, even knocked unconscious. I hate these consequences. *Mera dil bahut jaldi pighal jaata hai.* I quickly run up to my colleague to find out if he is all right. To me, it's just a game; I have no intention of hurting anyone. I too have been hit on the head once, so I know exactly how it feels.

I do know of some fast bowlers, though, who enjoy hurting people. The sight of blood makes them happy. I have heard them say—*theek hua, achha hua.* But hitting a batsman was never my goal. I just wanted him out and back in his dressing room. I guess hitting a batsman, especially a well-set one, can be a very satisfying feeling for a fast bowler. It is certainly pleasurable when a bowler finds his length and bowls exactly the way he wants to. The short rising bowl is one of our great weapons and once you hit someone, he remembers it throughout his career and you can play upon his emotions, keep him on the edge a little.

I know cricket is a gentleman's game, but it is a competitive one as well—tempers and nerves often get frayed. And sometimes, too much is made of this. For example, during the World Cup in South Africa in February 2003, Matthew Hayden and I got into a verbal duel. We had lost our first match and I was not in a pleasant mood. The next day, I went down for breakfast and Hayden was there too. I can't remember what triggered the argument, because we started the conversation by wishing each other a good morning, but then we got into each other's face. We were swearing at each other and I was pretty hot under the collar. Just before I lost it altogether, I remembered that he was physically bigger than I was. I thought *ke yaar*, back off, *isne mujhe utha utha ke marna hai*. I pulled back from what might have become a physical scuffle and thought I'd get back at him on the field instead. When we went to Australia in December 2004 for a three-Test series, I carried this memory and started tormenting him both on and off the field. To my delight, I got him out three times in two Test matches. I was fined a part of my match fee for signalling him to walk out when his wicket fell in the first Test. I remember telling him, 'Goodnight, sweetheart, go back to the dressing room and watch me bowl', among other things.

I wasn't being personal. Even if he isn't my friend, I think he is one of the finest batsmen in the world. And I do have great relationships with other international players. Most of the time, we leave what happens on the field, on the field. These things are part of a planned strategy as well. If I can get a batsman upset, he will play defensively and make mistakes. Most bowlers single out batsmen who are not comfortable playing against them and try to intimidate them further. This is a way to crank up the pressure on them. It is a way to keep a player out of form. And we all know that it can and does happen to us as well.

I love targeting the best batsmen. My game has always been aggressive and that's how I like it. I love taking a wicket and then standing at fine leg and looking into the dressing room at my victim biting his nails. At the same time, when they take my bowling apart, they enjoy watching me simmer at fine leg. The best part of the game for me is when there is no pain and things are going my way—rare moments when you place the ball where you want it to land and get the wickets your team needs for a win. That is priceless—a feeling that is indescribable. When *you* are in control.

Mind games are a part and parcel of cricketing strategy. Like what we did with Ponting in Melbourne. We kept needling him, saying, you can't pull the fastest bowler in the world who, incidentally, is from Pakistan, not Australia. He fell into the trap and pulled—we had a man waiting.

The batsmen also have their ways of throwing a bowler's concentration, as Hayden could tell you. The important thing is how to keep the issue from skyrocketing. We know our lines but sometimes we get carried away. I suppose the responsibility for keeping discipline and peace on the field falls on the captains. They need to know how to calm things down quickly before an incident gets out of hand, and this applies particularly to the captain of the fielding side. When this fails, the umpires step in. Some of the umpires are great at handling pressure. This is where their skill and judgment come into play. Like in any other sport, the blood is quick to rush through a sportsman's veins and we can get into verbal and even physical altercations. Cricket, in fact, is the least violent compared to say, football or ice-hockey. All it requires is a strong umpire who knows the game and the players to intervene and diffuse the situation, leaving the judgments for later.

When I look back, every year of my life appears to have been divided equally between six months of happiness and six months of uncertainty. When 2005 dawned, I was in Australia playing in the three-nation ODI series against Australia and West Indies and doing pretty well until I pulled my hamstring in the second match and was forced to leave the ground after bowling just 2.5 overs. From there we left for Sydney for our next match that was to start three days later. The management by then had decided that I was to be sent back home as I couldn't play the rest of the tour. The following morning, I woke up and tuned in to the local news on television and my jaw dropped. A young girl had alleged that a Pakistani cricketer had raped her. I hadn't yet closed my mouth when our team manager, followed closely by our coach Harun Rashid, burst into my room. Rashid saw me and blurted out, 'What have you done?' My response was clueless: 'What on earth are you talking about?' He hissed, 'This is serious—it's a rape case!'

Finally, I got it. My manager and coach had automatically presumed that I was the culprit! I was livid and yelled at them at the top of my lungs, ending my tirade by saying, 'Why are you talking to me about this? Get the hell out of my room!' When I calmed down a bit, I went back to watching the news and to my horror, I found that without waiting for the facts to emerge, or confirmation from any source, the entire international media led by the Pakistani media had fallen in with Rashid's presumption of my guilt and were pointing fingers at me.

Unluckily, I was about to be sent home for being unfit. This was good enough for them to work out that I was the rapist and was being sent back home to hush up the matter, or something to that effect. The news was on all the television channels, especially the Indian ones, and all of them insinuated that I was the culprit.

I was worried, really worried. I had never been given a break by the media and that wasn't about to change. I immediately made an effort to contact the girl in question. I got through to her spokesperson and heaved a sigh of relief when he said that the poor girl didn't even know me and it was another guy from my team. Eventually, the board found out the name of the player, but they didn't bother to send out a press note saying I was innocent. They got their act together and hid his name from the media—no such protection was offered to me, and I was innocent!

When I got back home, I was stunned when first my family and then my friends asked if the allegation against me was true. I was furious and hurt. Thanks to the media, I had to explain my innocence to everyone around me. I had a huge fight with my family and then I stormed out to take on my friends. I told them that I had nothing to do with the case. They believed me, of course.

As soon as I could, I went to the board to find out what was happening. I ended up having a big row with Shahryar Khan, who was the chairman at that time, because he refused to take any action. I wasn't asking him to name the person involved, all I wanted was somebody to tell the rest of the world that it wasn't me! But it was as if I didn't matter. I couldn't believe that they could do such a thing to anyone. In fact, the first question I asked him was, 'How can you do this to me?' He responded by insisting that it wasn't his fault, or that of the board, that everyone thought it was me and that it was the media who was responsible—media *chalareya hai sab kuchh*. Fine, it wasn't the fault of the board, but couldn't he have stopped or corrected them? Eventually, the news did get out that it was someone else but the board shielded him and never allowed his identity to be made public.

I went around like a wounded animal unable to get justice. I got to know who the guy was from other sources but chose not to confront him—he couldn't possibly speak out to clear my name, it would only get him into all sorts of trouble. Ultimately, the girl, who was a student in Australia though originally from Karachi, didn't press any charges nor did she mention the perpetrator's name because of the stigma attached to the issue of rape—the victim only gets further victimized.

Even now, when I think of it, I feel miserable and hard done by. I needed closure. If this had been done by the international media alone, I would have sued them but with the Pakistan media, there is no accountability for anything. They knew it was another guy but they made sure they named me. Others, of course, insinuated my culpability; they were intelligent enough to know that if they named me, I would sue them. The thing that annoys me the most is that the media had openly named me as the culprit but when the truth came out, no one, *no one*, felt it was important to apologize to me publicly for the world to see and hear.

One of the lessons for me from this unresolved issue was the realization that my integrity could be so easily doubted by almost everyone. There were enough people who thought I was capable of such a heinous act. Everybody got their

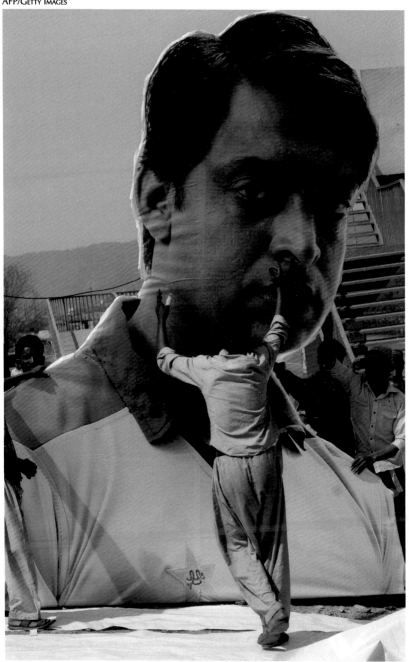

My murshid said I would be a star—and I was

Starting young

My thinking rock

The tree without djinns

On Eid, in new clothes, with strict instructions to sit still...

...still trying to sit still

I always go back to my old house when I visit Rawalpindi

My pillars of strength, my parents

© Shoaib Akhtar

Being on a
bike always
puts a smile
on my face

GETTY IMAGES

If I hadn't been born a human being, I would
have been an eagle, of this I am sure

Fast bowlers are naturally aggressive

Brian Lara, down and out

Bone shards and cartilage: funny how these little things can bring you to your knees

The prize wicket of Sachin Tendulkar

Odd man out: with Anwar Saeed and Inzamam-ul Haq

When we're good, we're great!

Crossing the 100-mph barrier,
not for the first time

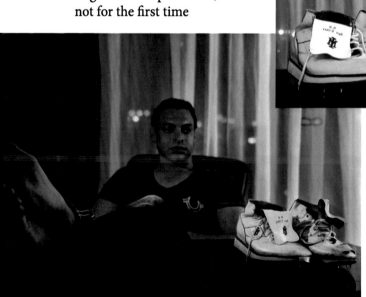

My
100-mph
shoes

Bowlers also win matches: with
Brett Lee, Muttiah Muralitharan,
Harbhajan Singh

Spearheading Pakistan

My fans keep me going

It takes a good coach to bring out the best in a player: with Daryl Foster and Bob Woolmer

Dancing to my
own music

Man of the match for the Kolkata Knight Riders: Shahrukh
ain't heavy, I can take his weight

'Star Over My Heart'—I always played my heart out for my country

© Shoaib Akhtar

© Shoaib Akhtar

I wish I had played with Imran Khan

enjoyment out of it. The media got its piece of sensational news to air. The board was able to draw everybody's attention away from their team's performance; somebody's captaincy got saved, somebody else's bad performance was overlooked. Everybody got away and only my name was tarnished—*sab bach gae; sab ne apna apna situation sambhal lita te mainu badnaam kardita—bas!*

9

Down But Not Out

There were trying times ahead. I was still nursing my hamstring when selections for the India tour loomed. We didn't want to take any chances because this was a big tour; as I have mentioned before, I can't bear to lose to India, so I told the board that I wouldn't go because I wasn't fit and I didn't want to spoil our chances. Once again, my decision annoyed Inzamam but they went ahead without me. Unfortunately, we started losing badly. One evening, Sheikh Rashid, a minister from Pindi, rang to say he had a message for me from President Musharraf and could I please come and see him. We met at PC Hotel in Islamabad and he informed me that I must go to India and play. I told him what I had told the board, that I was not fit and would be of no use to the team. My answer was not to their liking and my relationship with the President deteriorated. Once again, I felt Shahryar had let me down. He knew I was injured and could have supported me.

Meanwhile, the wind changed and we won in India, and all of a sudden they came to an understanding that they didn't need my services any more. Inzamam and the board dropped me for the upcoming West Indies tour—I wasn't even informed about their decision. It was quite painful but *main sochiya koi gal nahi*—I thought, never mind, I'll wait for my time. But the team was doing well, and I felt that my chances of getting back in were rather bleak. So when I was asked by Tom Moody to play for his club in Worcestershire, I took up the offer. Earlier, Tom had invited me to play for a charity game that he had organized. We had got to know, and liked, each other and he had asked me if I would be interested in playing for his county, for he felt the club would benefit from my experience. I hadn't thought of playing a county season at that time, I simply said, 'If you are there, I will play.' When I joined the team, he made me feel very comfortable, looked after me well and trained me for a week. Tom wanted me to assist in coaching the team's fast bowlers—teach the youngsters my trade, so to speak—and I did.

Later in the year, the management decided to consider me for the Afro-Asia Cup—after telling the media, of course, that this would be the last chance for Shoaib. And so I joined the team. I performed well and after the tournament was over, I went back to Worcestershire. But when Moody left to become the coach of the Sri Lankan team, somehow county cricket lost its charm and I ended up playing in fewer games. I must add here that nothing happened to upset me. My teammates, led by Vikram Singh Solanki, were a great bunch of guys but somehow I had lost interest and asked to be let off, and they let me go. I thought things had gone smoothly—why would the club want a disinterested player? So I was surprised to hear of a remark by John Elliot, the chairman of Worcestershire, that players like me were no good for the club. What is it about chairmen and me? I had claimed six wickets for sixteen runs for Worcestershire against Glamorgan—for his club, you know. Then he went on to state that I hadn't been any good for any club that I had played in because 'Shoaib is a superstar and does what he wants'.

All I can say is that it was nice of him to call me a superstar. I met John Elliot only once and that, too, in the car park. I guess he was upset with me because I hadn't wagged my tail around him. I had heard that he was a bit of an attention seeker who liked people to hover around him—not something I would ever do, so I guess he just got pissed off with me and made those remarks. He actually went around saying that I distracted the youngsters, I wasn't serious about cricket and was a bad influence in the dressing room, and stuff like that. I wasn't the only one who was surprised at these accusations. Worcestershire's captain spoke up in my support. When he was in Pakistan later that year, Solanki told the press that he was surprised at the chairman's remarks and that Shoaib had not been a bad influence and was very congenial.

By this time, my relationship with Inzamam had soured to such an extent that I didn't think I would get a chance to play for Pakistan as long as he was at the helm. So, when my name was announced for the World Series, I started preparing for it.

A lot of people within the ICC questioned my selection but the 'little master' of cricket, Sunil Gavaskar, took a stand for me. He said he didn't care what was being said about me, or how the Pakistan management portrayed me. He said *koi ki kainda ha uddi parvah nahin. Main te selector aan; main te dekhan ga ki Shoaib kiddan perform karda hai*—his job as chief selector was to ensure that the best players were picked, those with talent, and he didn't care about the rumours. So I was selected over other guys.

I was really looking forward to the World Series. It was exciting to play with different players, and face teams from different continents. But I quickly realized that no one took it very seriously, even though there was a lot of money to be made. Each one of us stood to make around US$100,000 but everyone concentrated on partying. We had fun in the dressing room even though we didn't know each other that well. I remember once, Sehwag was changing his shirt and Chris Gayle looked at him and quipped, 'Sehwag, man! I've seen a better body on an elephant.' It was strange to walk into a dressing room filled with all the big names, most of them with their fingers in their ears, attempting to block out Ntini's—supreme athlete though he is—singing. Ntini was crazy—he would sing loudly and dance wildly around us, often pulling others, including me, to dance with him. Chris would tease him saying, 'I could take you out of a jungle but I can't take the jungle out of you, Ntini.' You couldn't help laughing. It was the funniest dressing room I've ever been in. And it was almost inevitable that we lost the three matches we played in that frame of mind.

I had played two ODIs out of three, but refused to play in the last match because my knees were killing me. They were swollen and messed up, so I couldn't run. But I admit I was partying quite a lot, which was probably why the others, especially the English players, started saying that I was a very non-serious player and that I was one of those guys who was just lucky to be a star. I don't blame anyone for not knowing what a sorry state my knees were in because over the years I had got into the habit of hiding my condition from everyone. I did this because I knew that my board would not help me or understand, and I would have never got to play. Back home, if you say you have an injury, you are in trouble, so I hid it during the World Series and instead, listened to all the stuff that they said about me. Suddenly, the dressing room was not such a fun place to be in.

One day, I wasn't scheduled to play so I was lounging in the dressing room when coach John Wright asked me to put on my kit. It was no big deal, I would have donned the kit but I drew his attention to the fact that I wasn't playing, so maybe wearing civvies was okay. He didn't agree and yelled at me to shut up in front of everyone. I couldn't take that, so I returned the compliment. He didn't know that I don't let things go easily if I get riled. I kept on at him throughout the day, although he was quiet. So I left the World Series with a pretty bad reputation.

The very next month, England was to play Pakistan. They had won the Ashes and were on a high. I was once again given an opportunity by the board to play for Pakistan, despite my differences with our captain. The first Test was to be played in Multan and I remember clearly the first day of the match. I wasn't sure if I would be played and was only told on the morning of the match that I was indeed playing. Great, I thought. This was my chance to prove that I was a star bowler who could make it happen for the team. Nobody in the team was talking to me but that was fine as far as I was concerned, I have never bothered about others' behaviour towards me. Besides, what was new?

I must confess that there was a part of me that had distanced itself from the team. However, every game I play, I play with the same earnestness and intensity; if I don't, the batsmen will smash me all over the field and I can't tolerate that. Of course, my knees were as bad as ever, so for the seventh time in my career I took recourse to painkillers that were injected directly into my knees to numb the pain. I then went on to bowl my heart out in the Tests and won the series for my country.

Surprisingly, they gave the Man of the Series to Inzamam and not to me. I think everyone was taken aback by this decision. I had emerged as the highest wicket taker in the series with seventeen wickets. My slower deliveries had proven unplayable for the English and their captain, Michael Vaughan, acknowledged my skill by saying this was the best spell he had seen from any fast bowler. That too, on such dead pitches. 'Why is he not the man of the series?' he asked.

Then the ODIs started and they lost badly. My commitment on the ground was an eye-opener for some of the English players, especially Andrew Flintoff, who had observed me in the World Series in Australia. I had been out there having a good time and partying, and he probably didn't have any great respect for my bowling ability. One evening, we went out together and he confessed his bewilderment, saying it was as if I had two radically different personalities. One popped up in the World Series, a guy who was interested only in having a good time. 'And now I meet this Shoaib; so focused, and who can win games single-handedly and bring us back to earth. Who are you? I think I've met two different people in two months. Which one is the real you?'

I just smiled and said, 'Both.'

He continued, 'What are you made of? We were sure that after that series you would be dropped forever but you have come back to show the world what you can do. Amazing!'

Vaughan acknowledged my performance too, by remarking that he thought my presence in the Pakistan side was the big difference between the two teams. Balm to a wounded soul indeed!

My wounded knees, however, required urgent attention. But first we had a huge home series to deal with. India was coming to Pakistan and this time I wanted to be in the thick of the action. But I feared they would prepare batting pitches, dead pitches with no juice in them for the bowlers to use. Inzamam was the captain and I requested him and the management not to let this happen—but who listens to me? You have in your armoury the fastest bowler in the world, supported by some excellent pacers, surely that was something to work into your strategy. But no, we prepared perfect batting tracks. I told the management, what is the use of having me then? You know India is not comfortable against fast bowling.

It became a running argument between the captain, the management and me. I firmly believed that there was no need to be defensive but they preferred to make pitches on which the batsmen had plenty of time to gauge the length of the ball. Frankly, we made the pitch for Sehwag and he tore us apart.

We would have faced a humbling defeat in the series but for the fact that we reined in Sachin Tendulkar. What went in our favour was that Sachin was suffering from tennis elbow; this severely handicapped the great batsman. We managed to psychologically browbeat him. We bounced the ball at him and were able to unnerve him. I returned to the dressing room that first day with the knowledge that Sachin was not comfortable facing the fast and rising ball. And he was distinctly uncomfortable against me. That was enough to build on.

When we got back on the field, I bowled a particularly fast ball which he, to my amazement, didn't even touch. He walked away! That was the first time I saw him walk away from me—that, too, on the slow track at Faislabad. It got my hunting instincts up. In the next match, I hit him on the head, and he could not score after that.

After Sachin, there was not much opposition. I was the one who would pass by the bat and bruise the batsmen and Asif would pick up their wickets. At team meetings, we would pool our observations about the Indian players and strategize to contain them. It was only then that our lot realized that the pitch needed to be fast. After drawing two matches, we finally prepared a proper pitch, as I had wanted from the start. And we won, and how! We destroyed them. We could have had all the matches in our bag but captains tend to be picked from among batsmen who always think defensively and, to my mind, negatively, especially guys from the subcontinent. To me, making a slow track, without grass, is equivalent to being selfish—it only allows a batsman to get individual records. Thank goodness for all-rounders—win matches for us.

Another factor that perhaps the Indian team had to cope with was the presence of Greg Chappell as their coach. I felt sorry for India because I found him dour faced, with no sense of humour, and wondered how he infused enthusiasm in his team. He did have a talent for creating uncalled-for and unnecessary controversies though, and of course he questioned my bowling action. When Chappell opened his mouth, I immediately got in touch with a law firm and they said, if he does it officially, both of us will go laughing to the bank. To my great regret, the ICC restrained him; I would have been delighted to make some money out of him. In fact, I had been waiting for someone to report me and was ready to sue just about anyone; Greg Chappell would have done fine. Alas! Twenty-five million pounds—that's the figure that seemed to have nestled in my head—flew out of the window.

My bowling is my pride. By questioning my action, Chappell insulted me, and I refused to shake hands with him after the matches. Then he had a row with Ganguly and I remember talking to Ganguly about his attitude. Most of the players didn't have any respect for him. He never laughed—such a downer. And he was so cold. I know that people can be different but being cordial can't be so hard. Anyhow, I just can't respect a cricketer who tries to finish off another cricketer. That is what Chappell was trying to do by questioning my action.

What the opposition didn't know, but our management and team knew, was that I was playing with a hairline fracture in my fibula. I had been in pain so often that I was used to it, and I played two matches with the fracture. They put a needle into the bone to make it numb. During the second match, the hairline fracture widened. Then my knees started playing up. I was in such bad shape that even Inzamam got worried and actually asked me not to play, but I insisted. Finally the gap widened so much that I couldn't play any more. In fact, I couldn't even walk. Unable to ignore the problem any longer, I went to Australia for a knee surgery. This was my second knee surgery. I had already had one done in Pakistan, even before I made my Test debut in 1997, but I hadn't wanted to tell anyone about that. If I had, they would have said, *Ida pahle hi operation hogya, enu bahar kaddo.* He has already been operated upon, chuck him out.

So I went for my second surgery in 2006. It took me five months to recover but after that I began to feel better and was ready to play again. But I was dropped from the Test team; they said I wasn't fit. I felt very letdown by Inzamam. I mean, he had seen how much I was prepared to suffer for the game and how I had pulled my weight for Pakistan. But I was still left on the wayside. It was Bob Woolmer who took my side (and people think we didn't get along!). He insisted that I should be taken care of—Bob, our coach, not Inzamam, our captain. He acknowledged the service I had done for my country against England and India. This was what Bob brought to the team—caring and support.

You see, our management doesn't look after its players the way other boards look after theirs. Back home, if you are fit and perform well, everybody is your friend. But when you are down and out, nobody looks after you. I have never been able to understand this attitude and Bob was not prepared to accept it at all. So, thanks to him, I left for England two weeks after the Test team had left. He had organized a month's training schedule for me at Edgbaston, Birmingham, and put me up at the Marriott—at the PCB's expense, of course. I got back to the desired level of fitness and rejoined the team in time to play one T-20 match and then the ODIs. I did pretty well, too. I got some wickets and was even declared Man of the Match in one game. But in the last game, I got into another argument with Inzamam. I sat outside, and we lost the match.

The PCB now had a new chairman in Naseem Ashraf and at the beginning of his term, I thought we got along well. My first impression was that he seemed to know in which direction the team should move. Towards the end of the year, we headed off to play the Champions Trophy in India. At Jaipur, as usual, the Pakistan team was warmly welcomed by Indian fans, who seem to be especially fond of Afridi, me, and some others. We started having a great time, going out, eating great food, loving the publicity and attention we were getting, especially the attention of Bollywood actresses. I was bowling well and all seemed wonderful when one fine morning I got up and there was this news buzzing amongst the players that I had tested positive for drugs. I had failed the dope test along with Mohammad Asif. The two of us were immediately called back home and then the agony began.

Perhaps Naseem Ashraf had not intended for the news to get out. He had talked to his friend Agha Akbar, who happened to be the sports editor of *The Nation*, a leading Pakistani newspaper. In his very first statement after the fact, Ashraf said that it was an internal matter for the PCB alone and that he would deal with it without any interference from the ICC. I was very impressed—he seemed to be doing the right thing, he was being strong. If the matter had gone up to the ICC, they would probably have banned us for life.

Some people, of course, were delighted at my predicament. Intikhab Alam was one such well-wisher. He was our manager and was also on the committee that was dealing with the issue. And he made sure I would get it in the neck. While the hearing was in progress, he kept winking at me and whispering, 'It's okay, it's okay, you are good.' During a break, he even followed me to the bathroom to assure me that my case was very strong. The truth was, he was mercilessly back-stabbing me, feeding false information all around. Even as he reassured me, he was talking to the news media against me, saying ridiculous things like 'Shoaib's testosterone levels are very high because of the drugs, and he has a very active sex life'. He added for good measure that I had told him this myself! What kind of a man is he?

But Intikhab Alam was the least of my worries. I had a tribunal and a very serious charge to face. Nandrolone is a very controversial substance and its use is banned, though it is commonly used by athletes in all disciplines of sport—tennis and cricket included. It is an oil-based substance that lubricates the joints, it helps you gain muscle tone, and it's also an injury-masking substance. Studies show that its level can be increased in your body by using stuff like Promax 50, a liquid protein diet, TBbomb II or Viper, and the like. I had been taking protein substitutes for years in order to build up muscle so that they could support my joints and perhaps that had increased my natural production of nandrolone. That was all I had in my defence.

The tribunal was headed by Moin Afzal, a retired High Court judge and he ensured that during the hearings I was humiliated enough to satisfy everyone. I was made to sit for three hours outside the room, in the passage, and people kept walking by, gawking at me. Nobody even cared to offer me a glass of water. How ruthless they can get! If the PCB gets hold of someone, it really knows how to finish him off—*voh sochtein hain maar dalo saale ko. Ek star fass gaya hai, beizzati karo iski*. I was in trouble, so I had to swallow it all. It kept getting worse and finally I was handed a two-year ban. Strangely, Asif, the other guy who faced the same charges, got away with a year's ban. Different judgments for the same charges!

As I had been granted fifteen days to appeal against the judgment, I thought, let's try and pull some political strings to influence the board.

A short distance from my home lives a very influential man. I won't mention his name but he is a very, very powerful guy in Pakistan, well set with the President and everyone else. I rang and asked to meet him and said, 'Help me, sir! Help me get out of this mess.'

He said to come on over.

I immediately drove to his house and stopped the car at the gate. The guard walked over and said that I had to identify myself over the intercom so I got out of the car, picked up the intercom and wished him by saying 'Salam bhaiya'. In response, I received a string of abuses. Shocked, I cut in and said, 'Excuse me, sir, *aapne mujhe abuse hi karna thha to phone par kar dete.'* If all he wanted to do was to abuse me, he could have done it over the phone.

He kept right on and threatened that he would send people to kidnap me. I saw red and yelled back, 'You bastard, do it now. I came for help and you invited me to your door to abuse me—I'll remind you of this one day!'

He kept abusing me from indoors and I kept returning the compliment while standing on the road.

I knew that it wasn't easy for anyone to harm me—I am well-known in Pakistan. But I felt humiliated—I felt it deeply. I swung on my heels and started walking back home. Ramzan, my driver, requested me to get into the car but I just shouted at him to keep quiet. So there I was, walking down the main street, unaware of the tears of humiliation that were rolling down my face, while my car followed me. I guess people must have stopped and stared but I was too wrapped up in myself to notice. Some stopped their cars, shouting, do you need a lift; some were abusive. They knew I was in trouble, going through a bad time. Finally Ramzan stepped out of the car and said, 'Sir, I know you want to be alone but let me walk with you.' This was the first time since the trouble started that I had allowed myself to cry, and I couldn't stop. I remember Ramzan telling me gently, 'Sir, you are a very tough man, let it go.' I said, no, today they set fire to my heart. I needed to walk to regain control of myself, to understand what had happened, to get my bearings back. When I reached home, I went straight up to my room and did what I usually do whenever I feel down. I went to sleep and shut out all the terrible things that had happened to me.

When I woke up, I thought, this is it, this is the end. I set a date for a press conference to announce my retirement but that very evening Tauseef came over and took me to his home. He talked me into changing my mind and urged me to contest the ban. In my darkest and most difficult hours, Allah ensured that I had help. The two families that I had, one in Islamabad and the other, Tauseef's family in Lahore, gave me unstinting support, as did Meher Ali, a gentle giant whose sagacity I have come to depend on and, of course, my dear friends Shahid and Ijaz. All of them have stood by me stoically through thick and thin and have often taken up cudgels on my behalf. They never let go of me.

So I appealed against the order. In the meantime, Fakr-ud-din G. Ibrahim became the head of the new tribunal and my case went to him. I was fortunate to have Abid Hasan Minto sahab, a highly qualified lawyer who is greatly respected in Pakistan, to argue and ultimately win the case on my behalf.

As a postscript to this rather ugly business, I must share with you that I met Moin Afzal once again about a year ago. He was present with his family in the same restaurant I was in. I remembered how badly he had treated me and asked him to get out of my sight. His kids began protesting and I told them, 'Don't make me get up! Trust me, you don't want that to happen.'

10

When the Going Gets Tough

Even though the ban was lifted, I was not sure of holding my place in the team but I continued playing first-class cricket in the hope that it would happen some day. Naseem Ashraf came to watch me play one day and was impressed enough to select me against Inzamam's wishes. To my relief and great delight, I was back on board and heading towards South Africa to play in the three-Test series. I missed the first Test but in the second Test, in my very first spell, I took four wickets and succeeded in turning the match around in our favour. Unfortunately, my hamstring started acting up. But Bob Woolmer, for some reason, refused to believe that I wasn't fit—later, I had an MRI taken which showed that I had a second-degree tear in the muscle.

I have mentioned before that Bob and I had sorted things out between us. In the beginning, he couldn't figure me out, so yes, we had our share of disagreements. The one that made the most noise was when we got into an argument in the dressing room during this Test series in South Africa. Bob said I was faking injury and I argued that I was truthfully in pain.

This went on and on, with Bob pressing the issue even when we went out to the nets. Both of us refused to back down and Bob came right into my face, so I pushed him away. Cameras clicked and aired this moment on TV; once again, I was caught in a controversy.

What the media never bothered to air was that Bob and I soon found our equilibrium and became friends. Later in the year, I helped win a few games, and he realized that I was a fast bowler who could run in and win matches for him. In fact, it took him some time to understand the Pakistan team as a whole—its culture, if I may use the term here. It has never been about discipline or commitment or anything else; the Pakistan team is all about passion. Bob finally realized that he didn't have a team to coach and take care of, we were a set of individuals who needed individual attention.

I have always maintained that this game, at least for Pakistan, is about individuals. One batsman and one bowler coming into form is enough—that's how the Pakistan team works. Once Bob figured this out, I must say, the team began to play well under him. Unfortunately, he didn't have much time left. The team had to leave for the World Cup in the West Indies and I was unfit. He tried very hard to persuade me to join the team but I had memories of being careless the last time I was there and was adamant. I was unfit and was going to look after myself.

It was a terrible day for the Pakistan team when we lost Bob. He was a great coach, a caring coach. He was a good man, though misunderstood by a lot of people, and he gave a great deal to the Pakistan team. I recall that I was out dining at Avari Hotel in Lahore when I heard the news of his passing away. I was stunned. Bob had so much love and passion for the game. It meant everything to him. I have always thought it ironical that the game for which he had so much passion took his life. All of us mourned his death and for a long time, the dressing room felt strange without him.

I firmly believe, and this is because I knew Bob, that he died a natural death. He took on a great deal of stress because that was the kind of person he was—dedicated and intense. The way we departed from the World Cup was too much for him. Once again, the team had lost badly and were licking their wounds in the dressing room when the news came in that Bob had died. Some said he had committed suicide and then rumours began to do the rounds, of murder! When the team finally made it back from the West Indies, they had horror stories to tell. I was told by so many of them that when the news of his death broke, a shocked gloom settled upon the dressing room. However, nobody from the management came forward to support them, everyone left them alone. No one from the board came to their aid.

The media was having a field day, conjuring up whatever tale they chose, and there was no one to counter these or answer on behalf of the team. It was awful—sitting so far away from them, I felt their misery. They were harassed for a good twenty days more. I thank Allah that I was not a part of the World Cup team, otherwise I am sure the media would have charged me with murder—charged, not accused. The saddest part of it all was that Bob's body was not handed over to his family for a long time. He had to suffer even after death.

The airing of the argument between Bob and me was probably the proof that was required to turn Ashraf against me. Before this, he had been very supportive despite the fact that there were many around him who tried to poison his ears. Ashraf turned against me now and I was hauled up for disciplinary action. For a period of seven months in 2007, I was kept out of the team and it was only in September that I joined them in Kenya to play the T-20 Quadrangle. Ashraf had by now decided that he required a puppet captain to retain control over the team, so he bypassed the senior and more deserving players—Afridi should have been made captain in my opinion—and chose Shoaib Malik. Malik was backed by Wasim Akram and began playing games at the instigation of the PCB. I was trying to keep my head down until the upcoming T-20 World Cup—the first T-20 World Cup—but by now, controversies seemed to follow me around.

Our team reached South Africa to take part in the pre-matches. I was bowling my best in those days. I had honed my slower ones to perfection and by the time the first four matches that we played were over, everyone was telling me that this 2007 Cup belonged to me.

As usual, things spiralled downwards rapidly. One day, after a nets session in Johannesburg, I was in the dressing room and Afridi was pulling my leg and teasing me; just joking around. Not the best thing to do, though, when I've just come off a bowling spell. I am usually tired and aware of every muscle in my body. I got irritated. Asif was in the adjacent bathroom and found my irritation very funny. I got really cheesed off and picked up a bat—I don't know what made me do it, what was going on in my mind. I kicked open the door of the bathroom, pulled him out. He was jeering at me and said a couple of things that got my goat but I never thought I would react the way I did and especially towards a junior. Afridi was still aggravating the situation and I swung the bat at both of them. Afridi ducked but Asif couldn't get out of the way, the bat struck him on his thighs and he collapsed. I had lost it. I had never behaved like this, especially in the dressing room. I still don't know what happened. All I know is that it was incredibly stupid of me. Afridi did what he always does: he leaked the news. He is very friendly with the Karachi media, Geo television channel and others, and what happened in the dressing room became prime-time news. Initially, Asif denied to the press that I had hit him. Then, after a few hours, he told them that I had hit him and he was seriously injured. He really played it up in front of the media. I knew I had made a bad mistake and I knew I was going to get punished for it.

Unfortunately, Naseem Ashraf had turned out to be a man who used all sorts of methods to keep himself in the seat of power. He used controversies in particular and I kept supplying him with fodder. I became his scapegoat for anything and everything—did you know Pakistan lost the World Cup because Shoaib hit Asif with a bat?

I was sent back home, which was good for me in the long run because we did lose the finals against India and I wasn't there for them to pin the blame on. They would have banned me for life. Back home, I faced an inquiry. I was in the wrong and I apologized in front of the media. Once again, *mujhe zaleel kiya gaya*—I was humiliated. Same bullshit that I had been through at almost regular intervals—it was nothing new to me. I had to pay a fine of thirty-four lakh rupees and Ashraf imposed an indefinite ban on me, which was summarily waived when South Africa came to Pakistan in October. It seemed they needed me after all.

The irony didn't escape me. After they had banned me, our manager Talat Ali had been quoted saying gleefully, 'I have banned him and he has been fined, so what's his next punishment?' I was asked to play the last match but my fitness was suspect and our coach, Geoff Lawson, insisted that I bowl ten overs before the match so he could judge my fitness. I was taken aback and asked, fit or not, how could he make me bowl ten overs before a game? I had to play the next day. But he pressed me and I acquiesced.

I played the Lahore match and got four wickets but we lost the match because of poor batting. We had five wickets in hand but couldn't get twenty runs! Pakistan ended up losing the series but that particular match got me thinking that something was wrong. I have never had the kind of relationships within the dressing room that allow for confidences, so have never had concrete evidence, but this collapse raised a lot of questions amongst the South Africans as well. I spent that night alone in my room, brooding over the day's play, and all the while I kept getting phone calls from people who were angry and upset at the way we had lost the match. They were livid with the batsmen. So was I. I didn't feel like hanging around with the team after that, so I went home.

My relationship with Naseem Ashraf had gone downhill very fast. Neither of us could stand the other, and it only took a spark to set us off against each other. There was a huge personality clash between us. Ashraf wanted 'respect' but I cannot give respect to anyone who demands it; my respect has to be earned. Besides, Ashraf lacked any sort of grace. He used to come into the dressing room wearing Pakistani colours or the team blazer. To my mind, players earn their colours with blood and sweat; it is an honour to wear the national colours and they should be worn only by those who play for Pakistan.

Ashraf also tended to behave like a dictator by never explaining any action or sharing information with the team. He just threw his weight around and told us what to do. And he had a captain to enforce his rules. Before I left with the team to play in India, he warned me that if I didn't perform well, this would be my last series—and he didn't say it politely either. 'I'll screw you and finish you' is how he put it to me. I didn't like the way he spoke to me so I didn't go for the last meeting before we left for India.

I bowled well in India and got four wickets in the first Test. When the second Test began, I was running a temperature of 102°C but I decided to play. That, however, went against me because they started saying I was not fit. I would have thought that they would appreciate my commitment! The Indian team was very good and it met an opposing team that buckled under pressure and was filled with discontent—*ladaiyan, jhagde* and the usual leaking of team-meeting decisions to the media. Leaking team news to the media has become a habit—it's almost a cultural thing for us. The atmosphere just kept getting worse, primarily because of the games Naseem Ashraf's handpicked man, Shoaib Malik, the captain, played with the seniors in the team. This is how things routinely go wrong with us. Seniors get bypassed and are belittled. The juniors have no mentors and get corrupted. No one is there to look after them.

The result of all this was that in 2007 there was no coherence in the team and we lost the Test series appallingly to India.

And you can guess who was blamed for it all. Shoaib Akhtar. Incidentally, this was also the last Test match I played.

Towards the end of 2007, we learned that not one but two leagues of club cricket, the Indian Premier League (IPL) and the Indian Cricket League (ICL), were being created in India. This generated a lot of interest among the players. I was particularly attracted to the idea of playing in one of the leagues because I wasn't really sure when my board would cut my career short. As long as Ashraf was in charge, I wasn't going to be allowed to play peacefully. I was being wooed by both entities now and had to make a choice. The ICL was a rebel league that didn't have the support of the ICC and our chairman was persuading players to stay away from it. He declared that those who chose to play with the ICL would not play for Pakistan. That was something I didn't want, so I was inclined towards the IPL.

Shahrukh Khan, the Indian actor who owned the Kolkata Knight Riders, had got in touch with me to play for his team. I left for India again for the negotiations and was invited to Shahrukh's house for discussions. During our meeting, I got the feeling that it was Saurav Ganguly and not Shahrukh who wanted me on the team. Shahrukh wasn't sure about me, but Ganguly knew the kind of bowler I was. Then I met Lalit Modi, who had actively pursued me to join the IPL; he promised the heaven and the earth if I did. But when the bidding took place, I was disappointed. Bids are meant to be based on talent, and I genuinely felt that I was in a different league from some of the younger players.

The ICL, on the other hand, was offering more. Subhash Chandra and Himanshu Mody, who used to be a part of the

ICL meetings, rang me to say that I should let them know my terms; they were very keen that I join them. I was trying to be practical and think about my future for a change, and I knew I needed to make the right decision. I thought I might have to bow out of playing for my country, so I asked the ICL for an amount that would compensate for that and a bit more, and they were ready to give me what I wanted. Tony Greig was their main man and Moin Khan represented them in Pakistan. But I wasn't comfortable with the idea of never being able to play for my country again, and that finally swung the balance in favour of the IPL.

Shahrukh and I had talked about my not being happy with the money settled on me. I let him know that it was not just about the money, it was about justifying and acknowledging one's stature and talent. I told him, Look, I am letting go of a lot of money for you, so please compensate me for it; otherwise, please let me go. He tried to persuade me, saying, this is the first time we have tried bidding—we have an extra million for you. Somehow, even though I wasn't satisfied with the result of the auction, Shahrukh and Modi got me to agree. I remember Lalit Modi telling me not to join the ICL; we will eventually give you more money, he said. Please play for the IPL.

Meinu behla-phusla ke—I'll get this for you, I'll get that for you—they got me to say yes. Lalit Modi told me that I wouldn't regret my decision and that he would ensure that I made more money through endorsements and the like, but that never happened. I should have never listened to Lalit Modi and Shahrukh. All those who did join the ICL eventually came back and played for Pakistan. They buttered their bread on both sides.

Now here's the twist in the tale. I was prepared to accept less money in order to keep playing for my country; my board then slammed a five-year ban on me. I had openly declared my dissatisfaction with the PCB for not renewing my contract, preparing dead pitches and other stuff that got Ashraf all churned up and mad. He then had the gall to let me know that I would have to sign a contract with the board to go and play elsewhere. This wasn't right and I said, no, I won't, I have my own agent. I went back to Mumbai and signed the contract with KKR. The next thing I knew, the ban was in place.

This was the beginning of another difficult period in my life. Lalit Modi had a contract that didn't resemble mine. There was nothing in the contract that I had which indicated that the five-year ban by my board would be upheld by the IPL as well. But Modi declared that I had to be reinstated by my board before I could play in his league. So now, I had nowhere to go! I believe Modi's attitude towards me was influenced by his relationship with Naseem Ashraf. Ashraf wanted to ban me from cricket for ever—*Shoaib kahin ka na rahe*—and Modi was prepared to oblige. Shahrukh, however, remained committed to my playing for the Kolkata Knight Riders and wanted to help me but didn't know how to go about it. He had entered the cricket arena for the first time and it was also the first season of a newly formed league, so he barely knew the ropes.

Once again, I found myself running from pillar to post, trying to get some semblance of justice. When nobody on the board was prepared to ease things for me, I called up Mubashar, affectionately known as Moby the Duck, and told him about my problem. Mubashar is a wonderful man whom I had met in 2000 in Manchester; we have been friends since.

He immediately introduced me to Faisal Butt, who was a very close friend of President Zardari. I placed my problem in front of him and told him that Naseem Ashraf was jerking me around. Faisal Butt agreed to help me. The political wheels of our country were turning and President Musharraf was losing his popularity in Pakistan. Then Benazir Bhutto was shot and Zardari sahab started gaining strength politically so the tables were turning for Naseem Ashraf—he was Musharraf's blue-eyed boy but Musharraf's political clout was waning.

I had also made a call to Altaf Hussein sahab of the MQM party and requested him to help resolve the matter, suggesting that Rehman Malik (now Pakistan's Minister of Interior) was the man who could do it. Altaf bhai spoke to Rehman sahab, who at first didn't pay much attention to my case. Then Zardari sahab himself called. Rehman Malik belonged to his party, so now it became a party matter.

Two weeks went by. The controversy that surrounded the sacking of judges by Musharraf was at its peak. Zardari sahab was in Dubai and was neck deep in the matter. But he remembered me even in the midst of the chaos that our country was engulfed in. He called Faisal Butt and enquired about the situation. Butt told him that there had been no progress. Then Zardari sahab called Rehman Malik and insisted that the matter be dealt with that very night.

And so it happened that in the evening, I was running with Obaid, trying to keep my anxieties at bay, and later that same night I was being flown to Islamabad. At the same time, Naseem Ashraf was woken up and summoned to Rehman Malik's house. He was told by Rehman sahab that the problem had to be solved immediately. It has become a party matter now, and you need to get off his back—these are Zardari sahab's orders. If you don't lift the ban, there will be a new chairman in the morning.

Ashraf said he needed to discuss it with President Musharraf. Malik told him that President Musharraf had already been informed and he would not intervene.

So there we were, the chairman and I, standing in front of each other in another man's house, late at night. I could see defeat written all over his face and I will not deny that it gave me satisfaction. It was close to 2:30 a.m. when, dressed in white pyjamas and a red kurta, Naseem Ashraf had walked in rubbing his eyes, which nearly popped out when he saw me sitting with Rehman Malik. I was told later by Shafqat Naghmi, the CEO of PCB, that Ashraf had rung him after being summoned by Malik, to ask what he should do. Naghmi told him, 'You are standing in the middle of the road. A loaded truck is heading straight at you, you better move out of its way. Let Shoaib go.'

Rehman sahab invited all of us to stay and have a meal, but I said I didn't want to eat with someone like Ashraf. However, I finally did so out of respect for Rehman Malik.

Rehman sahab then wanted me to shake Ashraf's hand but I baulked. We sat in opposite corners of the room, not talking to each other, while Rehman sahab told us how he wanted us to walk out of there, if not as friends, then as men who had put the past behind us. Not possible! Rehman Malik stepped out of the room and I couldn't resist asking Ashraf what had happened to his code of conduct and discipline now? I must have continued in this vein for a while, before Malik sahab came back in and began coaxing me to back off saying, he is older than you, apologize to him. You had announced publicly that he wanted you to go through him for the IPL, so please apologize publicly. I nearly had an apoplectic fit at the thought of an apology but he requested me to do it and there was no way I could hold out for long, so a series of custom-tailored apologies followed. I still can't swallow what I had to do but we came to an arrangement that allowed me to play in India and later, the ban was lifted. I owe President Zardari for standing by me and am deeply grateful to Mubashar and Faisal Butt. I will never forget what they did for me.

My first match in the IPL season was an emotional one, for I had come through a nightmare year and was still raw. I was mentally so low that for the first time in my life, I didn't feel like playing cricket. I just wanted to get away from it all. In fact, I nearly pulled out of the IPL because I wasn't sure about myself—I lacked confidence and felt broken inside.

My friend John Buchanan also believed that I was not fit enough to play the match, which happened to be against the Delhi Daredevils. I have noticed over the years that I only have to hear someone tell me I can't do something and I immediately get the burning urge to prove him wrong. Between you and me, I had had no practice, no training, as I had been caught up in the battle with Ashraf and had been under a huge amount of stress, wondering how to find enough money to pay the fine levied on me. But John only had to sneer at me and I told him that I was more than ready for the match. Ganguly and Shahrukh had, at the same time, told me that they needed this game badly so I said, play me, let me run for you and I will get you the match.

On the eve of the match, I willed myself to lose all the

baggage of the immediate past. And when I heard the crowd roaring my name, everything fell into place. I thought to myself, you wanted to be here, you are here. Listen to the crowd that's behind you. They are standing as one for you, so enjoy it. When I got on to the ground, I heard the crowd getting behind me and when the wickets started falling, I shook off every care. That first match was one of the highlights of the season and I was bowling fast again. We were defending a low score of 133 runs. After facing my first delivery, Sehwag said, 'Oh shit! You look like you're in the mood today.' I grinned and got myself 4 for 11 from 3 overs, a performance that earned me the Player of the Match award—a slap in the face for Buchanan. We had restricted the Daredevils to 110 runs!

Then we partied till six in the morning—Ganguly, Sehwag, Shahrukh, and all the rest of us. Back home, people started questioning the board's actions. The media said, look at the way you treated him and look how he is playing away from you guys, outside the country. I began to hear good things being said about me when at one stage I had thought that it was all over. So it was a very emotional comeback for me and I can only thank my supporters and fans, especially the fans of Kolkata Knight Riders.

It was also a great experience for me to interact with the Indian public. This time, I was just a cricketer in their eyes, not a Pakistani cricketer. I had always felt loved by the Indian public, particularly the people of Kolkata, and I consider Eden Gardens one of my favourite grounds. Everywhere I went, I felt that I was supported—the crowds really backed me, they seemed to want me out there. That night, when I won the match against the Delhi Daredevils, people jumped around and danced in the streets. It took us ages to reach our hotel from the stadium. The accolades were like a balm to my soul. A few people broke the safety cordon around us and carried me on their shoulders to my room. Not something I was used to in India, as a Pakistani player!

They treated me as their own, and it felt wonderful. I had never expected it. Before the game, I had wondered how the crowds would respond to Pakistani players and to me in particular. It was unbelievable. I laughed and soaked it all up. I knew I had been popular here before the IPL but after this, it was like we had touched each other's hearts. The IPL made me feel connected to Indians—it was a unique feeling. But of course, with me, nothing lasts. After playing three matches, I got injured again, and couldn't play any more.

I must say that the IPL was a terrific experience. It was good to play with and against some of the best players in the world and I enjoyed myself immensely. I feel though that the IPL, and especially the club boards, should be more transparent in their money transfers, and must most certainly honour their contracts. It's the players who bring in the crowds, so they need to be looked after. But then, it is a relatively new format for India and I am sure they will clean up their act, and this will benefit the good players. If it can successfully look after the players, this event is a good thing and it must be nurtured carefully. In fact, I think more boards should follow suit. This is going to be the future of cricket.

Unfortunately, on 26 November of the same year, the dastardly Mumbai attacks occurred and relations between India and Pakistan deteriorated. No Pakistani cricketer was picked for the second season and it doesn't look like we will be

invited back anytime soon. I can understand the club owners'
response to some extent. Among other things, the media
showed images of a few people in Pakistan—an insignificant
minority, I may add—dancing in the streets after the blasts.
I recall thinking in horror, people die in Mumbai and you
celebrate! Are you human? Don't the people of Mumbai have
red blood like yours?

I hate all this. My life is half over and we still have this
immovable wall of distrust between our countries. When will
it change? The people of both countries want peace and the
freedom to visit any city in each other's country, whenever
they wish to. If I could help resolve our differences, I would
gladly walk barefoot from Lahore to New Delhi—or whatever
it takes. I despise terrorism and the harm it has done to my
country and my people.

11

I'm Still Standing

I was home after playing the first season of IPL, awaiting the lifting of the ban on me. I had become an untouchable, thanks to the vendetta led by Ashraf, but wasn't about to let anyone know that I was worried. Ashraf and I happened to pass each other one day in Lahore and I told him that while he was still the chairman, he would pick me for the team again. He went away laughing, but I was convinced it would happen.

At this point in time, however, I was being ignored, so when an opportunity arose for me to play for Surrey, I grabbed it. And here's a funny story. Usually my agent looks after all my travel documents. This time, however, when I flew into Heathrow, I was stopped by Immigration for not having proper documents. I recall one officer telling me quite sympathetically—he probably followed cricket—'Look, I know you have to play for the county but I'm afraid you don't have the requisite documents, so we will have to deport you.' This was at 2.30 in the afternoon and I was sent back on the next flight.

I landed in Islamabad at 9 p.m. and went to the embassy as soon as I could to process all the paperwork and get a visa.

Then I was back in Surrey. Meanwhile, the headlines back home screamed, 'Shoaib deported'—big deal!

Finally, in October, the ban was lifted and Ijaz Butt oversaw my selection for the T-20 series in Canada. But the PCB was still hoping to get rid of me once and for all, so they called me in for a random dope test in the hope that I would get caught again. But I tested clean and went on to Canada with the team. We did quite well in the tournament and reached the finals, but lost to Sri Lanka in King City. The important thing for me was that I was back in the reckoning again, against all odds.

The year 2009 began with the PCB putting me back on a central contract, which defined a fixed salary per month for a stipulated time period, besides match fees, bonus, etc. Needless to say, it had to be dragged out of them, and for this I have to thank Younis Khan and Abdul Qadir. Once again, my knees were really messed up, and I had let everyone know that I wouldn't be able to play a Test match in the state I was in, so the PCB wasn't keen to induct me. Younis, however, was insistent and argued that I would be useful in the shorter versions of the game. He pushed hard and I found myself on board for the home series against Sri Lanka, to be played in January. I am grateful to Younis for his faith in me but my knees let both of us down and I was dropped for the last ODI game.

The year was an insignificant one in some ways, except for the terrorist attack on the visiting Sri Lankan team. The terrorists chose to fire upon their bus as it was leaving for the match venue. I believe that while this was obviously the result of a security lapse by the police, it was also because of the negligence of the board. We had such an incompetent bunch of guys organizing the tour. The director of operations, Zakir

Khan, had been a cricketer once—though he barely played two or three matches for Pakistan—and he knew little about management. Yet he was given such a responsible position by the board. This was courting disaster and disaster occurred. If I remember correctly, six of the Sri Lankan players were injured; Thilan Samaraweera and Tharanga Paravitarana received serious injuries. We were lucky that none of them got killed.

In Pakistan, terrorists regularly inflict huge damage to life and property and it is usually innocent men, women and children who get blown up in the marketplaces or at shrines and mosques. No one seems to be able to stop it, so much for the bullshit war on terror.

The attack on the Sri Lankans was the worst thing that could have happened to Pakistan cricket. We lost everything—being unable to play at home is dreadful. By Allah's mercy, no fatalities occurred. And we will always be grateful to the people of Sri Lanka and their government for their dignified and far from acrimonious response to what happened to them on Pakistani soil. My Sri Lankan colleagues could have lost their lives and many more could have been seriously hurt; indeed, they were fortunate to escape with their lives. Yet, how bravely they reacted. They took bullets and yet they didn't say a word against Pakistan—our ties have been further strengthened by their gracious behaviour.

I know it's not news to the world that over the last few years, Pakistan's politics and economy have become deeply fractured. I also hope it's no news to the world that ordinary Pakistani citizens like me are terribly anxious. The war on terror has affected every aspect of our existence and not just cricket. Everyone in this war follows their narrow agendas and the Pakistani people suffer. It is my opinion that until the war in Afghanistan comes to an end, Pakistan *mein sakoon nahin hoga*. Peace is necessary for everything. This may be a naïve point of view but perhaps the best way to go about bringing peace to the second decade of this century is for governments and countries to leave each other alone and get out of each other's space—else this region is going to drag everyone down with it.

Everybody needs to start looking at the bigger picture. So much money, so many lives are being wasted but the war on terror seems to have no end, no solution. Unless there is stability in the region, Pakistan *mein cricket wapas nahin ayega. Aur jab tak yeh* so-called war of terror—I don't know what it's all about, *kaun si war Pakistan ladh raha hai aur kiske saath?*— it will be very difficult for cricket to survive in Pakistan. For a long time, we players felt that cricket had nothing to do with what was happening around us and then the Sri Lankan incident happened. Cricket became a victim of terror. We lost everything—Pakistan wasn't considered as a co-host for the 2011 World Cup.

The perpetrators of the attack on the Sri Lankan cricketers were never caught and yet the Sri Lankan government and the team's attitude ensured that Pakistan found wonderful friends in the worst time in its history. The Sri Lankans understand that it is a rare minority that wishes so much harm on another human being. How can you stop suicide bombers and the like? Because of them, Pakistan cricket continues to suffer. Our home series will now be played in host countries like Abu Dhabi, Dubai, Sharjah and England. We can only be thankful to them for enabling Pakistan to remain a part of international cricket. Our bowlers will get an opportunity to use lively green wickets that help seam movement but nothing can make up for not being able to play on home soil in front of the home crowd. Strangely, such serious matters do not seem to affect the workings of the PCB. Cricket in Pakistan is being threatened, yet they continue to mess around with the players, indulging in petty politics and pursuing personal agendas.

I had been selected for the 2009 T-20 World Cup to be held in the UK. However, I knew that despite a new chairman—Ijaz Butt had taken over from Ashraf—the board and the management were waiting for an opportunity to drop me, especially Yawar Saeed, who has been the manager for nearly four decades now. Saeed has ruined Pakistan cricket by indulging in all sorts of dirty politics and concocting intrigues and controversies out of thin air. He manifests no desire to nurture and promote talent; on the contrary, he has no problems getting rid of talent when he doesn't like someone personally. He was mainly responsible for making Younis Khan suffer by throwing him out and keeping him out of the team for a whole year. Butt went along with it because they were friends. And Saeed, of course, had problems with me.

We had just returned from Dubai after a series with Australia when things started going wrong again. A preparation camp for the T-20 World Cup was held in Bhurban, Islamabad. Unfortunately, I chose to get medical attention just before the camp and was unable to attend. When you play, you sweat profusely and this, more often than not, causes skin problems. Even if you shower several times in a day, when skin rubs against skin, you develop all kinds of painful rashes, rough patches and skin tags—acrochordon is the medical term. I needed to pay attention to the condition of my skin but picked the wrong time to do so. Nobody was pleased and I was back in the PCB's blacklist. Three days before the team departed for the T-20 World Cup, I was dropped. I had been treated at Mayo Hospital by Dr Ishtiaq Ahmad, who is also a professor attached to King Edward Medical College. The report that he forwarded to the board stated that I had been successfully treated for skin tags. However, the medical panel of the PCB twisted or tweaked that report—I am convinced this was at the behest of Zakir Khan and Saeed—and told the board that I had been treated for genital viral warts! The PCB then called a press meeting and announced to one and all that I had this disease and was unfit to play. I was shocked. This was literally hitting below the belt and I didn't know how to fight back. They actually used this false report as an excuse to get rid of me—how desperate they must have been.

Zakir Khan is a complex and insecure person who gets threatened by the popularity of players. Men like him want players to hover respectfully around them while they boss them around. I am not one of those diplomatic chaps who can listen to such rubbish and I hold these two guys responsible for the way in which I was abused. While they were patting themselves on the back for having successfully got rid of Younis Khan and me, our chairman kept silent. Presumably, it all happened with his knowledge. It is difficult to believe that he couldn't have stopped them if he wished to.

Initially, Dr Ishtiaq Ahmad and I thought of suing the board for defamation but better sense prevailed. Once I did that, any cricketing opportunities that were left for me would also disappear. Besides, those around me advised me to let it go as quietly as possible—media *mazaa lega, chaddo*. The selected team went ahead and won the championship; Mohammad Amir emerged as one of the star performers. The team was lauded upon their return and then they travelled onward to Sri Lanka and I was ignored. I guess they didn't feel the need to disturb a winning combination.

I wasn't getting to play so I thought, let's pay some attention to my knees, and went in for surgery. I had to scrounge for the medical fees because Ashraf had slammed a defamation suit of twenty-two crore rupees on me, over the IPL issue, which later was brought down to seventy lakh. Now, I didn't have that kind of money to spare. Even though I had a contract, the board withheld my dues because of the pending court case. Finally, they did release my wages, minus the seventy lakh of course. So I spent that year pretty tight for money. Eventually, when 2010 arrived, they did not renew my contract. Abdul Qadir actually resigned because he felt that the board's treatment of me was unduly harsh—board *ne ziyaati kitti mere naal*.

So that's how the year 2009 passed: I was dropped, maligned and fined. It's not that I took it all lying down. I tried defending myself against them and when that failed, I tried pulling strings to get them off my back. I tried seeking help from everyone I could think of, including the prime minister's office, and I was even thinking of approaching the President. Difficulties seemed to be coming at me from all sides and I got nervous and depressed. But the day I gave up and left everything in Allah's hands, my name was included automatically. The lesson to be learnt here is that it's best to relax, keep your mouth shut, not go complaining from pillar to post, and remain alert for opportunities. There is a solution to all of one's problems but they will appear in their own time, so one must learn to sit it out and stop panicking.

So I looked at myself and thought, if I want to continue playing, I need to get my knees fixed. I hadn't earned any money for over a year but I flew to England and checked into Lister Hospital for another knee surgery. After the surgery, the doctor told me in no uncertain terms that I needed to start thinking about saving some strength in my knees for my old age and that I couldn't keep punishing them the way I was. I now knew that the time had come for me to decide about my future. The truth was that there was very little mileage left in my knees but I wanted the 2011 World Cup so I promised myself that, given the chance, I would give my very best and then bow out. It wasn't an easy decision. I love this game and it has given me everything I wanted. But I did want to retire with dignity and not be shoved out in disgrace. So I came back home and spent the next six months going back to the basics. I clamped down on my anxieties, continued training, held on to my belief in Allah, and things started getting better.

This is how it has always worked for me. Whenever I have left everything in his hands, I have benefited. Before the Asia Cup 2010, I was asked to take a fitness test. Later in the evening, I became a bit restless but I took a deep breath and told myself, let it go, and went to sleep. When I woke up, I got a call from the PCB informing me that I had been selected. I said, thank you very much. I also told them that I would only be available for the T–20s and ODIs, and they played me in those formats.

It was good to be playing again. Slowly I started getting back into my rhythm and form and began doing well enough for people to notice and say nice things about me, although in a rather surprised tone. My speed, despite a shortened run-up, was okay but I aimed to rev it up even more. Playing for your country is always a great feeling and playing my first match in Sri Lanka in the Asia Cup after a long lay-off was great. We won at Dambulla and I got three wickets for forty-one but eventually we lost the tournament. Sri Lanka has become one of my favourite places for a visit. They are a lovely, warm and gracious people, very humble and big hearted, and a great cricketing nation.

Besides, the crowds enjoy watching me play. I never get booed like Ricky Ponting does. And I have great respect for the talent within their team. It is the batsmen from Sri Lanka, with their fearless batting, who showed the world how to play the one-day game. They were the ones who got runs within the first ten overs and brought life into the game. Jayasurya led the way and Jayawardene is another superb batsman, as is Kumar Sangakkara—they have a very talented batting line-up. They need to produce good fast bowlers but, of course, they have Murali, who is the greatest of all spin bowlers. Of a hundred balls you might face from him, you are bound to miss thirty. He is a master spinner. The ICC, however, has never truly recognized what a great talent he has and, more often than not, has hindered his progress. He has got eight hundred wickets—what a feat—a feat worth honouring him for. Why hasn't that been done? Murali is a tough cookie and has never let all this get him down, and for this I admire him.

After bowing out of the Asia Cup, we set off immediately for England. The English cricket board had very graciously agreed to play host for our home series against Australia, after which we were to stay on and play England. We played two T–20 matches against Australia and, to our delight, won both. Since I wasn't playing in the Tests, I returned home for that duration and flew back for the next set against England, and that was when the British news channels began airing match-fixing allegations. Once again, everything became messy. I hadn't expected this from the newbies. *Main soch raya si ki kis kism de ladke nain?* What kind of guys were these? How can they not take pride in their game and their integrity while playing for the country? It was all very frustrating. These constant allegations of match fixing are so embarrassing that sometimes I feel like I am standing naked on the field. This was not the comeback I had hoped for. Instead of enjoying myself, I had to walk around hearing awful things about my team. I desperately wanted us to play well, especially in preparation for the World Cup, and was knocking myself out for it, but I was also fighting to stave off demoralization. I had started by trying to become a mentor to the youngsters but now I didn't know whom to trust. My team was crumbling around me.

At Lord's during an ODI match, Paul Collingwood walked up to me and said, 'Shoaib, are you blind? Your whole team is involved in match fixing!'

Exasperated, I replied, 'Paul, if you know something, tell me.'

He replied, 'Shoaib, we have always respected you as a player because you never cheated the game, but your team does.'

I kept repeating, who does? He was clearly bitter and claimed that I was being totally blind. Later, I watched in despair as Jonathan Trott hit Wahab Riaz on the face and called him a fixer during a net session. The team management wanted to lodge a complaint with the police but didn't because things would have deteriorated even further and the tour would have been called off—as it is, it was hanging by a thread. The English players were very upset with us and called us fixers even during play. *Bade anxious halaat mein hum khele voh tournament.* I only wish we had won. We were fairly hopeful when we were 2–2 in the series. I kept telling myself, do your best, put everything you have into it and don't get distracted, but it was hard. I wish *ki hum jeet jaate toh hamaari badnaami thori kam ho jaati.*

After the allegations became public, the management clamped down on the team. We were like prisoners, not allowed to move around freely. I became very nervous. I had just about managed to get back in and I became paranoid about somebody trying to do me in under cover of all this confusion. I was worried about dope tests and refused to eat or drink at our hotel, and began squeezing bottles to ensure they were not punctured or injected with something that might end up in my blood. I would get a friend to order food from a particular restaurant, rush there, swallow the food and rush back to the hotel. This was because there were strange people all around us, guys who had nothing to do with the team or the management. I remember discussing with a few other players how uncomfortable we were with the situation and how suspicious it all was. We were even afraid that the house-keeping girls might put rape charges on us.

You might raise your eyebrows at this but that's truly how uncomfortable we were. One member of the team after another was hit by match fixing allegations and the English players were not very happy playing against us. We didn't know whether the tour would continue, there were rumours of it being called off. Finally, it was only because the English board would have lost a lot of money that the teams played on. As far as I was concerned, it felt as though the tour had actually been called off. I didn't know if I would ever be considered for the team again. We were shit scared and yet we had to play on.

I must say that all through this, the three boys who were under the ICC scanner stayed in their rooms and refused to eat or drink. Everyone got nervous and our security in-charge, Major Najam, was asked to keep an eye on them. He was with them almost 24/7 for thirteen days, just in case they attempted something foolhardy, perhaps even suicide. He literally had to force open their jaws to throw water down their throats.

Major Najam shared an observation with me about this time which was interesting. He said that two of the boys, Salman Butt and Mohammad Amir, looked tense and upset, while Asif Mohammad was the calmest of the three. I wasn't all that surprised to hear this because Asif had been caught previously for wrongdoing—he had a criminal record. He remained calm and kept saying, *chaddo ji, koi masla nahin hai.* Forget it, there's no problem. When he got back to Pakistan, he didn't appeal like the others did.

Butt told me that he couldn't believe what was happening and that he felt he was living a nightmare. I told him, no, this is happening for real and if you are innocent, face the ICC squarely and blast everyone. So far, he hasn't taken my advice. The ICC, I may add, finally took a stand and imposed a lifelong ban on the three of them.

Our management became so careful after this that in Dubai, during the South Africa series in November 2010, they put extra cameras in the hotel hallways. One night, I returned to my room ten minutes after curfew time and was fined US$500, but funnily enough, Zulqarnain, one of the boys in our team, managed to abscond with his luggage. He later surfaced in England.

The saddest thing was that cricket took a back seat during this time. We hadn't won a single series yet and that worried me more than anything else. There seemed to be very little desire to reach for the skies and the World Cup was around the corner.

But adversity can often bring out the best in people and that's what happened to us. The seniors in the team, and this included Afridi, Umar Gul and myself, sat down with Asad Shafiq, Azhar Ali and a couple of other youngsters and said, let's save Pakistani cricket. We began talking and encouraging each other and started making special efforts to raise the morale of the team. There was a full season ahead of us and the much coveted World Cup to play for. We told them, we've got to put all this behind us and play to win. Personally, when the World Cup trophy was unveiled later in the year in Dubai, my mouth watered, I wanted it so badly. It had been put into a box and placed at the bottom of the largest freshwater tank in the world, which happens to be in the Dubai Mall. Dale Steyn and Morne Morkel dived in and brought it out. The organizers had asked for one player from our side to dive in as well and I would have jumped at the opportunity, but no one told me about it. I do remember thinking that winning the Cup was possible if we strategized effectively and played fearlessly.

We went on to New Zealand after this, and things started settling down. I was visiting New Zealand after a gap of six years and had memories of a wonderful tour in 2003, especially of the Wellington match in which I had taken eleven wickets and won the match for Pakistan. I wanted to bowl my best again. And I didn't do too badly. The media started drawing everyone's attention to the fact that I was still a wicket-taker for my team.

We were good about supporting each other as a team now, even though Intikhab Alam continued to distance himself from us, not telling us what was on his mind but letting outsiders know that only those who did well on the tour would go on to play the World Cup. The PCB did the right thing by retaining Misbah-ul-Haq and Shahid Afridi as captains for the Test and T–20 teams respectively. Misbah is a well-grounded team-man and his presence greatly helped steady our morale. We didn't win but we didn't let ourselves down either. Slowly, and at times painfully, the collective will to do our best bloomed in the dressing room.

Our team was in Sri Lanka when the terrible news of the earthquake in New Zealand came through. It took the lives of many and destroyed the properties of even more. I recalled enjoying a delicious lamb steak at a very pretty restaurant in Christchurch, looking out at the peaceful landscape, and was grieved at the thought of so much devastation and pain.

The battle for the 2011 World Cup was finally upon us. As I have said before, I had made up my mind to retire after the World Cup and yet spent many sleepless nights before informing the management of my decision. On the morning of 17 March, just before net practice, I told the boys that I was bowing out. It was a very emotional moment for me. Cricket had transformed my life, it had given me everything, and walking away was proving very hard. Everyone there knew

I had fought tooth and nail to get back into the side, so my announcement caught them by surprise. I thanked Alam for giving me the central contract and Waqar, of course, but when I continued to thank individual members of the team, I noticed tears on the cheeks of Misbah, Gul and Hafeez, and nearly broke down myself. I hurriedly stuffed a handkerchief in my pocket and walked to the media centre, where I announced my retirement to the world. It is difficult to describe how I felt at that moment.

I'd had a dream of breaking my own record, just for myself—to feel like I was the fastest again. I had already crossed 97 mph in England in 2010, without even getting into my rhythm properly. I was feeling fit and ready and knew that if I was able to truly find my form, it wouldn't be difficult. During the match against Sri Lanka in the World Cup, I had clocked 159 kmph and while nobody else paid much attention to this, I began to think, 'If only I could do it in India! What a nice place to achieve something like this. But most of all, Pakistan should win—everything should come in a package. The Cup, and also me breaking my own record.' Hey! I can dream, can't I? And nothing is impossible in cricket. That is the beauty of this game. I kept telling myself, 'Let's cross it once again for old times' sake. No competition, just for myself.' Alas, it wasn't meant to be.

At the semifinals in Mohali, we faced a team that performed superbly as a unit. We, on the other hand, seemed to have lost the plot towards the end. This was sad because we had worked so hard to keep it all together. Our win against Kenya and then Sri Lanka had brought about a change in the dressing room. It had fanned a hunger, a belief that we could go all the way, but *ehtiyad rakhna zaroori tha*—we had to continue to be careful and not get into any more controversies.

The pundits at the World Cup called us the dark horses and seemed surprised that we had played so well in the games preceding the semifinals, but we had found the will to shrug off the past. There was no dearth of talent in the Pakistan dressing room; all we had to do was to keep it together. Our management continued to crack the whip, threatening rather then coaxing us to play our best, and kept their thoughts to themselves. But that was not unusual, so we were able to ignore the silence of our manager, Intikhab Alam, who firmly believes that uttering an encouraging word to boost a player's morale is not a part of his job profile. Of course, this also meant we didn't know what he was thinking, which didn't help at all. As far as I was concerned, our coach, Waqar Younis, had no problem telling the world that he wasn't sure I was fit or had the stamina to play ten overs, though he had to admit I wasn't bowling too badly. Again, this was nothing new, for he had been talking about me in this vein since I had been selected for the side in 2010. It was another matter that I kept telling everyone that I was fit and ready and was taking wickets for the team.

Finally, before the match against Australia, both of them asked me how my knees were and whether I would be able to play. I answered, 'You guys should know that I am fit, you've got me jumping hurdles, literally, and training hard, haven't you?' And boy, were they making us work. We were lugging weights, jumping hurdles and even boxing, if you please. Nobody thought it was important to give the body time to rest. In fact, a couple of youngsters complained to me that they were being over trained just to force me into proving that I could keep up. And still there was no sharing of ideas or any meaningful communication at all from our manager and coach.

Gradually, the silence began to permeate the dressing room too. I felt a keen sense of déjà vu. My last day in the dressing room felt just like the first time I had joined the national team, when nobody talked to me if they could help it. I felt just as unsure and nervous as I had then. The only difference was that nobody was shouting at me; I was a senior member of the team after all. All the attempts made by us to pitch together as a team had evaporated like ether. I couldn't understand why there was such a sense of unease around me. I mean, the management should have been relieved, for they had always wanted to get rid of me. Perhaps they didn't know what to do with the fact that I wasn't being slung out by my ear, I was walking out on my own steam. But I *was* leaving.

Their silence, the refusal to share any decisions with the rest of the team so as to avoid taking on board their inputs, made everyone nervous and by the time we reached Mohali, the atmosphere in the dressing room was no longer conducive to victory.

Once again, it was a combination of the coach, the manager and a willing captain that had ruled against me but they kept it a secret because almost everyone around us had begun to say that Shoaib should be played. Waqar was a great cricketer but a terrible captain and coach. He wanted to play his own man, Wahab, and worked hard to keep me out. And, of course, I was never told in advance if I was to play the next match or not.

I sat on the bench, dressed in Pakistan colours, and watched us defeat Australia. I sat on the bench during the quarter-finals and watched us knock the West Indies over. I fought the disappointment by telling myself, *koi na*, I was still a part of a winning team. Then I sat on the bench in the semifinals against India, watching hope slowly slip away. The not-knowing was what had hurt the most. Afridi had chosen to tell the media that I was not playing in Mohali before he felt the need to tell me. The morning of the match, I had walked out to hand some passes to a friend, who broke the news to me. For a few seconds I thought my heart would burst, everything went blank, because I had been led to believe that I was in the squad. And then I shrugged off the descending darkness and went back to support my team. I would have shared in the glory if we had won the World Cup, whether I was on the field or in the dressing room, just as I now shared the disappointment of our loss. I will, however, forever carry the feeling that perhaps the result could have been different if they had played me.

Needless to say, we took our loss hard. The younger players were crying in the dressing room and Waqar was sulking as usual. Afridi and I had spent the day avoiding each other. When we were climbing into the bus that was waiting to take us to our hotel, he walked up to me with a long face saying, '*Yaar Shoaib, yeh kya hogya*—how did this happen?' A younger Shoaib would have had a lot to say in response, but that day I just gestured that he should move away from me.

Back in Islamabad, my family and friends gathered in support. That night I fell into a deep sleep from which I awoke feeling fresh and relaxed. A phase of my life was over. I had lots of things to wrap up though, and Pakistan had lots of things to say about me. Very kind and loving words came my way from my fans, my friends and even the media. We met the prime minister, who singled me out for generous praise, complimenting my bowling skills and saying that I had served my country well and with honesty. He added that I had 'contributed a lot to Pakistan cricket, even when you were in pain'. In fact, for weeks after our return, the public and the press continued to heap praise on me, until even Waqar seemed to feel he had to say something. He ended up saying many splendid things about me and my bowling ability and claimed that I was 'irreplaceable'. It would have been nice if he had said all that to my face. It would have been nicer if the PCB had given me a farewell. It would have set a much needed precedent for the team.

12

Soaring High on Broken Wings

Many of my well-wishers and detractors have commented on the fact that I should have played more than just forty-six Test matches and 163 one-day internationals in a career spanning eighteen years. What they don't know is that I have spent my life running on swollen and painful knees and it is a wonder that I can play at all. If you saw my knees, you'd understand what I am talking about. They bear the scars of three knee surgeries, the skin is puckered due to the insertion of tubes through which fluid has been frequently drained out and there are innumerable puncture marks from the pain-killing injections. I am called the Rawalpindi Express, fast and unstoppable, but I have struggled with asthma and am flat-footed. In all these years, I can't recall a single day when I wasn't in physical pain. To all my fans and friends who wonder why I didn't play enough and to youngsters who wish to play cricket, this chapter is for you.

People think I am unfit now, but I was always unfit. I never had access to proper coaching or a physical training instructor. In my self-designed training schedule, running held

a prominent place. I ran excessively and it ruined my knees.
By the time I entered the international cricket arena, they were
already in bad shape. Of course, I knew something was wrong
with me and I even showed my knees to a local specialist, Dr
Ahson Farooq, in Lahore a couple of months before my Test
debut in 1997, and I underwent a surgical procedure on his
advice. Dr Farooq watched me wince as he tapped a pencil
against my knee and then proceeded to tell me that I shouldn't
consider playing cricket as my knees would not support me.
My professional career would barely last a couple of years,
he added. I was young, just about to enter the national team,
and over the years I had discovered that I could endure more
physical stress than most people, so I didn't pay attention.

Bowling fast is a hard job and the physical demands of the
fast-bowling action can have a damaging effect on a bowler,
especially to a self-taught one like me. With no one to explain
the various techniques, I learnt to bowl by observing other
pace men—and that, too, mostly on television. It was many
years before I understood the principles of fitness and the
consequences of ignoring proper training practices. I felt the
physical stress, of course, but it was much later that I found
out that each time I landed on my back foot, I was shifting a
force measuring eight to ten times my body weight, through
the joints below my waist, on to the front foot.

So much cricket is played today, the season seems to last
a whole year, and bowlers face a heavy workload, which is
detrimental to their physical health. A bowler continually
repeats an explosive action that places great strain on the
body. This is true for all bowlers but fast bowlers are especially
prone to injury as their bowling technique calls for a very

high intensity. The most common injuries, according to a study by the Australian board, are to the knee and lower back, followed by injuries to the shoulder. The study also talks about the 'other' injury group that includes injuries to areas such as the groin, face, heel, toes, stomach and wrist, and I have experienced the whole gamut. Pain, I was to learn, is a constant in a fast bowler's life and my knees have always been in a miserable state. Some of my recurring injuries have been injuries to the right shoulder, hamstring injuries, rib injuries, injuries to the quadriceps, a fractured right fibula, a calf muscle strain, a sore back, and bilateral mediscus. Yes! As a journalist has so astutely written, 'the whole caboodle'.

In spite of all this, what makes us carry on? Athletes, especially fast bowlers, are in a state of denial. You have to deny all the aches and pains in order to finish your allotted overs. Pace bowling demands a measure of physical endurance that can only be built up over the years and it's also about self-abuse. Everything hurts. Your back hurts, your shoulders hurt, your feet hurt, your ankles hurt, your legs hurt, your lungs are filled with fire and, of course, your knees hurt. I refused to acknowledge the pain I was in because if you wish to compete at the highest level, you cannot afford to give in to pain.

And so I ignored Dr Farooq's advice. Nothing and nobody was going to stop me from playing cricket. He, however, knew what he was talking about, for in 1998, during my one-day international debut in Zimbabwe, my knees caved in—the left knee in particular was spectacularly mangled. I really thought I was finished.

In 1996–97, Dan Kiesel was appointed as the physiotherapist for the Pakistani team. Of German Jewish descent, Dan is one of the finest and most knowledgeable people I have met but unfortunately, these qualities were never appreciated by the board, so he quickly moved on. While he was still there, however, I was the new blood in the stable and he began keeping an eye on me. One day he called me over and said we had to have a serious discussion about my future and that I was to start taking care of myself.

'I take great care of myself and am very diligent about my training,' I replied jauntily.

'We'll discuss your training later,' Dan said, and then tried to explain the mystery of my aches and pains. He told me that there was hyper mobility in my joints. They moved too much and caused excessive friction, which led to a build-up of fluids and considerable pain. My joints were subject to a lot of wear and tear, he said, and at the rate I was going, I had only two or three years of cricket left in me. You are going to have to play some matches and sit some out, he finished. Now, this I didn't want to comprehend. I was young and raring to play everything that came my way and here was Dan telling me I had to duck out of games! And that, too, without letting the board know what was going on.

Dan had seen the state of my knees during the South African series of 1998. My problem was, and continues to be, that my knees frequently fill up with fluid and broken pieces of cartilage and need to be attended to. This means going to a clinic the morning before the match and having a syringe plunged into my knees, to draw out about half a cup of the stuff from each knee in order to bring down the swelling. Dan took me for my first draining at Durban and by evening my knees had started swelling up again. No wonder he was concerned. I maintained this schedule before every match. My knees would swell up and I was, more often than not, in agony, though I didn't let anyone know.

Some days, my knees got so bad that I had to crawl to the bathroom. I would crawl into a hot-water tub and soak my knees in order to lessen whatever stiffness and swelling might be building up. Then I would pack them with ice and take an anti-inflammatory tablet and walk on to the field as if I had no worry or pain to contend with.

Dan used to make us take an ice bath and was very particular about me taking it. I hated it with a passion and still do. I used every trick I knew to avoid it; often, I did so by getting into the room first and pretending I had just got out of the ice bath. I would then hang around and make sure no one else missed the treat—it was fun watching them moan and shiver. But Dan was very concerned about my knees. If the board overplayed me, I would do incalculable damage to myself. So, basically, I had to outsmart the PCB and still play. I had no idea how I could do this, neither did he. I was to find a way to secure my place in the team and yet avoid playing too much. I was in a quandary, for if I lied and got caught, I would get thrown out.

There is an uneducated school of thought within the Pakistan cricket management that the more you use a bowler, the more you make him bowl, the fitter he will be. The reality is that an express bowler can't be made to play continuously for very long stretches. The physical consequences are too severe. But they believe that a bowler must bowl his legs off.

Take me, for example. They knew that I was their fastest bowler, a match winner, and that over the years I had become prone to injury. Yet they would have me bowl from morning till evening. We were taught that the more you bowled, the fitter you would be. As a result, for most of us, the wear and tear began much earlier than it should have and we broke down at our peak. I was no exception.

Before we start playing at the international level for Pakistan, half the mileage is taken out of our knees. There are many examples of players becoming unfit at their peak. I can give you the names of six bowlers, a couple of them quicker than I was, who are nowhere to be found today. Mohammad Zahid was the quickest bowler the world had ever seen. He is now working somewhere in England. Why did we have to lose him? Brian Lara said that he was the fastest bowler he had seen in his life, but his own country's management failed to nurture him.

It could have happened to me as well; actually, it should have happened to me, given the fact that I have this weird body. I was made to run so much in domestic cricket—*saari mileage pehle hi nikaal di mere ghutno se*, even before I could make my debut for the national team. There is a mileage coded into your knees that allows you to play only up to a certain extent or for a certain number of years. In our country, they use up that mileage very early, making you work harder and harder, bowling incessantly in the nets and on dead pitches that require you to exert more force, so naturally the body starts giving up. The height of foolishness is not understanding that fast bowlers should be given a lighter workload so that they last longer. Other cricket boards have come to realize that the most serious injuries occur in bowlers with the highest bowling workloads. When these bowlers continue to bowl while injured, they end up risking even more serious injury.

Get your hands on the December 2008 issue of the *South African Journal of Sports Medicine* if you want to know something about fitness and injury linked to this sport. The journal has presented findings of a study by the Australian Cricket Board that indicates that 'fast bowlers at first-class level significantly increased their risk of injury when their bowling workload exceeded more than 20–30 overs a week. Junior bowlers are at a greater risk of sustaining an injury and then becoming re-injured in the same season, as they are still maturing and developing.' Most of us are in, or have barely crossed, our teens when we join the side and the physical demands of such activity begin to take their toll on our immature bodies, resulting in 'overuse-type injuries'. Stress fractures, shoulder dislocations, lumber discomfort, groin injuries, all begin to add up and before you know it, you are spinning in and out of the side like a yoyo.

A sportsman knows his body better than anyone else does and learns to listen to it to survive. He is best qualified to identify his own weaknesses with regard to physical performance and to find a way to counteract these weaknesses. Therefore it is necessary to involve the bowler while setting his workload schedules. If this is done, each bowler will legitimately work towards ensuring his own individual fitness and thereby reduce the risk of injury. The PCB doesn't listen to you though, so you learn to camouflage real injury with minor ones and make enough noise about these to give yourself some healing time and still retain a berth in the team. For me, most of the time, the rest and recovery period was never enough. I had to get back or I would never get to play, so the injuries would resurface and I would often play when I shouldn't have.

Over the years I have had to inject pain-killing injections in my knees—fifteen in one knee and sixteen in the other, so that I could move around. I have for many years been able to play because of my willpower alone and I have done my hardest to ensure that the board never got a glimpse of my knees. I even got my knee operations done without letting anyone know. I expended considerable energy trying to hide my injuries and my pain from my board, for fear that they would throw me out. I also didn't realize in the early days that I was asthmatic; hot and humid weather ensured that I couldn't breathe normally. Initially, I thought I was fatigued or something similar. Other people often thought I was acting—*drama kar raha hai*. To add to my woes, my ribs kept breaking, and my shoulder, my fibula—there isn't a part of my body that hasn't been injured. I have been cut open and sewn up so often that, believe it or not, it doesn't bother me any more. All these injuries have left scars all over my body; they could be mistaken for tattoos. But nothing could dampen my enthusiasm or take me down. Once, I remember, I broke my tendon and they strapped it up, but I couldn't sit still, so I went out on a biking trip.

I don't mind syringes either, because they give me desperately needed relief. I'm actually very cheerful when I go to the doctor. I think my family suffers more than I do; they think I am abnormal. I have gone abroad for two surgeries in 2006 and 2009 and will probably have to undergo another one soon. That doesn't worry me. My friends find this a bit macabre. I tell them that in the 'normal' state I am in so much pain that I love the feeling of numbness that comes with anaesthesia. No, I'm not nervous about surgery at all. The only part I don't look forward to is the procedure for the removal of the tubes used for draining fluids. When they took out the tube after my first surgery—I had had a major reconstruction of my knee, which will probably soon need a replacement—I nearly passed out with the pain. My doctor advised me to have mercy on my knees. Leave some strength in them to play with your children, he said.

In 2006, they tell me, I nearly gave the surgery team a heart attack. They had put me under for what they thought would be a period of four to five hours but I woke up midway through the operation. I don't remember it but the doctor told me that I got up, struggled and fought with them. My knees were open and bleeding, and I was trying to touch them. They had to get help to hold me down before they put me under again. When I was back in the recovery room, I flirted with the nurse. Apparently, I even grabbed her hand. She sat with me till I went back to sleep. When she left, they tell me I got up and, with thick drainage tubes stuck in my knees, was spotted walking down the corridor looking for the toilet. Finally they tied me to the bed, gave me sleeping pills and made sure I slept for two days. For good measure, they locked the door on me. I was clearly their nightmare patient.

I was again up too soon during my last operation in 2009. Andy Williams, my doctor and a very fine man, said that I got up and started fighting with those around me. I gather I was very aggressive but I have no memory of it.

People think I'm crazy but when I come out of anaesthesia, I feel very hungry. After my last knee surgery, I ate seven pieces of KFC chicken and two burgers. I did throw up, but after an hour I ate again.

If our training and coaching programmes hadn't for years

ignored new scientific procedures for enhancing players' capacities, perhaps I wouldn't require so much medical care. Can you believe that I was one of the first in the team to use a gym? Nobody else did; some of them didn't even know what a gym was. The gym culture came to our team as late as 2001, but I had been using one since my college days, thanks to Shahid bhaijaan. The Pakistan team started using the gym as a part of their training when they became aware of my hydraulic training, in 2001.

I believe in using the gym as much as possible. During the Asia Cup in 2010, a journalist commented that I looked more like a wrestler than a sprinter. I would like him and others of his opinion to know that my joints won't hold up unless my shock absorbers, my muscles, are built up. My shoulders, my biceps, triceps, tummy—if they are weak, all the stress would go to my joints and due to excessive hyper extension, they would almost twist over on themselves. Fusion occurs, and fluid builds up in them. I need to strengthen up and not lose muscle tone.

Youngsters who are getting into the game should take me as an example for how not to train. I ran like mad and bowled till my knees gave way, even before I entered the Test arena. My advice to them is to study their body carefully. Use a gym with a trainer who understands body mechanics. Training has to be individually directed. Everyone has different needs and a good coach should know that. He should be willing and prepared to give each player the individual attention he needs. The trainer should know who requires to shed weight, gain weight, build up muscle, etc., and which part of the body needs special attention. Time has to be invested in water training as well. Swimming is most desirable because you exercise without straining your joints or harming your bones. These are training methods that teams the world over use regularly, unlike us. The day after a match, going to the gym is a must. It restores energy and recoups strength. A batsman requires one kind of attention, a bowler another. Fitness can be successfully achieved by using the gym with due care, by eating right and, of course, match practice. I believe that real training occurs only at match practice. You have to play matches, even net practice is bullshit. Camps exist merely to get everyone together, but the real workout occurs when you play a match.

When you are young, you don't realize the importance of training right. The body almost looks after itself till the age of twenty-five. After that, it demands attention. It is crucial for a sports person to know this. If you need protein supplements, take them—they help build and repair cells—but only upon professional advice. Do keep an eye on the chemical components of medicines and stuff that you eat, in case you end up imbibing something illegal. If you don't take care of yourself and if you do not have a proper coach and trainer to guide you, you will end up abusing your body.

Your coach will always know what your fitness level is and if he is a good coach, he will use you properly to get the most out of you for the benefit of the team. If he doesn't, it can lead to plain and simple abuse. Some players need strength training, some need flexibility. Every athlete is a unique person with unique needs. My board doesn't understand this. I never got the proper attention that I required until I met Tauseef.

The team coach has to be very shrewd and accurately gauge how much workload is to be given to which bowler.

For example, when I was playing county cricket in England, my coach told my captain to give me fourteen overs only, not more. They used to make me bowl 12–13 overs in a match. They knew that anything more would be too much for me and then I might be lost for the whole season. The Pakistan management made me bowl 22–24 overs in a match. I was bound to become unfit. I am a fast bowler, and express bowlers run out of steam quickly. If you ask them to bowl continuously, you will destroy them. Ironically, nobody else takes the blame. It all falls on the broken-down bowler. I used to tell each and every one of them—the coaches, the captains, the management—let me do this much, let me do it my way, and you will see that I can do wonders for Pakistan. No one listened. So I lost interest in listening to them. I did my own thing and that, of course, annoyed everyone.

My country is a sports-loving nation with little means to sustain the industry. But it is vital for our future generation of athletes to avail of new training techniques and learn how to take care of themselves so that their performance does them and their country proud. Schools should have personnel equipped with such knowledge, who can then make it available to parents, coaches and cricketers. If they are educated about the risk factors for injury, injuries can be avoided or taken care of in time. This is the only way to prevent the early onset of injuries in the young and promising fast bowler, thus prolonging his career.

As for me, I knew from the beginning that my body was not fit enough to play cricket the way everyone expected me to. If I put myself through that much strain, I would not have been able to survive. So I said, let me find something new. Let me bowl fast. If I bowled fast and got batsmen in trouble, everyone would notice me. So I knew exactly what I was doing. I always bowled fast and well, but really quickened my pace when I knew the time was right. If I had shown my hand before the right time, I wouldn't have made it through. I settled on the big stage—the World Cup in 2003—and then I took off. The batsman who touched my first ball just fended it off and it flew past everyone for a six. The world exclaimed, Oooh! This is Shoaib Akhtar!

I believe I knew what I was doing at every stage in my career. But when I walked on to any playing field, any ground in any country, there was only Pakistan on my mind. All my passion came to the fore and I felt that even if I got physically shattered in the process, I must contribute something to my team—*Main tut javan, lekin main kucch de ke javan.* I gave the last bit of energy that was within me, even if I was injured. That is the only thing that drives me—doing something worthwhile for my country.

In 2010, once again, I got a chance to play for Pakistan. Afridi, our captain, knew that he had to use me intelligently and started the season by accepting my suggestions on when I could be played and when rested. Consequently, my performance was good. Waqar, our coach, suspected my fitness—he made me take a fitness test before the Asia Cup. He wasn't happy even when I got three wickets in four overs against Sri Lanka. My knees continue to remain swollen and tender but I performed decently in England and didn't do too badly in New Zealand either. I was focused on the 2011 World Cup. As for pain, to hell with it! No sportsman worth his name seeks sympathy. If I was in pain, I knew that the others were in their own private agony as well. We were all too busy constructing an aura of invincibility designed to intimidate our opponents to admit to being vulnerable ourselves.

And yet, fast bowlers are like big babies, they respond better if they are pampered and cared for. You might ask, why do we need to be pampered? Because we are doing an abnormal job! Our bodies undergo incredible stress. Our joints wear out; the entire body suffers tremendous wear and tear. Most fast bowlers are also a bit high strung. Look at me—I get upset quickly and I come around even quicker. I think this temperament is universal to fast bowlers. We are usually on a short fuse and are restless by nature, full of energy and very aggressive. When I bowl, my heart rate jumps to over 170, the blood rushes through my veins, my body temperature shoots up to over 102°F. We also lose body weight dramatically while playing. No wonder we are touchy, ready to hit out and get into scrapes. Other players tend to understand this. They too are dealing with different physiological pressures, so plenty of steam gets let off when we come up against each other. Bragging is natural to us, sledging is done deliberately, to throw the opponent off his game. The cricket pitch is an arena where some of what happens resembles a small war. But nobody takes it to heart.

So much has changed of late as technology has brought the pitch closer to people's sight and hearing. I run in feverishly, my heart beat races to 180-190 (this is when doctors would suggest bedrest and warn of a stroke!), but that's what the game demands from a fast bowler. At this time, if somebody makes uncomplimentary remarks or even if a batsman moves away because a fly is obstructing his vision, I can't stop myself from reacting aggressively.

This is how I think of it: the fast bowler is a rare breed that requires special care. I mean, you do take great care of racehorses, pamper them to keep them fit; Formula One race cars require the attention of a large team of workers to perform their best. Why not look after your fast bowlers? A fast bowler is not a stock bowler. If you push him too hard, he will break. According to our management, however, the fast bowler is to be used but not taken care of. The result of this lack of care and attention is that most of us become self-centred. We decide when to play and when to hold ourselves back. I accept that this is not good for the game. But what can one do? It has happened so many times to me and to others: we become unfit and the board doesn't even bother about us. This has been going on for a long time. I know of bowlers who have been neglected by the board and when they come back to play, they have deliberately underperformed in a weird form of protest or revenge.

Take a look at our cricket history. Players have been dropped and played at the whim and fancy of the board. When they don't play, they don't earn; they starve. Only if a player is secure will he go all out for the team. Once again, it all boils down to economics—a man has to eat! I don't know why this simple fact is overlooked. Give the player something to live by when he is not playing and make him want to do his best for you. We all know that if we get injured or unfit, nobody is going to look after us. So all of us play carefully—*bach ke kheltein hain.*

Pain is something that I can hide from the world but not from my parents. They see it on my face. I have often woken up to see them sitting on my bed, gazing down at my face. I

keep telling them not to startle me like that, it's not the way
I want to start a morning; they don't listen. But I believe that
I am able to walk, run and play because of their prayers and
blessings. My whole family—my parents, my brothers and
sister—prays for me and Allah hears their prayers.

Eighteen years are more than enough. It's a long, long career,
especially for somebody with an abnormal body like mine.
Those who started playing with me have become family men
with kids and have settled down; I continued playing with my
broken knees. I thank Allah for keeping me strong. What counts
is one's spirit, heart and mind. You must have the will to never
give up and keep working towards your goal. I have always
admired people who fight back against all odds. Great leaders
like Qaid-e-Azam Jinnah, Nelson Mandela, Mother Teresa and
Gandhi, who were prepared to fight for their beliefs.

Life itself is a great teacher. I learnt that making a name in
one's field doesn't happen by fluke or by luck, it requires hard
work and dedication. One can win if one is strong, clear headed
and clean of conscience. If I can succeed with this abnormal
body, anyone can. This I believe. And I have run my fastest,
bowled my fastest, later in my career. In 2003, I became the
world's fastest bowler. This was not at the beginning of my
career but after seven years of playing. People tend to slow
down as they grow older, but I managed to bowl faster and
faster—once again, not normal.

I would like to say this to aspiring young cricketers: identify
your talent so that you can nurture it. If you have the talent,
don't let anything or anybody stop you from reaching your
goal. Hold on to your convictions and believe in God. And
ensure that you train right. The right way of training is what

will make it a little less painful. You won't damage your body the way I have mine. And believe me, if I can pull through, so can you! That's what I would like to have this book do: inspire young people to believe that anything is possible, if only you put your mind to it. *Meri zindagi ek khuli kitaab ho jo har kisi ke leye ek misaal-e-rah ban jaaye.*

There are many pitfalls on the road to success and the trouble with fame is that it invites you into an illusionary world where one can lose one's grip on reality. If deprivation can be used as a catapult to success, it can also lead you astray. Look at my life, at my mistakes and my struggles. Avoid the first and take heart that I, despite my weird body, made it. I hope young aspirants can learn from what I did and also, what I didn't do. The truth is that money can be made legitimately and shortcuts will get you into trouble and bring others down with you. Choose the harder, longer route—*usi mein sakoon hain, usi mein neendein hain, usi mein sab kuch hain.* I have seen the condition of those who have chosen the shortcut—match fixing—and I can tell you with conviction, *koi sakoon nahin hain unke paas*—they have no peace, no sleep, and nobody is loyal to them. The payback is inevitable.

Identifying the right path is your duty, not God's, and after having identified it, you need to stay steady on it. If you stumble, pick yourself up and keep going. Believe in God and in yourself, and He will help you out with everything, *nek aulaad, paisa, sakoon.* Do not corrupt yourself with ugly money. I didn't, and I'm still standing.

13

The King and I

The males in my family are very dominating, they don't listen to anyone. I don't listen to anyone either, so I guess altercations are inevitable. I can be very aggressive and stubborn—very, very strong-headed. If I don't want to do something, then all the great teachers, the ustaads, can try and explain or convince me but I tend to resist them. There are lessons that I have to learn by myself and when I don't and disaster strikes, it's nobody's fault but mine. I accept that. I have always done things the way I have understood they should be done, not by blindly adhering to rules and regulations—*yeh qayda, voh qayda*. It seems to me that people just keep moaning about discipline and rules; they never question them.

The Pakistan Cricket Board rules our career and therefore our lives and the chairman rules the board. It has been our greatest misfortune that more often than not, we have had uncaring chairmen; men who did not care much for Pakistan cricket and even less for the players. There were exceptions, of course. We are fortunate to have had Khalid Mahmood, who was a good chairman and handled things beautifully. In 1998–99 Mujeeb-ur-Rahman, the blue-eyed boy of the government of the time, became the chairman. He tripled our wages, which was a move towards some sort of fair treatment to the players, and he lost his job in no time. Then there was Dr Zafar Altaf, one of the nicest men our team has known. If he had stayed on, things would have really brightened up for us but he left within three months of taking up the position to pursue his first love, agriculture.

In my opinion, the board that actually promoted the cause of Pakistan cricket was the one headed by Lt. Gen. Tauqir Zia. He was the best amongst the chairmen during my time and his tenure was beneficial for Pakistan cricket as a whole. During this time, many new cricket academies were established, old venues were upgraded, new grounds were built, and central contracts for players were initiated. He was proud of his players and believed in backing us in times of need.

Nobody can question Lt. Gen. Zia's capabilities. He set about ensuring that the PCB had good relations with the ICC, because of which its chairman Jagmohan Dalmiya backed us completely. We toured India and the Indians came over as well. He was able to oversee damage control after the bomb blast in Karachi, just before the second Test of the New Zealand series in 2002. Many international teams began to raise the question of security for players touring Pakistan but he was able to reassure them and several teams, including India, came over regularly to play with us. If we had won more matches, perhaps he would have stayed on longer. But we lost so many that he had quite enough of us. Unfortunately for us, after him there came a string of chairmen who were and are responsible for, in the words of an eminent sports journalist, 'PCB being a basket case'.

After Lt. Gen. Tauqir Zia, it seems to me that anyone who joined our cricket board underwent a strange transformation, a complete metamorphosis. Before joining, he would be a fan of the players. The moment he crossed to our side of the fence and became the chairman, oh ho! He felt he was the biggest star and would start throwing his weight around. So, let's dominate Shoaib Akhtar! How? By putting him down and getting him to grovel. If initially the chairman was inclined to do some good for us, there were plenty of people within the board telling him, Just look at him, sir. He thinks he is bigger than you are, sir. You are the boss, sir. *Bas!* Match on! Shoaib must bow down or go. The chairman didn't care what I had or hadn't done for the Pakistan team; he only knew that I refused to buckle down to him. I am sure others had to face this kind of harassment too, but I can only speak for myself.

A shining example of what could happen to you if you didn't play the game, as it were, dates back to 2008 when Naseem Ashraf was the chairman of the PCB. The gentleman would want me to give him some net practice, and I was also expected to wine and dine him. I responded by telling him, *Allah ke bande*, I have served Pakistan for over ten years, *itna naam kamaaya*—earned a reputation for myself by winning Test matches and series for Pakistan. Am I now just considered fit to wash the PCB chairman's dirty shirts, give him net practice?

That was it, the battle began. His demands were amazing. He told me that I had to go through him if I wanted to play in the IPL. Was he my agent or the chairman of the cricket board? I said, no, I beg you to leave me alone, my connection is directly with Allah, let me be. He did not; I was banned from playing for Pakistan for five years! On what pretext? No prizes for guessing—'discipline'. There was a period when allegations of match fixing cast their shadow over the whole team with the single exception of me. What was I collared with—being undisciplined! What did I do to deserve the tag of being undisciplined? I didn't kow-tow to others, I didn't grovel. Sadly, despite the blatant unfairness of it all, there was no one to question the legitimacy of the board's actions, or those of the chairman. Why? Because he had President Musharraf's ear. Incidentally, he resigned within a couple of hours of President Musharraf's resignation in August 2008.

Please keep in mind that anything can happen where the PCB is concerned; there is virtually no accountability. If you have strong connections in the right places, you can get away with anything and do whatever you want. I, however, come from a certain social background that never had the backing of people in power, so we as a family have always looked after each other—we shared the good and the bad times together. In the early days of my career, we were rather scared and worried about all the allegations that were flung at me. When I proved myself on the ground, a lot of people, including some political heavyweights, began to side with me but early on, we brothers and sister only had one another to depend on and we faced several anxious moments. We knew we were vulnerable, anybody could use or abuse us badly. The PCB chairman, our management and captains could scare me with threats of kicking me off the team, which they did. I paid fines and sat out matches regularly but never learned to play that particular game.

The post of the chairman of the board is very important. He should be selfless, knowledgeable, and must love the game. That is essential. I can tell you honestly that most of the chairmen we have had till now have barely had a backbone. They were fence sitters, unwilling to initiate any action, and most of them had huge chips on their shoulders—don't ask me why, but this is what I have experienced. The only thing they seem to want is for players to suck up to them, and then they spend the rest of their tenure seeking revenge on those who don't. A big man can take big decisions; you can't expect big decisions from petty people, or for great things to happen during their tenure.

Take a look at Shahryar Khan. He acted like a nawab but couldn't take decisions like one because he was weak. He made no effort to keep the media off my back or support me when I was injured. All he could say was that he was helpless! Look at how badly he handled the ball-tampering allegations made by Darrell Hair at that infamous Oval Test match of 2006. It was the right decision for us to walk off the field but I don't agree with what happened after that. We had made our point and should have gone back and played but nobody could take a firm call on what to do. The chairman was standing there watching the captain leading his team off the field and not bringing it back on even after registering the protest. What kind of a chairman does that make him? What about his responsibility towards the game?

Pakistan cricket's tragedy has been that Shahryar was followed by Naseem Ashraf, who was followed by Ijaz Butt—it was downhill all the way. Basically they were an uncaring lot who corrupted our country's cricket with their mind games. I would call this the darkest age for Pakistan cricket. If such people lead the cricket board, how can you expect any improvement in Pakistan cricket's ratings? It won't happen, it's not possible, and if this state of affairs carries on, cricket in Pakistan will continue to deteriorate. After we—and by this I mean the senior players on the team—retire or leave, within two years we will lose against a team like Bangladesh. Mark my words! I say this sadly and find no satisfaction in expressing these views. I have played with the team that has beaten the world, so there is no joy in me when I think of such a future, only grief.

With a bunch of incompetent and self-obsessed guys on the board, it is a wonder that any work gets done. They came through recommendations, *sifarish. Rahi–sahi kasar unhoney nikaali!* They only look to their own survival and as a result, so does everyone else—the players and the captain. Zakir Khan has been one constant in the PCB for many years now. He is barely literate but is retained because his personal relations are so good with the top guys. Once, the ICC wrote him a letter asking him to send reports that were lucid and in correct English—there were too many errors in his correspondence with them. And he is our Director Operations!

Actually, there is only one person who does any work within the board and that is Subhaan. He works there in multiple capacities—as a typist, executive, tour organizer, etc. He does all the work and no one else does anything of use. They don't even know how to work. They can't speak, read or write English, so they are unable to communicate with other boards properly and yet, they comprise the PCB. So how can you expect the privacy of the players to be protected? You are surprised that my medical report suddenly landed up in the hands of the media, all twisted and untrue. When I protested and asked them to at least retract and apologize in public, they refused, saying, we will apologize to you in private, take it if you want to continue playing!

The other problem has been that all that the PCB cares is about winning. It doesn't matter how an individual may have performed—no win, no forgiveness. But the fact is that a team cannot always win and when we didn't, the PCB would single out certain players to punish. They never understood that players are at their most vulnerable at such times. We would have to face inquiries and accountability cells in which the management would try its hardest to lay all the blame for a loss on us, so that it seemed as if we went to play a match with the deliberate aim of losing. That is the heaviest burden we have had to bear. Who wants to lose, for God's sake! But nobody is spared. A captain comes in, gets thrown out so that the board can keep the critics at bay, and the players all run around blindly in circles, not knowing what to do or how to protect themselves. Cricketers with a mind of their own become the target of all sorts of politics. Most of our coaches face the axe as well and are so scared of losing their jobs that they spend their time keeping the board happy, joining their politicking and perfecting the art of becoming yes-men.

Wasim Raja was one of the strangest coaches we had, a very angry man who lost his cool at regular intervals. Fortunately for me, I was injured during his tenure. From all that I have heard of his time with the team, I'm quite sure I wouldn't have been able to understand what he wanted from us. I was in the team, though, when Javed Miandad became the coach and I believe he was one of the main reasons why I lost much of my match fitness. I had to look elsewhere for answers to my queries, in journals and especially consulting coaches from other academies like Daryl Foster and Ian Pont. In general, our coaches have had nothing to offer Pakistan cricket, nothing apart from playing dirty politics. They just wanted to earn some money and travel in their old age—*bas*! You should listen to them talk about the game, about life, or just about anything; I have often been embarrassed. Imagine what they would have been like in their younger days, when they were playing. Take Intikhab Alam, for instance. He has played for our country, has been coach to the team, and therefore has been around for nearly forty-five years. Yet, he is the most illiterate man you could meet. He has no clue what coaching is all about and can't distinguish an in-swinger from an out-swinger, but he gives advice to the Pakistan side! He doesn't understand the intricacies of the game either, so has no useful inputs in strategy. Most of the time, he dozes off or sits around or makes us do yoga—that's all he does.

Of late, Intikhab Alam has been saying to me that he is sorry for everything that happened. He tries to make his peace with me and actually asked me if I felt he had done me wrong. He said that he knew I held him responsible for a lot of things. I said, 'Yes, you have messed things up for me but I have survived.' I told him that he had been quoted making statements about my private life, my sexual proclivities, which I wondered how he knew about. He denied it all and said that he would tell me who was actually behind my character assassination. I think he considers that an apology, though I am still waiting for him to spill the beans.

All this has led me to believe that for us, a coach is a useless appendage. Today we use our coach as a fetch-and-carry boy, fit only to get things for the players from outside the hotel. Yes, if there was somebody like Daryl Foster or Tom Moody, it would make sense to have a coach. These gentlemen know their cricket. In particular, they know how to use a bowler to the team's best advantage, how much to bowl them, when to rest them, and when to get work out of them. If you don't know anything about your players, what is the purpose of coaching them? Are you going to teach me to bowl at this stage? No, you need to understand my temperament and get the best work out of me, for the benefit of the team.

I was amused when Shane Warne dryly informed me that John Buchanan took credit for the victories of Australia and announced that he was the best coach going around. Hello, friend! Look at your players. Adam Gilchrist, Ricky Ponting, Shane Warne, Glenn McGrath and Justin Langer, to name a few. Give this team to Zimbabwe and they will win.

It goes without saying that if the PCB takes credit for the team's success, it is also largely responsible for our deterioration. Having observed its functioning closely over the years, I have given some thought to what changes are necessary within the board. The root cause of corruption, actually, is the way in which the board is selected, not elected. If members were elected to the board, they would be answerable to the governing body and would take their decisions carefully. There would be greater transparency, democratically elected members would have more freedom to do things, and they wouldn't be under the chairman's thumb.

I also believe that the PCB needs to get out of the control

of the President, prime minister and other high-ranking politicians. It should be an independent body. The board would then become a stable entity which could function free of political pressure and that would be beneficial for the players and for Pakistan cricket. A stable board would bring stability to the team, which in turn would help us win more consistently.

I remember how, at the start of our 1999–2000 Australian tour, a new chairman was brought in, only to bow out midway to another, and then came Lt. Gen. Zia. So we had three chairmen in the course of one tour. That was something the players didn't need to deal with.

The other important change that needs to be rushed through is that whoever gets selected (preferably elected) to the board should be given a minimum term of three years so they feel secure enough to do some work. Right now, the governing body is full of honorary stakeholders, from the chairman downwards. If you wish to give honorary jobs, they should be given to achievers from the corporate world, who are already receiving good money and are highly educated. These guys wouldn't be in it for the money or the attention or any such thing. The PCB's future is very bleak. Pakistan cricket *hogi toh Pak board chalega*—there can only be a cricket board if Pakistan gets to play cricket. As the matches dry up for us, the board is feeling the pinch and I wish they would do something about it. Already, they have had to axe a few positions.

To my mind, a crucial step towards a healthier association is for the PCB to start respecting players. The PCB should remember that it exists because of us. Players do not need to be involved in administration but they should be privy to decisions that directly affect them. The PCB should to more transparent about sponsorships and contracts to the players. This is a big problem—corporate endorsement contracts like with Pepsi and others are not explained to us and our opinions are certainly not asked for. This is unjust—we should be in the know as to who gets what, and not be presented with a done deal.

When I look at the state of Pakistan cricket today, I feel sad, but also angry, especially with the men in the PCB. Even now, with all that is happening around us, they refuse to change their ways. The game is not about the ICC, PCB, BCCI, IPL, it's about the players. They have to be endorsed. Look at Shane Warne; he is a fantastic ambassador for the game, promoting both Australian and world cricket. We should be thankful to Shane Warne and Murali because their achievements endorse the game and inspire youngsters to try and spin the ball. Look at Wasim and Waqar—what amazing bowlers they were. Vivian Richards, Sunil Gavaskar, Brian Lara, Inzamam-ul Haq, Sachin Tendulkar, Ricky Ponting, Adam Gilchrist, Justin Langer are all-time greats who caught the imagination of the world. When they batted, their skills attracted more and more admiration for the game, drew more people in. Because of them, cricket became more interesting. If Imran Khan had not played for Pakistan, Pakistan cricket would have died. Before him, nobody had been able to create a world-beating team.

So the PCB has to understand that you cannot continue to belittle players and then expect great things from them. Despite our differences, I hated to see the way Wasim was pushed out. Indisputably, he was a great fast bowler—a talent that emerges rarely. His talent alone should have earned him respect, and

Pakistan and the world owe a great deal to him, but he went through some harrowing times because of the board. Look at the way Waqar and Inzamam were treated towards the end of their careers. Forced into unplanned retirement, they were handed some money, a car, and packed off. The board should have retired them with honours, in full public gaze. Instead, they were insulted and thrown out. I didn't want this to happen to me. I'd had enough trouble with the board anyway and was determined to leave with grace—and I did.

Now is also the time for the PCB to get its act together and start finding a way for us to have more matches to play. And by this I mean we need to play more and more Tests. I agree that T-20 cricket has brought money into the game and that is a good thing. IPL, for example, has been a boon for new and previously unknown talent. But most of the players are in it only for the money. They grab a few contracts and that's it.

Some lines need to be drawn. As far as Pakistan cricket goes, T-20 is destroying the game. Quick batting, quick matches—nobody has the temperament to play one-dayers, leave alone Test matches. We were already a very aggressive team and are now playing in a more aggressive format. The Test format requires us to have patience and discipline. T-20 has ruined the techniques of the batsmen in particular, so it is not surprising that we tend to collapse in the longer format. Excellence eludes us, and no great players are emerging. That is my objection, my reservation about the T-20 format. It's good for senior players who don't have to bowl too many overs. But it's not good for youngsters who have just started to play.

I firmly believe that youngsters should be given more Test matches to play so that they can develop true and complete skills, learn patience and the art of the game. Playing a Test is like receiving an education. You learn every skill, persistence, mannerisms, technique; everything can be acquired when you play Tests. It's a test of character and is an absolute must for a bowler. He develops in every sphere—line, rhythm, ball control—and he learns to use all the elements around him and above all, patience. This format alone separates the men from the boys. Shorter versions of the game do not help you master the game. Besides, records set in Test matches are valued more, and rightly so. Every wicket and every run taken in a Test is valued; therefore, those who are good cricketers in the Test format are and should be valued more. The PCB needs to wrest as many Test series as it can from the international calendar if Pakistan cricket is to stay alive. And the players need to remember that this is the best form of the game.

The way Pakistan cricket is going will affect the future of cricket itself, but I wonder if the ICC cares. Surely it has some stake in not losing a member country from a handful of nations that play the game? Surely it should realize the need to assist in stemming the decay in Pakistan cricket and bringing it back to health? No doubt, finding alternate nations to host our home series is a very good beginning but I can't help but feel that the ICC should have invested more time and money in promoting cricket around the globe. Cricket remains barely a ten-nation game. Why? Recently, the ICC spokesperson let everyone know that it couldn't manage fourteen teams and the next Cup would revert to ten nations playing. Instead of moving forward, the ICC wanted to move backwards. Thankfully, they seem to have changed their minds now.

Frankly, promotional matches are of no use. What is

required are Test matches and one-dayers in which the best teams participate. Bangladesh's success story is due to the fact that consistently, over the years, its team has had opportunities to face stronger teams. There is a huge support for the game in Canada, for example, yet the ICC has not been scheduling big games there. It has a lot of money and should invest in starting and nurturing clubs in non-Test playing countries. As a result of poor distribution of finances, the game is starved and is played only by a few nations. I don't know why only a very few countries from Africa play. There's a continent's worth of talent there. The ICC really needs to think global.

I feel that it is not just the players who set up a game but the umpires as well. It is important for players to acknowledge this and maintain good relations with them. There is no doubt that umpiring can make or break a game, or players, as we all have seen. Today, of course, umpires have been stripped of a lot of their decision-making power. Perhaps it is not really a good idea to take away so many of their responsibilities and hand these over to a camera. Human errors made by umpires actually make the game more interesting and add to its uncertainties. Though it can be very frustrating when they don't give a catch off an edge or accept an appeal for an lbw, it all evens out in the end. As far as the referral system goes, I don't really support it as it undermines the umpire's decisions and makes the game too prim and proper, like a well-covered lady.

I have always tried to maintain good relations with umpires, including Dickie Bird and David Shepherd, to name only two. They were thorough gentlemen. Steve Bucknor is one of my favourite umpires along with Rudi Kirsten, Simon Taufel and Aleem Dar. I used to go up to them before a match, shake hands and give them a hug. I'm not saying that I got wickets because I got along well with them; I'm just saying that I got along with them and respected them. Some umpires, poor chaps, get easily pressurized. They just don't have it in them to resist us, and very often we could influence them through heavy and consistent appealing. But these particular guys were very confident and stood their ground under all sorts of pressure, and that I respect. Steve Bucknor was so much in command that he could calmly diffuse the ugliest of situations, such as when two players got mad at each other. He had an eagle eye and both bowlers and batsmen felt safe with him. Moreover, he is a very nice man and was never harsh with his reports. Umpires like Bucknor seem to understand the problems fast bowlers face because of the rigidity of the ICC rules, which appear to be in place only to restrain us.

Rudi had a great sense of humour and was a very strong man. You couldn't push him around. We used to arm wrestle and kid around with each other. Whenever I passed him on the field on my way back to my bowling mark, I would pull his shirt out of his trousers. He always took it in the right spirit but he used to tell me to stop, because there were so many things in his pocket that something might fall out. I guess it is not with everyone in a position of authority that I get into trouble!

And then, of course, there was Darrell Hair, a very cold man, dull and dry, with no sense of humour. He was one of the umpires who twice called me for chucking and reported my action. I asked him why he kept doing it. 'Do you have a personal agenda against me?' I got no response. Finally, the ICC curbed him but I was rankled by what I had to undergo as a result of his calling me a chucker. Once my bowling action got cleared by the ICC, I am not sorry to say that I started heckling him. And it was not only I who had trouble with him. Hair's rather oppressive and negative attitude towards our team on the field made us all feel insecure. He didn't bother to hide his contempt for us and we all felt it, whenever he was on the field. Our constant worry was—would we get fair decisions? In my opinion, he has always been harsh with teams from the subcontinent. He has had problems with Murali, with me, with Indians, Pakistanis and Bangladeshis—all of us. And, in turn, he is the least favoured umpire among players from our part of the world.

During the Oval Test fiasco in 2006, we actually felt that Hair had crossed the line. It was very difficult to get him to agree on anything, especially when we wanted to change the ball. Then, of course, he was penalized for the way he handled the walkout. On the fourth day of the now infamous Test match, the Pakistan team refused to take the field after tea in protest against accusations of ball tampering. The umpires then deemed that the team had forfeited the Test. I am told that Hair came to the dressing room and asked if they were coming out to play. No one responded, so he left. Finally the team did go back in, but delayed the decision far too long. It was weak management at our end. I am glad I wasn't part of it; otherwise I bet they would have found a way to blame me.

While the ICC should be assisting in promoting the game throughout the world, back home the PCB should be worrying about what might happen if the game dries up for us. How can we retain the popularity of the game within the country? What happens these days is that if you win the World Cup, people start watching and playing. It shouldn't be like that. We need to pay more attention to children playing the game in residential colonies, in galis and mohallas. Grassroots cricket must be organized and nurtured so that the sport remains in the hearts and minds of people. Encourage youngsters playing colony games; put it on par with district cricket. Day-and-night matches are played on the streets during Ramadan. These should be encouraged as well by instituting a trophy or a prize. If the PCB focuses at this level, they will find many young fast bowlers who are seventeen or eighteen years old and ready to take on the world. They should also encourage club cricket— they will discover that a huge talent pool is at their disposal. The PCB will then never have to struggle to find new talent like, say, Amir. He is out of the reckoning now and there is a great need for pacers. There are many like him and, given the opportunity, they too will shine.

Three years back, I had talked to the board—and this was before the IPL had started—about creating our own six teams and starting league cricket. Organize matches, offer good contracts. I have had this on my mind ever since I played for Mossman Club in North Sydney in 2002. My friend Kamil Khan had spoken to Mossman Club to invite me over. Brett Lee was also playing there and he too suggested that I should be asked to play with the club. So I went. It turned out to be excellent competitive cricket—I was actually taken aback to see that club cricket could be so competitive. It was all very enjoyable. Sydney is a beautiful city and I ate at some wonderful restaurants. I had a great time—we played hard and partied hard. We won lots of matches and generated a great deal of publicity for Mossman during the 3–4 weeks that I played there and I always wondered why we didn't have something like that back home. I told the board that I thought it imperative that we start a league because the way things were going for us, in the coming years nobody would be interested in playing against us. Sadly, this is coming true.

The big teams have said they don't want to play in Pakistan, so what is left? The matter is beyond urgency. I have suggested often enough that we need to have at least two big tournaments in a year and these could be held on neutral grounds, say, in the UAE, where they have beautiful stadiums. Get a new group going that invites the current Asian teams like India, Sri Lanka and Bangladesh and then invite others too. Afghanistan should be given more opportunities and why isn't Nepal playing, they love cricket there. I know this to be true because I was recognized everywhere I went in Kathmandu. If all the SAARC countries get in on it, cricket in our region could develop further and if there is good prize money and it becomes a success, the rest of the cricket-playing world will want to join as well. If the PCB continues to depend solely on the ICC, it is doomed. *Khuda na khasta agar aur controversies nikalti hain toh*—if there are any more controversies, my gut feeling is that Pakistan may be banned for two or three years. *Usse pahle aap apni tayyari kar lain.* In that case, we need to be prepared.

Is anyone listening?

14

The Dressing Room

If the Pakistan Cricket Board resembles anarchy, things haven't been very different in our dressing room. What people don't know is that our dressing room resembles a place where wild animals are packed together and it has been so for some years now. When I got angry with Mohammad Asif and had to face disciplinary action because of it, I recall wondering why so much was being made of it. Over the years, I have seen fistfights, knives flashed around, bats swung at each other—it never got out because everyone was doing it. For me, of course, an exception was always made—*koi maafi nahin hai, aur jo marzee kare.* I was given no leeway. Someone else was facing a rape allegation, his name was kept a state secret, and my name was sacrificed. And look at what the world media is saying about us with reference to match fixing! The result of all this negativity is that parents do not want their children to play cricket, to get involved in what they perceive as filth. All of us, including myself, the captain, the media and the cricket board are responsible for having corrupted Pakistan cricket.

We are all responsible for the state we find ourselves in today. No one has beaten us on the field. We have done it ourselves, thanks to our myopic vision.

The first time I walked into the Pakistan dressing room, I was stunned by the reception I got. The atmosphere was vicious and almost every senior player, when not yelling at me and other juniors, was either whining about how they were being ill-treated by the management or swearing at them. As far as I was concerned, the PCB had selected me, and Majid Khan had enough faith in me to threaten throwing out half the senior members of the team, including the captain, if I wasn't played, so I had absolutely no problem with the board and will always be grateful to them for giving me a chance to pursue my dreams. When I began to realize that all this negativity was the nature of the dressing room, I chose to mentally detach myself from my surroundings.

In the beginning I was just so happy at having achieved my goal of playing for my country that almost nothing could dampen my spirits. Later I realized that this alienation was necessary for me to remain sane and so I stayed away from the politics in the dressing room. So did other junior players like Shahid Afridi, Azhar Mahmood, Saqlain Mushtaq, Shahid Nazir, Abdul Razzaq and Saleem Elahi. We gravitated towards each other, forming lifelong friendships. Over the years, we spent so much time together that perhaps we got to know each other better than our families knew us.

We had some good times together. I used to play tricks on them, especially during practice or at the nets. Silly things like pulling down their trousers when they looked up to catch a ball. The poor chaps would take their eyes off the ball in the air to grab their trousers and would get hit. They would also get yelled at by the coach.

Afridi loved his naps and would invariably find the only corner in the dressing room where one could take a nap without anybody, especially the captain, catching him. Once, after a particularly taxing morning's play, I wanted a snooze as well but it wasn't easy to get Afridi to abandon his spot and it wasn't an easy task waking him up either. So I shook him awake saying, 'Wasim bhai is looking for you.' Not wanting to draw our captain's ire, Afridi jumped up almost immediately and I quickly took his spot.

Some of us loved massages and used to hog the masseurs while the rest would have to wait forever for their turn. This had to change, I thought, and the next day I bought some itching powder, put it into the massage oil and sat and waited for the fun to follow. You should have seen how quickly those guys swore off massages. I did get caught though, and received an earful.

Good times, those! We all loved beaches and swimming in the ocean. I used to hide among the rocks or corals and then proceed to duck people under water, much to their irritation. I would swim under them and grab their legs; I guess they thought a shark had got them—you should have heard them scream! I found it very funny, they didn't. But they gave as good as they got and I too was at the receiving end of many practical jokes. Once, the whole lot of us suddenly decided that we needed a suntan. Don't ask me why—Allah has already given us a nice bronze colour. We threw away our clothes at St. Lucia and swam, went for walks and slept on the beach nude. After two days of this, we looked pretty much the same except for the fact that our backs were covered with huge blisters and sleeping had become synonymous with excruciating pain. I spent those sleepless nights waiting for one of them to drop off and then I would put his hand in warm water just to get him up again. Now we diligently use sun block—lots of it—no matter how ridiculous we look.

I remember a particularly funny episode involving Saqlain Mushtaq and Javed Miandad. Saqlain had been playing really well but had also heard rumours that he would be dropped in the following game, so he rang the coach to find out why. He got no satisfactory answer from Miandad, so the next morning we saw a very sullen Saqlain sitting in a corner and glaring at Miandad, who was unusually quiet. We knew what was going on and were looking forward to some interesting moments. Sure enough, when he could no longer hold back his anger, Saqlain jumped up, yelling at Miandad to give him a good reason why he was being dropped. He grabbed a bat and ran towards Miandad, who fled for cover. Miandad took off towards the chairman's office, followed by a bat-wielding Saqlain. All of us started running in a line after them, doubled up with laughter.

Led by Miandad, one by one we burst into the chairman's room, Saqlain with the clear intention of hurting Miandad, whose ego was already suffering. We weren't helping the matter by laughing our heads off. Just when we got some control over our laughter, the good gentlemen of cricket, Inzamam and Saeed Anwar, joined us and tried to calm Saqlain and asked him to forgive Miandad. They did so by quoting various hadiths. *Voh hadith suna suna ke samjha rahe the! Yeh hadith hai, is mein yeh kaha gaya hai ki aap maaf kar dein.* An indignant

Miandad kept asking if there was a hadith that took his side too, for he was the injured party. They very seriously replied that there was one that stated that as he was the older man, he must forgive Saqlain—'yeh hadith hai ki aap badein hain, aap usey maaf kar dein.' We just cracked up again.

Then there was the mandatory reading of the namaz together, as a team. It was funny to see how quickly guys disappeared from the dressing room. Some dove into the bathroom and some remembered urgent appointments. My poor knees would be locked after the day's play, so I was also one of the many who would try to avoid kneeling. A very determined Inzamam would, however, go from room to room, collecting everyone who was absconding. Some guys would walk in straight from the club and join the early morning namaz and get their brownie points.

There was another funny incident involving Miandad. He came storming into the dressing room one day, shouting at us, saying we had fixed the match. Perplexed, we answered, 'But Javed bhai, we won the match!' He pointed to some players and kept pressing the charge. It was so ridiculous that we all collapsed with laughter. This was in Sharjah, where we were playing against England, and I had done very well. We went on to win the tournament but he stuck to his claim that we had fixed the match.

The dressing room was the best place to be when the team was playing well and winning. During the 1999 World Cup, our spirits were so high that we didn't feel the need to go out anywhere. The dressing room was a happy and happening place. The seniors were relaxed and looked benignly at us when we got up to mischief—chucking water at each other, joking and teasing each other. We actually wanted to be together even after the match and went out to a club or for dinner. I must say that we had some of the best wits amongst us. Wasim, Waqar, Moin had a terrific sense of humour and were game for anything. We had great times outside the dressing room and usually forgot any issues that had cropped up amongst us.

At St. Vincent, in the Caribbean, Wasim, Moin and I took a bet that we could swim the kilometre stretch between two islands. We took off, determined to outdo each other, but lost steam halfway through. Suddenly the distance seemed never ending and we began to look at each other rather anxiously. I recall that the three of us kept encouraging each other to carry on—*Koi na! Shabaash! Agge barh.*

Somehow we reached the beach, hauled ourselves out of the water and fell on the sand, utterly spent. It took us a while to get our breath back and gain control of our quivering limbs. It was only then that we began wondering how on earth we would find our way back. When we got the strength, we started waving, jumping up and down on the beach and yelling, 'Please help us get back.' The rest of the team assured us many times afterwards that it was a funny sight to see us hopping around on the far horizon.

Another time, in the West Indies, I was jet skiing and Wasim was riding pillion. I had taken the ski quite far from the beach when it bounced on a wave and his sunglasses fell into the water. Wasim wanted me to stop and jump in to retrieve them. *Maine kaha, 'Wasim bhai, aap ka dimaag theek hai? Gehra samundar hai, kya ho gaya aap ko?'* I pointed out that we were rather far from the coast and these were deep waters. Finally, I did jump in at his insistence, and so did he. After looking in vain for his glasses, we gave up and turned back towards the jet ski. It had floated far, far ahead of us.

Then there was Mushtaq Ahmed. He enjoyed playing cards. One night, he rang Moin, asking for a loan because he had lost all his money at the blackjack table and wanted a chance to win it back. Moin responded, 'It's two in the morning and we've got a match to play later today. What on earth are you doing playing cards at this hour?' But Mushtaq kept begging him to loan him some money so Moin said, 'Okay, come up to room number 201 on the second floor.'

So there was Mushtaq at two in the morning, banging away on the door of room number 201 on the second floor and yelling, 'Bhai, open up, I'm here,' only to hear a voice from within roaring, 'Who the fuck are you, banging on my door at this hour?' An ever hopeful Mushtaq yelled back, 'Moin, gora mat ban—Don't pretend you are a white man, open the door.' The gentleman did just that. Later, Mushtaq told us that a giant opened the door and he fled, muttering apologies over his shoulder.

Yasir Hameed, or Badshah as he was affectionately called, was the funniest of them all. He had virtually no short-term memory and got himself and us into a lot of trouble because of this. Once, the whole lot of us were at a beach resort, taking a short break during a tour, when Badshah and Kamran Akmal decided to jet ski. Akmal was tempted to take a dip and told Badshah he was jumping off for a swim and that he should hover around nearby and pick him up later. Badshah swears till date that his intentions were honourable but he forgot all about Akmal and headed off in the opposite direction. Fortunately, there were others in the vicinity, who fished out an agitated Akmal—*beech samunder mein bechara haath hila raha tha ki Allah ka vaasta hai mujhe bacha loh.* The poor chap was waving his hands frantically to draw attention to his plight. Later, a rather tearful Akmal asked Yasir, '*Oye Badshah, tu ne mere saath aisa kyon kiya?*' Why did you do this to me? An abashed Yasir answered, 'I'm so sorry, yaar! I forgot about you.'

Another time, during a Test match in Bangalore, Yasir suddenly stopped Ishant Sharma from bowling to him. When Ishant asked him what the matter was, he said, 'I forgot to wear my abdominal guard.' The match had to be stopped till Badshah was properly protected.

On every tour that we went, serious love would bloom in the dressing room. There were always at least five to six ashiqs in love. They would get so involved, they would promise marriage and togetherness forever. These Romeos would sit around sighing, reading love letters and stuff, only to fall in love again with another girl on the next tour. In Sydney, I remember we had eight boys crying their eyes out in the dressing room and sixteen girls crying outside. This heartbreak would be enacted at the airport as well. One player received a letter from a girl, written in her blood. He promptly set about writing back, using his servant's blood. *Maine usse kaha, yeh kaun sa tareeka hai yaar, kam se kam murgi ka khoon istemaal kar.* I told him it just wasn't fair, at least he could have used the blood of a hen.

There were five or six stalkers who kept chasing me, and I would set them after Afridi or Saqlain. There was a particularly determined lady who cornered me in our hotel corridor one day. I somehow convinced her that Afridi was her man and helpfully gave her his room number. As I fled from the scene, I could hear her yelling outside his door—Afrriiiiidiiii! For quite a few days afterwards, I had to avoid being alone with him.

We were a loud and boisterous lot, so injuries occurred regularly in the dressing room. Sometimes they occurred when we won and began hugging each other—someone would jump on you and a muscle or a bone would give.

During Inzi's captaincy, the whole lot of them realized that I was the adventure loving member of the team who knew the best places to visit. From then onwards, I was asked to organize all our trips in England, New Zealand, Sri Lanka, just about everywhere. The tours were usually relaxing and fun and the team bonded, away from the pressures of the dressing room. Sometimes, even if we went out in the evening for a party or a meal together, we would carry the dressing room with us. But if we were outdoors, in the fresh air, we were able to shake off the baggage and enjoy ourselves, whether we were fishing or swimming or just horsing around.

As I have said before, Wasim, Waqar, Inzamam, Moin all had a great sense of humour, and the dressing room would ring with laughter when they were in a good mood. It was also the worst place to be in when they were under pressure. Tempers always soared when we were not doing well—the guys ended up hitting each other, the security guys around us and, for good measure, any policemen hanging about. Since our seniors were the ones losing their cool, we followed their lead and most of the time, the captain didn't intervene. If the PCB and our coaches were uncaring, our captains were no better. Our governing body has a habit of changing the captain if the team fares badly. They did this frequently and arbitrarily, so, naturally, every one of them concentrated more on trying to hold on to the captaincy than anything else. To hell with nurturing or leading the team!

The government puts its own man in as the PCB chairman and he does what it wants him to. In turn, those who wag their tails before the PCB are made the captain. As a result, we had a number of uncaring men who rose to captaincy though there were other, more deserving players, who might have been better suited for the job. Take the terrible decision made by the board in 2007, for instance. Afridi deserved the captain's cap but was bypassed, and following Wasim Akram's advice, it was given to Shoaib Malik of all people. The board now had a *ghulam*—a slave who would jump through hoops for them. It seems that the main objective in making Malik the captain was to get rid of the senior players, guys who had a mind of their own. They dropped Razzaq for the T–20s, and this was a man whose game was tailor-made for the format. Afridi nearly followed suit, after he lost his temper with Talat Ali, the manager, over the way in which he was handling the team. I had developed a habit of keeping out of others' fights but had the good sense this time to step in. We stood together and Afridi stayed in the team.

I wish we had started getting together on issues earlier. We should have got behind Razzaq. In fact, all five of us—Mohammad Yousuf, Younis Khan, Afridi, Razzaq and I—should have resigned and walked out in protest against the unfair treatment meted out to us at the hands of the management. In hindsight, our lack of unity was a big mistake that we talk about with regret today. Malik set about doing his utmost to get rid of all of us and kept at it till he was dropped. He was a puppet in the hands of Ashraf and scandal after scandal kept breaking. How could our team progress and meet new challenges? It is the captain's job to throw out jealousy, back his players and coax them to play better. Dressing room *mein gandh nikaalna hota hai, dalna nahin hota.* You need to get rid of the rubbish in the dressing room, not add filth to it.

Teams are made in the dressing room and their success depends almost entirely on the calibre of the captain for it is he, not the chairman or any other member of the board, who has the maximum influence on the players. For years we have lacked a strong and, more importantly, a caring captain at the helm. Actually, what we needed was a father figure, whether captain or coach. We didn't get that.

The Pakistan team is mostly made up of players who have come from economically challenged backgrounds and have been deprived of an education. So we learn everything from cricket; it is our educational institution. We learn to speak English, drive cars and conduct ourselves. Therefore, we are very vulnerable and need good, strong mentors to protect and take us in the right direction. Somebody like Imran Khan, for instance, who in my opinion has been our greatest captain. He was a fabulous bowler and all-rounder who nurtured some of the greatest Pakistani talent like Wasim and Waqar. Selfless and hardworking, Imran was an example to us all and he dedicatedly put together a team that was fearless and victorious. However, when I became a part of the Pakistan team, the feeling of team spirit was almost non-existent. It didn't take a rocket scientist to figure out why. There was too much politicking and back stabbing; it was a group of people struggling to survive each other's onslaughts. The thing that saddens me is that this mess was often created, or at the very least encouraged, by the captain. I am amazed that even after having a mentor like Imran Khan, a stream of uncaring captains held sway—some of them had played under him.

After observing the way the PCB and its managers deal with captains, I can understand the pressures they have to face, and I know that only a very strong and resilient man can stand up to it all. Wasim had the quality, the calibre to take over from Imran, but he stumbled.

Inzamam, at one point, did manage to keep the team united. He and I didn't get along but that didn't affect the team—we did well under him for a while. However, a strange thing happened to change the mood in the dressing room just about then.

It is my opinion that the namaz is the duty of every Muslim. Every Muslim knows this, and he also knows that if he doesn't do the namaz, he will be held responsible in the court of the ultimate judge, Allah. To force grown-ups, as though they were children, to do the namaz or *zikr* seems a bit strange to me. The problem begins when someone feels that now he has got on to the right path, he must make everybody else do what he does. I think that's missing the point; it's also a form of arrogance. If you can find the right path and correct yourself, so can the other man. If you impose your will, Allah's benevolence and kindness are ignored.

But some people thought that this was the way to take the team forward. Roza, namaz, tabliq were to be compulsory team events. Guys were taken to task if they wished to pray in the solitude of their room. Threats were used; if you don't pray with the team, you will be thrown out. I can guarantee that ten of those praying with the team were doing so because they were scared of being thrown out. I mean, to go around telling all of us that if you recite the namaz with the group, you will be selected and will be in our good books, is the strangest thing. *Namaz saadda zameer hai*—namaz is our conscience—but Islam has also given us instructions on when and how to pray. *Islam da adda hissa pakeezgi hai!* When the whole team got together for namaz, the bathroom floor would become wet and filthy, with tissues strewn all over—it was disgusting. Islam is all about purity, cleanliness. You can't dirty your environment and consider yourself clean.

We began praying on airplanes, if you please, although it is absolutely clear that if you are travelling, you can be excused from namaz. And the toilets—oh my God! Once, the team made the water flow out into the aisles and there were complaints all around; they stopped us from praying on that flight. It wasn't safe, either. All of sudden, a whole team would start moving about, jostling each other, trying to pray. You can sit or even stand to do the namaz, but you have to be considerate to others. Islam insists that you care for others.

I firmly believe in namaz—it is every Muslim's ornament. One should wear it with pride and with a pure mind. However, you cannot ignore the other duties that Allah has ordained for you. A cricketer's primary duty is to play cricket. If you feel that cricket is less important, leave it—go out into the world and preach. I'm sure you will be of greater use there.

When religion came into our dressing room, I thought, what hypocrisy! These guys tell lies, do wrong things, and then they read the namaz. I believe that namaz stops you from doing shameful things, yet here we all were, praying and then immediately going back to being shameless. You are not true to the game, you get out deliberately and indulge in other similarly hateful activities. *Us namaz da Allah nu ki fayda?* Of what value is this namaz to Allah?

I, for one, don't believe in showing anybody how pious I am. I pray in my room or at a masjid and I think that is the proper way. I never felt the need to show them I was praying, so I was never popular. Some of you may be scratching your heads and wondering what all this has to do with cricket—so did I. When they would question my truancy, I would say, I'm a Muslim, I'm doing everything I should, I don't need you to tell me what to do. I know it, I have learnt it. But you guys, one moment you pray and the next moment you roll up your prayer mats and start swearing at each other. If you read the namaz, you should forgive your enemies. We would be praying together and then some ghastly rumour of wrongdoing would pop up. I think it made a mockery of prayer.

In 2003–04, Lt. Gen. Zia was keen that I take over as the captain and he was backed by Aamir Sohail. I was performing well and frankly, there was nobody else around. Rashid Latif had been banned, Inzamam was making a comeback, they didn't want to give it to Younis, and they felt that Afridi was not ready yet. But what did I do? I ran away to England instead. I wasn't interested in taking on any additional responsibility. This was a big mistake on my part. It would have been good for the team and me. I would have learnt to be more responsible and certainly would have fought for my team. But I wasn't ready for it. I didn't think it was my job. I was running alone, winning matches for the team, and I felt that was enough. I wanted to be free and without any stress. I realized too late that I was being extremely self-centred and selfish. Pakistan cricket needed me and I guess I let it down. We were an immensely talented lot—Wasim, Waqar, Afridi, Saqlain, Razzaq, Azhar, Elahi and I, among others. Each of us could, and did, win games single-handedly. But to win big tournaments we needed great leaders and that's what we lacked.

' I was happy when Younis Khan became captain because he is a great team player, but he wasn't aggressive enough with the management. At long last we had a good man, a great teammate and a good cricketer at the helm and we won the T–20 World Cup. It was as simple as that, but did the PCB care? Look what happened to him. The chairman didn't like him and he got dropped, faced inquiries and struggled to find a place in the team. Later in 2010, we won the series against Australia so they said we won, we don't need him. How sad is that! Talent and experience were made to sit outside and he had to apologize for nothing, just to appease the egos of the board members, before he was allowed to play again. This is not how teams are made. You need a combination of experience and new blood that works together.

A couple of years ago, I became aware that the younger members of the team liked hanging around me. This was because I gave them the respect that was their due. I was like an elder brother, a mentor to them, I made them feel that they belonged—that they were stars in the making. Some did not listen to my advice, that was their choice. I felt that it was my responsibility to warn them of all the pitfalls that could come their way. My intention was not to crush their spirit. The idea was to correct them when they misbehaved, for their own good. I always offered my own example and told them, 'Don't do this; I did, and look at the trouble I got into.' Most of them hailed from very poor and uneducated backgrounds and clung to me when they travelled. I instilled confidence in them and encouraged them to go out. How else would they learn to communicate with people from other cultures? *Jab aap unse laad karenge to voh apse laad karenge.* If you want the younger players to respect you, you've got to respect them—it's as simple as that. Give them a chance to grow.

Unfortunately, our seniors were the most corrupt people I have known in my whole life. Barring a few like Rashid Latif and Moin Khan, the rest indulged in activities that certainly didn't help the game, yet most of them were let off with fines. The fact is that I can't point to any one player and say, this man steadied our team—*isne Pakistan cricket ko sambhala. Pakistan cricket ki jo tabahi hai, voh Pakistan team ne khud ki.* Always leaking our disagreements to the media, devising devious schemes to throw this one or that one out, in-fighting, not allowing young talent to grow and thrive—this was the state of our team. So it was not the board alone that ruined Pakistan cricket, it was the team itself. Players often took their issues to the press. Some, mind you, did it to sell a story and make some money. Some did it for mileage. As a consequence, relationships within the dressing room broke down badly. Rashid Latif, Aamir Sohail, Wasim Akram, all ended up with extremely bad relationships within the team. Moin Khan stepped down from vice captaincy. He was banned from entering the dressing room and even the ground. What a way to end a career!

I write all this not because I want to whine about it, but because I know that we could have done so much better, reached much greater heights, for we had the talent to do so.

But other than Imran, I'm sorry to say that I haven't met a single cricketer who put the game before himself. This is my personal opinion and I stand by it.

While we were destroying ourselves, the media took up the responsibility of creating more trouble. I am not saying that they should have looked the other way, but surely one should wait to verify facts. It saddens me that they took it upon themselves to distort Pakistan's image in the cricketing world. Because the captains were not strong willed, they couldn't handle things either. Like the match-fixing scandals that never seem to stop. I also wish the media would stop projecting them as mere scandals; it's more serious than that.

Every piece of news that comes out of our dressing room or team meetings takes on a sensational spin and is reported to the world every day. In my opinion, our media has had a huge hand in destroying the reputation of Pakistan cricket and hasn't learnt that their counterparts around the world mostly take care not to tarnish their country's image. Your country matters, boss! Sport is a national matter and we should be supported when we are going through trying times, not harassed and humiliated.

15

Where Do We Go from Here?

For most cricketers, the game is also their bread and butter. And everyone knows that a sportsman's earning time is limited and the game is physically debilitating, but who cares! Till 2000, Pakistani players were paid PKR 18,000 (approximately US$200) as fees for a Test match. For an ODI, it was PKR 12,000 (approximately US$150). Even today, we are probably worse off financially than any other team in the world. People say there is a lot of money in this game; yes, there is, but not in Pakistan.

A bowler of my calibre in India would earn fifteen crore rupees or over a million and a half US dollars in a year at the very least. This is, however, the total amount I have earned during my entire career, including sponsorships, advertisements—everything I have ever done. This is how much money a big 'star' like Afridi or I get in Pakistan, so you can imagine what the others earn. There is good money in first-class cricket and even in the Ranji Trophy in India. If you come from a village and can play 15–20 matches at this level, you can take back at least fifteen lakh rupees, which is good enough to build a pucca home in the village. I understand that India's economy is larger than ours, but even Bangladesh pays better money than us.

There doesn't seem to be an alternative, however, for most players, for jobs are drying up fast in Pakistan and those that exist pay a pittance, so if a player doesn't get to play, how is he going to survive? The white man is safe. He has alternatives; he can work in other fields. Indian players are also better taken care of. Sanjay Manjrekar, Navjot Singh Sidhu and several other players have found jobs that help them earn a living with dignity. *Pakistan mein koi channel hi nahin hai. Aur jo hain, woh kehte hain muft karo. Aur jo dete hein voh 10,000–15,000 per interview dete hain.* Our top match commentators hardly make ends meet.

The result is the total lack of security faced by a player even at his peak. Combined with the shenanigans the PCB indulges in, this leads to a strange problem, of a player's need for revenge. Players, great players, have chosen the wrong path because they have wanted to get back at the board. They have been humiliated so many times that they don't care about the consequences. The problem arises when the player becomes insecure or is treated badly, like I was by Naseem, and starts thinking, well, they are going to throw me out after a few games but if I ever manage to get back, I'll show them! A strange desire for vendetta sets in. When they regain their berth, they make sure they hurt the PCB in some way, even if it means fixing a match. This may sound strange but it's true: most of the time, these things get done not out of greed but because they want to hurt those who have hurt them. And, of course, they make a quick buck in the process. This is what I have observed with Pakistani players. Bitterness is the main motivation for match fixing. The constant insecurity and financial strife lead to depression, which turns to anger, and anger leads to match fixing.

The pressure is enormous. Most of us are the sole, or main, earning members of extended families and we are surrounded by people who seem to offer a way out, even if it is the wrong way. Given the lack of financial security, when an opportunity to earn money arises, some slip up and grab it. Unfortunately, such opportunities have come our way frequently and before you know what is happening, the deed has been done and the tracks have been covered. The question is, why doesn't the management ensure that the team is not exposed to bookies? We don't go to them, they come to us. In fact, they are always around us. I find it ironical that the board enforces curfews and restrictions on players when they are on tour but have no problem with these guys hanging around us all the time, abroad and at home. We don't usually know who they are to start with. They are introduced to us by other acquaintances. They are present at the parties we go to and are on first-name terms with almost everyone we know.

'What will you do after cricket?' Everything starts with this question. We shouldn't need to be doing anything at all! This is our bread and butter; we should be able to retire with our old age secured. It's a professional game after all. The question is usually asked by someone who has been allowed to interact with us. We are like sitting ducks, insecure ducks at that, always surrounded by rich people—guys who like to call themselves our friends. They watch a player closely, trying to assess his needs and leverage these. There is a sister's wedding to think of, we can take care of it. You've got old parents, allow us to take care of them. The temptations are innumerable. Fancy cars, hi-tech phones, girls, big houses, drugs—cocaine lies on the coffee table. And it's party time, all the time. In the course of my career, there have been so many scandals and allegations involving players. Many of them were forced to retire and now we have these new boys getting banned as well. So there is a problem, right? But nobody has bothered to find the cause and address the problem.

Remember that cricket keeps us away from those who could have anchored us in safe waters—especially family and friends. It's lonely out there and if you are not mentally strong, things can go horribly wrong for you. We spend so many nights alone in hotel rooms, away from our families, either passing time watching TV or sitting in the dark brooding about all the problems that surround us. Nobody is there to help or advice us, we have to go through it all on our own. Our personal commitments are huge because most of the time, the entire responsibility of taking care of the extended family rests squarely on our shoulders. In an ideal world, the family would make every effort to earn their own livelihood and not depend on one person to the extent that, instead of concentrating on the game, he ends up worrying about how to earn enough for everyone. Often, the result is that the player neglects himself physically and emotionally. Here you are finding it difficult to buy bread; how can you afford the personal trainers, nutritionists or doctors that you so badly need and most sports people in other countries take for granted? We are paying to maintain a large family back home and trying not to have a nervous breakdown. We can't afford shrinks.

Now, if Mahender Singh Dhoni is earning 100 crore rupees

per annum, he can afford to surround himself with educated people who take care of his health and career. They shield and mentor him and warn him if he is tempted to stray. Back home, we have to guide ourselves—*kee aiyashi nahin karna, bure kaam nahin karna.* I have seen many Pakistani players go through mental trauma. *Bahut saari rate kali hoti hain, bahut saare lamhe kale hote hain. Har waqt aap accha perform nahin kar sakte aur log baitthein hain gaaliyan nikaalne ke liye.* If they walk out of their rooms, they face abuse and stress from the board. Friends ask questions, families do too. We have friends who are friends only as long as we are in the limelight and drop us like hot potatoes when the first signs of failure become visible. The same friend who dined with you a few weeks ago, starts abusing you. So the sportsmen pop pills. I have seen players who are on sleeping pills 24/7; some take Xanax to keep calm. You are alone in times of trouble. And if you aren't strong—I will not name them, but I know of some players who have wanted to commit suicide. I have seen them tottering on the edge because they have financial responsibilities and can't survive. Once they had fame and now they have nothing.

If you are a celebrity, life is just that much more difficult to handle. Everything happens so fast; you eat fast, you speak fast, you stop appreciating the simpler things of life. You hear the laughter but don't see the smile. As a result, you start to change.

In my experience, celebrities are fragile people the world over and get knocked over very quickly. Many end up trying to cope by taking recourse to crutches like drinks, drugs, anything to alleviate the feeling of loneliness. They are often suicidal; you hear of so many succumbing to an overdose of drugs. In our country, they deliberately get into fatal accidents. We are surrounded by goodtime friends and the press alternately ooh's and boo's. Those whom we get close to spill personal details to the press for money or their fifteen minutes of fame. Sometimes, they cook up juicy scandals and serve them to a hungry media.

When you reach the pinnacle of success in your career, it's downhill from there on. One gets so used to packing in so much in a day that when the time comes to hang up your boots, a celebrity doesn't know how to handle the change in pace. That's when drugs come in. Look around you; all the celebrities you see are vulnerable because they are alone and depression is the only constant. A sportsman's physique is of great importance, for it is the vehicle for him to achieve his goals, yet when depression sets in, the physical abuse begins. First it's cigarettes, then alcohol, and finally hard drugs— cocaine and heroin.

Being famous in Pakistan has never been easy. Being famous is about fun and laughter but it's the harbinger of depression and pain as well. On top of this, we have a non-cooperative, unhelpful board and bad management. In retrospect, I understand why we youngsters were dealt with the way we were by our seniors. We were knocking out their future. I have groused a lot about how I was treated by them but when I was coming into the side, I was young and couldn't understand how much pain they were undergoing. I guess they reacted to me the only way they knew how. Towards the end of my career, I saw youngsters making a beeline for my berth. It was hard for me at first but I welcomed them, and hoped they would play with integrity and commitment for their country. Don't get me wrong, fame also brings positives. You enjoy your life as well, but the end of the story should be a good one. Film *khatam ho rahi ho aur hero mar jaaye. Aise to end nahin hona chahiye.* It's a very sad truth that our players mostly end up in a bad state because of a corrupt system that does not support them in any way.

Everybody on the board and in the dressing room knows this, yet no measures are taken to change the way the game is run. Nobody warns or counsels the youngsters who are the most vulnerable, yet there are enough people to mess with their heads—to take them out for dinner, invite them to their huge, beautiful homes and say, you too should have such a house with wonderful things in it. My own feeling is that the situation is so fraught now that perhaps before selecting players, the PCB should also do some psychological profiling.

Some time back, I talked to Amir about the life that awaited him. He was the youngster earmarked for the change of guard, to take over from me. He was juggling three phones in his hand and was swinging a set of earphones around. I told him, *Kadam dhyan nal rakheen, phoonk, phoonk ke kadam chalain.* Be careful, stop staring at the big tree, you will lose the view of the jungle. I sensed that he was getting into bad company and told him not to shift to Lahore, for it's a party house for cricketers and can be very distracting. I told him not to do what I had done, or he would suffer. He didn't listen to me.

The truth is that players are being forced to gamble because the system allows them to gamble. A player has to eat; the fallout is that a whole nation stands vilified. Amir's whole family depended on him. They had just got a glimpse of a better life. Now they are banned from looking ahead for five years at least. It's as simple and as raw as that. And it's going to haunt him for the rest of his life. What a waste of talent!

But if he had been allowed to play in the World Cup in 2011, would justice have been served? Yes, he is very young, but so are all those who stayed away from the temptations. I was about the same age when I was first accosted by these guys. This was in 1999 after a Test match at Kolkata. I didn't understand what they were talking about. How on earth did one fix a game? They explained that I was to bowl normally till I got a pre-arranged signal for no-balls, wides and stuff like that. They would place people in the audience, dressed in a certain colour, and I would be told in advance about the slots during which I had to perform badly. It didn't sound right to me so I told them I wasn't interested and didn't think I would ever be interested. They told me that half my team was doing it. That really made me mad but I replied that I didn't care, I wasn't going to. To my surprise, they just said, okay, think about it. We'll come back again. You never know, you might change your mind.

Sure enough, when I was back there a month later for the three-nation ODIs in March, once again I was asked to bowl badly and was offered 1.3 million rupees for each game. Actually, whenever we played in India, we were almost invariably approached to participate in match fixing. During the 1999 World Cup, I was approached before our match against Bangladesh, and yet again, before the semifinal against India. The price was 2–3 million rupees per match.

During the 2003 World Cup, they left a bag outside my hotel room. The moment I saw the bag, I went back inside and locked myself in. I called Azhar Zaidi, our manager, and told him that there was a bag outside my door, I don't know what is inside it. I said, please have it removed immediately. The ICC later asked me about this incident and enquired why I had not reported the matter to them. I told them that I did report it to our manager. Wasn't it his responsibility to take it further?

Everyone wants the players to reveal names, but the guys we meet are small cogs in a very big wheel. The kingpins are the mafia and we have no one to protect us or our families. So we take the fall alone.

In the beginning, I wondered why I was being singled out. I had no idea that they targeted all those who came from needy backgrounds. Most times, I knew these guys because they had ready entry into our world and hung around us during tours. Yasir and Najeeb Malik were two of the familiar faces, as was Rajeshwar. They would offer cars and houses as nonchalantly as one might invite an acquaintance to a meal. It was so casual and happened so consistently and openly that I thought it was a joke. I would tell them, *'Yaar! Aaisa mazak na kiya kar mere saath'*—Stop trying to pull my leg. Or a disbelieving *'Achha, hor kinna doge?'*—How much more money will you give me? And they used to get very upset with me saying, *'Yaar tu seriously kyun nahin layta. Tere baaki dost kar rahein hain'*—Why don't you take us seriously, all your friends are doing it. I would say, *'Bakwas, jhoot bolte ho'*—You lie! When they continued to approach me, I started getting irritated and shared my reservations with Afridi. I remember the look of concern on his face as he told me, 'Listen, don't pay any attention to all this bullshit, keep your distance.' I guessed then that he too was being pestered.

The last attempt they made was before the Jaipur ODI in 1999. I recall grabbing the guy and pushing him around roughly to drive home the point that I wanted nothing to do with them. But they are very persistent and no longer wait for us to go on tours either. These days, I'm not too sure if something is a set-up or a sting. I don't want to know.

After every conversation with these men, I would end up feeling extremely agitated. If people had approached me, they must have gone to others as well. There can be no smoke without a fire, and so I began to scrutinize videos of matches very carefully and found they were right—it happened often and regularly, usually in the shorter versions of the game, and at the IPL and ICL in particular, though I have no concrete proof.

Match fixing has taken such deep roots in Pakistan that everyone seems to be involved. In 2007, I was training at the nets in the Cricket Academy at Lahore when I was approached by a servant working there. He told me, 'Sir, if you want to get in on the action, let me know.' I was taken aback and asked him what he meant. He answered, 'Sir, I have a contact in Sialkot, and he wants you involved.' I was appalled to know that even a hired help could be mixed up in all this. I told him that if he wanted to keep his job, he should never approach me again and if I found out he was approaching others, I would make his life miserable.

Most of these allegations occurred in the period between 1995 and 2003 and as a result, I lost respect for most of my seniors. I have never been able to comprehend the management's stand either. Nothing was done to keep these guys away from us and nobody was proved guilty and punished. They knew that fixers were talking to us; why did they give them access to the players? And if you can't provide any proof about an incident of fixing or the persons involved in it, why cast aspersions? As it turned out, most of those accused or suspected have been forgiven and let off the hook. As for the players, well, the question is—why did their names appear in the press? Why wasn't my name ever included in such allegations? I never went down that murky street, so no fingers could be pointed at me. When Shane Warne and Mark Waugh admitted in front of the media that they too had messed up, I remember wondering, what were these guys thinking, to do such a thing? The difference between them and us was that they confessed and apologized and promised never to do such a thing again. In Pakistan, some players paid a fine but nobody ever owned up.

I have a personality that is aggressive. It threatens people. Because of this, some people hate me with a passion and I doubt that their opinion will ever change. Others who meet me, especially those who do not have a vested interest, are often surprised at what they find. I'm friendly, easygoing, and I love to laugh. I never retaliate, never notice those who back-stab me, and I never clarify anything. People write so many things against me. They misinterpret my medical reports. I don't care. I know I will ultimately prevail, come what may. I am a very, very lucky man. You can try it yourself—take a lottery in my name. I was a lottery for my family. So I have not and will not lose my understanding of what is right and what is wrong for the sake of money.

But in my country, those who follow the right path are treated so badly that they leave it all behind them and leave cricket as well. Most of them have chosen to leave Pakistan and live in England or elsewhere. At least five of my friends—Rana Qayyum, Naseer, Shakeel, Irfan and Alamgir—accepted the fact that they had to leave everything behind, including cricket. We have played together and I can tell you that they were good players—they now ply taxis in the UK. Then there are those who didn't leave the country, like Zahid Fazal, and still refused to take any bullshit from others. He was one of our finest batsmen, yet he has been wiped out of public memory. No one knows where or in what condition he is.

Despite our rotten system, great players have come up in Pakistan, but does anyone know what happened to them after they retired? Playing for pride is all right but pride doesn't feed you. I have seen good cricketers starving. I have seen players who have got over three hundred wickets struggling to make a living. I can't name him, but there is a famous cricketer who sits on the roadside and sells chana. I know of a former Pakistan captain driving a taxi in England and it is heartbreaking for me to know this. Amongst us, perhaps the only thing we can be sure of is that given a chance, our dignity will be stripped from us. Yet, nobody does anything about it. A retirement plan should have been in place years ago. I don't think any board has such a plan actually, but there is no reason why the PCB can't show the way. Contracted players do have a pension policy but not those who do not play regularly. Perhaps they could take five per cent of the match fees and create a fund—at the end of the year, the money could be given to former cricketers. We have often passed the hat around amongst ourselves when we learned of the plight of an ex-player. So many players who have bowed out voluntarily or have been forced out have come to me and asked me to give them two meals a day. *Yaar, hume khaana khila do, do time ka. Itne level ki poverty hai!*

I foresaw all this happening to me as well, a decade ago. In 2000, after the chucking allegation, I thought that my career had ended and immediately called up some friends to help me find a job—I was terrified of not being able to make ends meet. When I got back into the game, I used my earnings to build homes for my family. I invested wisely, and today I sleep soundly at night.

16

Being Shoaib

As a child growing up in a backward district of Rawalpindi, there was not much by way of entertainment. There were movies, of course, and I loved watching them, but other than that, there was not much to do except hang around on the street, visit a dargah or fly kites. My parents were very strict about my getting back home on time, so I hated the evenings and couldn't wait for the sun to rise.

When fame came to me, I was young and happily grabbed it with both hands. I found a whole new world to explore and I just wanted to go out and experience everything and that, too, in a hurry—*ki baad vich koi naa pucche ki tu ae kita, oh kita?* I didn't have to go to bed early and discovered that I loved the nighttime. Come evening, I brightened up, felt refreshed and more energetic, friends found me more talkative and, during my younger days, open to any sort of adventure. I bowl my best during the sun-warmed mid-afternoons in winter but I loved the nights and all the excitement and activity they heralded. These days, I find the nights ideal for reflection. Everything is peaceful and calm. There are less people crowding you, no traffic to deal with, so I feel free of the pull and push of life, of all the tension, and I come into my own.

Today my idea of a good time is lounging on a comfortable sofa and dining on seafood with an iced Coke in hand while watching documentaries on National Geographic, Animal Planet or Discovery. The images they beam make me marvel at the amazing creations of God. Man's inventions are just not that spectacular and I often wonder, what was Allah thinking of as he created all this? What were his reasons?

This doesn't mean I stay in all the time. It is my belief that if you have the means, you must enjoy the one life you have, and what use is money anyway, if you can't enjoy it with friends and family? I guess my idea of enjoyment has changed over the years. I'd rather have dinner with my friends at home, or with their families, and chat a while and then call it a night, or at the most visit a favourite restaurant. The younger Shoaib, however, needed to experience everything, he didn't want to miss out on what he thought was a good time. The thing is, I always liked excitement around me. And it's the journey to a destination or a goal that has always attracted me; when I achieve something or finish a set task, I get bored and move on to something else. That's why I love cricket, it's always changing, something new keeps happening on the field. Every day is not a good day; some days you bowl well and some days you lose your rhythm. The uncertainty of this game has continued to hold my interest.

As a teenager, when I was playing in the Under-19 team, I was considered to be a little 'over the top'. I worked harder than anyone (they called it acting), I took everything to the extreme—training, cycling, running or any other form of exercise. Then I would go out to watch late night movies, and visit clubs. I love music and dancing. In 1996, when I was in England, I danced the nights away in clubs. But I also loved and still love running on the beach, especially in the beautiful city of Cape Town, at the water's edge and some times deeper. I love the sound of the ocean, the waves crashing against the rocks, I love chasing the waves into the sea and then feeling them surge and slap me on the chest. It's the best feeling in the world!

When I entered the Pakistan team, I found that the players never stayed in their rooms so I took my cue from them and enthusiastically joined any excursion. I remember parties that lasted all night long. We would make friends at a club and they would come back with us to our hotel and the party would continue. I was the upcoming 'star' and was living under the media's eye but I didn't care. I never liked my movements being questioned even by my parents, though they had the right to do so, and I didn't think my private life was anyone else's business. It was naïve and idiotic of me, I guess. I loved all the attention I was getting from people. While everyone around did the same, they did it discreetly; I didn't. If I went out with a girl, I did so openly. The media was watching, so what? I wasn't committing a crime! Before I knew it, I had got myself this 'party boy' image. I hadn't done anything different or worse than the others but the media glare had settled on me for all the good things I did and especially for what they judged were the bad things.

I think I was only doing what normal kids of my age do. As far as I was concerned, it felt silly staying indoors after seven in the evening. In the beginning, I went out with my cricket mates—Afridi, Saqlain, etc.—but when they chose to stay indoors, I went alone and met up with other friends. Frankly, I have encouraged youngsters on the team to go out as well because I believe that they learn so much more by meeting people, going to different places. It's also important because you are able to understand the way people from other cultures think, and you learn to value your own. I never stopped going out even when I was going through a bad time. It wasn't in my nature to mope; when I did, it was a sign that I had succumbed to the stress. I had to get out, whether I was staying at home or in a hotel. If I didn't feel like company, I'd run on the beach alone. I would often go on animal safaris or jungle treks in order to disappear from the scene. *Main jata bahut kam tha aur rola zayada par jata thha.*

As for dancing, I dance all the time; everyday in the bathroom I dance and sing. I did so even in the team dressing room—my teammates probably thought I was crazy. I keep clicking my fingers and singing to myself as I get ready for a game. I'm in my own zone; it's the way I prepare for a match and my way has always been different from others'. My friends have never lost an opportunity to tell me that I'm not normal. Well, if normal means not having an inner rhythm, being boring, then I am happy not being normal.

Though many of my senior players and colleagues went clubbing, or to a party, almost every night and some of them even turned up on the field straight from a night out, it was my picture that was flashed in tabloids and elsewhere. Even today, if I go to one party in a year, my picture ends up in the news and as a result the public tends to think I am always at a party. As my popularity went up, I had the opportunity to meet several celebrities; I was a starry eyed youngster and was flattered that they wanted me around. I made genuine friends from amongst a galaxy of icons in the sports and entertainment world and enjoy being with them. Even now, when I meet Imran or even Wasim, I feel very happy and proud to be around such people.

As a kid, I loved watching films, so it was a pleasure meeting film actors. It was even more pleasing to realize that as sports persons, we were valued more and actors liked being around us. It felt good that the people I admired admired me in turn. It's still a great feeling. If I am in India, I end up meeting some film stars. Salman Khan, in particular, is straight after my heart. He is generous, likes to help people, is a straight talking guy, and I get along with him very well. But the media insists on portraying me as a star struck kid who likes to party in Bollywood and wants to be an actor.

I guess it all began in 2005 when Meera, the well-known Pakistani actress, told me that Mahesh Bhatt, an acclaimed director of Hindi films, wanted to meet me. I was attending a cricket camp in Karachi and he flew in with a film script. Mahesh wanted me to play a role in his film *Gangster* and I was tempted. It was a great script and I have always enjoyed movies but I didn't accept the role for a couple of reasons. The PCB was on my ass and was threatening to ban me—if you do the film, we will do this, we will do that. Secondly, everyone around me was against my doing a film. If you want to play cricket, then don't do it, it's not possible to handle two professions, they advised me. I didn't want people to think that I was a non-serious cricketer—*movie bhi kar raha hai*, like Mohsin Khan.

Gangster was a terrific film and it did very well at the box office. Offers continued to come in from Bollywood and from movie makers in the UK as well, but cricket won hands down because it was my first love. I still have no regrets about turning those offers down.

When I was younger, I would take my motorbike and hit the road as often as possible. Much later, driving Formula One cars, sky-diving and ocean-diving became my favourite things to do. I made friends with those who were good-natured, smiled and laughed a lot, and loved adventure. This is true for the girls that I knew as well—some of them were crazier than I was. There was this girl in Australia who took me to feed sharks; it was an amazing adventure.

I am fascinated by big cats and can spend hours in the jungle. I once hung out with a crew that was making a documentary on the Namibian desert lion and it was the experience of a lifetime. One night—hunting time for the lions—we left the safety of the prescribed track because we had heard that there was a possibility of finding lions. I recall thinking that perhaps this was not a very smart thing to do, but I would have happily led the way if I had been experienced enough. We came upon a big pride of lions that night. I was surprised to find that the lionesses were more aggressive than the males. Their roars seemed to go right through one's soul and could be heard three to four kilometres away.

During the 2011 World Cup, the morning before our win against Kenya in Hambantota, I went on a leopard safari. No one else from the team was with me but Wasim Akram and Rameez Raja came as well. For me, the interesting thing was also that I got to ride in a helicopter and see some of Sri Lanka's beautiful countryside. Lions, tigers, jaguars and leopards are some of the most beautiful creatures on earth; the tragedy is that they are in constant danger from man. Nature's gifts of strength, speed and flight to animals fascinate me. If I had not been born a human being, I would have been an eagle, of this I am sure.

You couldn't keep me away from extreme sports even if you tried. I just naturally gravitate towards them. As a child I ran on roof tops, clambered up trees and did everything that could have physically damaged me, with absolute abandon and enjoyment. I haven't changed one bit. When we were in Zimbabwe, we visited the Victoria Falls. I saw a place from where one could bungee jump and promptly went up to try my hand at it. Before anything else, they made me sign a form that said that I was not to hold them responsible if I suffered a heart attack or something else happened during the jump. I blinked but said, 'Okay, tie me up.' Then I looked down and my mind said, No! Please don't! But I took Allah's name and jumped. The free fall was terrifying. Those three or four seconds were the most frightening of my life. I began praying, 'Allah, please save me, I won't do it again.' I went back the next day for my second jump. Since then, bungee jumping has become one of the top few things to do on my list.

In New Zealand I discovered sky-diving. I have a love for speed in any form, and especially for high performance cars, but flying fascinates me. I have flown a Cessna, a Spitfire, and have sat in the back of a B52 bomber. I enjoy jets and make it a point to visit air strips. If I had not chosen to play cricket, I would love to have been the pilot of a fighter aircraft.

I have always enjoyed living on the edge. That is why I often broke rules. The risk-taking, the feeling that I might get caught—

that's how I enjoy life. Sometimes I would sneak out after the team had turned in and saunter back in at two in the morning. Or I would just roam around and not come back at the given time. Of course, there were times when I got caught.

You will never get me to confess that one should outgrow the college tradition of bunking. But, and this is important, I never went out before an important match and certainly did not miss curfew as often as is alleged. These escapades did, however, leave me open to controversies; for example, the management said I went out before the 1999 World Cup final. Bullshit! I wanted that Cup!

Very early in my career, I was labelled the 'bad boy' of cricket. Bad boys do bad things but I have not done terrible things to the game, I don't hurt people. Your past shapes you, whether you like it or not. My background, my journey to the present, has made me what I am today. I never used or harmed anyone on the way and believed in seeking guidance and help only from Allah. So my method of fighting problems is different from that of others. When I left home, I was very young and had no idea what I was getting into. I had a lot to learn, and said and did some things that I shouldn't have, but I wasn't trying to be a non-conformist, I was one. You don't want to think about your adolescent resentments when you are racing towards a batsman or are facing hostility from your own team, but I grew up with multiple chips on my shoulder, because of which I just couldn't be pushed around and always gave as good as I got. I rebelled against what was considered to be the norm because I didn't agree with it and that didn't raise me in the popularity charts with the self-declared kings of the game. As a result, I often stood alone and did what I thought I should do.

I was all raw energy and had no trouble with sledging or trash-talk. In fact, I relished, and still do, taking on a side that is more than willing to use their mouths as a tool. If Harbhajan was caught on camera yelling at me, it could just have been a reaction to my needling. I knew that retaliation was inevitable and I could be at the receiving end as well; therefore I never carried any ill-feelings towards my colleagues. At least, I never judged them on these grounds but if I caught a whiff of racism, then things were different.

Most of us leave our grouses on the field where they belong but non-players continue to talk about it forever and this often has a whiplash effect on players. We'd get fined and banned, of course, but the evening news would at times incite spectators to start a running feud that detracted from the game.

I always find it hilarious when well established sledgers, guys who are masters of this art form, whine when they are at the receiving end and publish accounts that they disliked certain guys who were doing unto them as they did to us. My methods seemed to work on the field, so I chose to carry on the same way, but perhaps that wasn't good for the game or for me. I often look back with a degree of impatience at the raw young pacer and person that I was but I also feel some sympathy.

I made enemies and kept getting dragged through one controversy after another. I hate being questioned and can never get press conferences right. So I guess I came across as boorish, if not arrogant. I never bothered to defend myself and still hate talking about my private life. And unfortunately, I still don't have enough patience with people who can't talk sense, be it friends, family, the PCB, or the prime minister. If I know something is wrong, I have to interrupt, to speak out and knock the idea down. I am brutally truthful and it hurts me. You can imagine how much trouble I get into at press conferences. I try to hold it in but I can't keep quiet. These uncontrolled statements that just shoot out of my mouth have cost me dearly. Often, I have been forced to retract statements and that hasn't elevated my reputation either.

It was hard enough to deal with the mess I kept getting into without the media highlighting all my frailties and ignoring my strengths. Most of the time, I was in some row or the other with the management, which had no compunctions about telling their side of the story to the media while I would let things ride because I was busy trying to find money for all the court fees and fines levied on me.

By nature, I don't like being negative or talking about negative things—I've spent most of my life fighting them off. My family knows that I don't like gossiping either. I dislike telephones and never call home when I am on tour, which doesn't make things easy for them. The sad truth I have to live with is that my family suffered a great deal because of me. All the accusations that were levelled at me were to an extent borne by my family as well. There was nothing much they could do to help but they hung in there with me, right till the end. I know that my mother has become diabetic partly because of the stress on my account. Her son was suffering and she suffered with him. She felt his pain. I know I am largely responsible for her ageing faster than she should have. She always says that I am her youngest son but I never stayed at home. My sister and brothers empathized with me as well. I noticed that whenever I performed well, my family was jubilant, there was happiness all around; when I struggled, they felt the pain.

My economic background and its incumbent responsibilities left me with no other option but to play cricket. In a way, cricket has taken away my family life. I missed so many family occasions, including my brothers' weddings, I missed a large part of my sister's growing up and then the birth of her first child. In fact, I haven't really got to know my nephews and niece; and I couldn't look after my mom and dad the way I wanted to. The game, to some extent, has also taken away my peace of mind and trust in people. I have become so aggressive that I startle even myself. The nature of my job is to wrench the game away from the opposition, hurl the ball at them like a missile—not exactly conducive to a gentlemanly deportment. The sport has also taken away the strength of my knees. I walk like an old man and feel every movement.

Cricket has shattered so many illusions. If I ever get married and have children, I would never encourage them to join this profession—it can take so much from you. Yes, it was an honour and I would do the same again, but I know it hurts like hell and I can take it but I wouldn't want it for my kids. I would instead encourage them to become useful world citizens.

Because it gives us everything we dreamt of and more, we get emotionally attached to the sport we play. In my country, cricket is a sport that keeps families and the nation together. It is also a sad truth that within our community, when a child does well, the parents are lauded, but if the child fails or strays, or is like me, constantly besieged by controversies and scandals, the family is ostracized. It took us many years of heartburn to realize that one has to disengage from the environment, not feel forced to respond or defend. In the early days, I used to take all the allegations to heart. Over the years, I learnt how to cope and carry on playing. My family, however, used to get very upset and hurt. Every incident was discussed threadbare. If I did well, they would be elated and congratulate each other and if things went wrong, they would be nervous and upset and want answers from me. A day came—this was after the 2003 World Cup—when I told everyone at home, 'That's it. From now onwards, no one talks about cricket when I am around. No congratulations, no questions, nothing. Let's keep cricket out of the house, please!' It wasn't easy but I kept insisting that cricket had nothing to do with my relationship with them. To them I was a son or a brother and nothing else, and after many relapses, we finally threw the baggage out of our lives. And then we could move on. They understood that yes, cricket is a part of my life, but the biggest part of my life is my family. Whenever I visited them, we had a rule that cricket was not to be discussed. There was so much else to catch up on. It was the same with my friends. Cricket stayed out of our equation and I confess to having dropped friends who seemed more interested in Shoaib the cricketer and less so in Shoaib, their friend.

Many journalists liked me because I was different and made good copy; I was 'colourful'. The others seemed to be more interested in my private life—I was fodder for gossip, which surprises me because I haven't spoilt the life of a girl or something like that. I have a large fan following all over the world; there were girls who chased me. I now look back and feel awful about the way we treated the girls who used to continually hover around us. They would take us out, buy us gifts and dinner, and then we would move on. I was one of them, but I never lied to them or led them on. It could be quite the opposite sometimes; there were crazy fans, girls who pushed themselves forward to the extent that they reached my home and proposed to me. This has happened a few times. My harassed family has had to ring me when I was on tour to tell me that there was a girl standing before them and to ask, *Tumhara uske saath kya tallukaat hai?*—What is your relationship with her? I used to tell them, you are now talking like the media. I don't even know who she is.

And then there were those who hung around us and sold their stories to the media. In fact, it took me some time to figure out that most of these girls loved to talk to the media. They would go out with us and sell highly embellished accounts of their meetings with us to the press. Many such inventive stories about me were published, especially when I was in England in 2000–2001, which I didn't care about enough to insist upon a clarification.

Cricket has given me everything I have wanted and a great deal more that I never thought I would get. Pain, physical torture, mental torture, and of course the frequent media trials that have given me a bad name. I have been humiliated by a few for their own reasons. But I have a large number of fans who love me. I can feel their love and am grateful for it. And then, of course, I have all the love and support of my family and friends; people who actually mean a lot to me and who I am concerned about. Amongst these I must mention Iftekhar, my cook, Ramzan my guard and driver, and my gardener. I spend a lot of time with them and they take care of me, come what may. They have never complained about my awkward timings, my cricket schedules. I respect and admire them and acknowledge that I would not be able to function without their care. *Voh mere bahut saaree raaton ke saathee hain jab mein akela hota hoon.* And I am very lucky because they really love me. Good times or bad times, they never change, and I can always expect genuine criticism, the kind that is meant to help me. Very often, I walk in to be greeted with a critical and mildly annoyed query: *Yeh aapne kya bowling ki aaj?*—What were you trying to do with the ball today? I tell them, *Yaar hogai aaj, kya karoon*—It wasn't my day, what to do? And they respond with *Accha koina, aggle game vich yaad rakheen*—Okay, never mind. Just remember what you did wrong, for the next game. And then Iftekhar places a delicious dinner in front of me to ward off bad memories of the day's play. I live away from my folks and these guys are my surrogate family.

Over the last few years I have changed, and I know it. It took me all these years of playing cricket to realize how important family is. I was always a rebel; I preferred to be outdoors, away from home. *Jab bura waqt aata tha* I used to keep to myself and never shared my concerns–I hate being at the receiving end of sympathy. But I learnt that those who care for me want to help. Like Sudesh, my friend from Delhi, who offers me good advice. There are a few people I can trust and I have learnt to value them. I now prefer to go out with these friends and their families. Yes, most of my friends are married now. Tauseef treats me like his younger brother, a member of their family, and I like this sense of belonging. His wife and parents give me great support and have stayed with me through thick and thin. And then there is Lt. Gen. Tauqir Zia's family to count on as well. I have been through some very frustrating times but they never left my side.

Yes, I've done it all, I partied and fought battles and had fun. Maturity has set in—well, at least I hope it has—and I know now that I could have done things differently, a bit differently. I know now that life is all about balance.

, It is time to start thinking of the future, time to give back. When your conviction in Allah grows, so does your self-belief, and if you are hard working, you get to your goals faster. I never gave up on him and he has held my hand. My attitude has given pain to me and others; only those who know me intimately can understand that I don't want to, or mean to, hurt anyone. My family recognizes this but can't fully understand it either. No one can, but that's just the way I am. It is this attitude that has made me millions and cost me millions.

Index